ACADEMIC RESEARCH WRITING

Ahmed H. Hamid Fadlalla

PARTRIDGE

Copyright © 2019 by Ahmed H. Hamid Fadlalla.

ISBN:	Hardcover	978-1-5437-4924-3
	Softcover	978-1-5437-4923-6
	eBook	978-1-5437-4925-0

All rights reserved. No part of this book may be used or reproduced by any means, graphic, electronic, or mechanical, including photocopying, recording, taping or by any information storage retrieval system without the written permission of the author except in the case of brief quotations embodied in critical articles and reviews.

Because of the dynamic nature of the Internet, any web addresses or links contained in this book may have changed since publication and may no longer be valid. The views expressed in this work are solely those of the author and do not necessarily reflect the views of the publisher, and the publisher hereby disclaims any responsibility for them.

Print information available on the last page.

To order additional copies of this book, contact
Toll Free 800 101 2657 (Singapore)
Toll Free 1 800 81 7340 (Malaysia)
orders.singapore@partridgepublishing.com

www.partridgepublishing.com/singapore

ACADEMIC RESEARCH WRITING

Data Methods; Writing Process; Language; Style; Punctuation; Common Errors; Citations; APA, Harvard, and MLA Referencing Styles; Editing; Proofreading; Formatting; and Submission

Ahmed H. Hamid Fadlalla

To my family who have been a source
of comfort and inspiration.

ACKNOWLEDGEMENTS

I am grateful to a number of people and entities who helped me in different ways in the course of writing this book.

I am grateful to my colleagues at the English Language Institute of the Royal Commission: Mr. Abdul Karim bin Adam, for undertaking a complete review of the whole book during the holy month of Ramadan last year; Mr. Ibrahim Yabagi, for reviewing the chapters on language; and Mr. Alfred Wilde, for reviewing the chapters on writing introduction, body, and conclusion.

My gratitude is due to the Royal Commission in Jubail, and the Colleges and Institutes Sector for their support and encouragement of research and writing in the sector generally. In particular, I thank the English Language Institute management for providing me with a flexible teaching timetable, which helped in utilizing my time in carrying out this work.

CONTENTS

Academic Research Writing v
Acknowledgements ix
List of Figures xxi
List of Tables xxii

Chapter 1 Introduction 1

THE PREPARATION STAGE

Chapter 2 Reading and Evaluating Sources, Data Types,
and Treatment 15

2.1. Choosing and focusing the topic 16
2.2. Reading as a necessary first step to writing 20
2.2.1. Preliminary overview reading to select suitable sources ... 21
2.2.2. Evaluating print and electronic sources 21
2.2.2.1. Evaluating internet sources 22
2.2.2.2. Evaluating URLs before reading 23
2.2.2.3. Criteria to evaluate URL sources 24
2.2.3. Developing an effective reading strategy 27
2.2.3.1. Reading for overview: 27
2.2.3.2. Critical reading and source annotation 29
2.2.3.3. In-depth reading and note-taking: 30
2.3. Preparing an outline 31

Chapter 3 Methodology and Data Types 35

3.1. Methodology 35
3.1.1. A Combined Qualitative and Quantitative Approach 36
3.1.2. Merits of a combined qualitative and quantitative
approach: 37
3.2. Data Types 37
3.2.1. Secondary sources of data 38
3.2.2. Primary sources of data 40

3.3. Methods of data collection 41
3.3.1. Interviews 41
3.3.1.1. Types of interviews 41
3.3.1.2. Types of ambiguous questions to avoid 42
3.3.1.3. Requirements and ethical considerations for
   conducting interviews 45
3.3.1.4. Advantages and disadvantages of interviews 45
3.3.2. Observations 46
3.3.2.1. Observations: definition 47
3.3.2.2. Uses of observation 47
3.3.2.3. The role of the observer 48
3.3.2.4. Advantages and disadvantages of observation 49
3.3.3. Surveys 50
3.3.4. Questionnaires 52
3.3.4.1. Requirements for good questionnaires 52
3.3.4. 2. Merits and limitations of questionnaires 54
3.4. Data Quality 54
3.5. Data Treatment 55
3.5.1. Processing 55
3.5.2. Presentation 56
3.5.3. Data Analysis and Interpretation 57
3.5.3.1. Numeric Analysis 58
3.5.3.2. Textual Analysis 59

Chapter 4 Ethics of the Academic Community 63

4.1. Initiation into the Academic Community 64
4.2. Academic integrity rationale: education for good
   citizenship 69
4.3. The place of virtue ethics in religion, philosophy,
   and psychology 70
4.3.1. The place of virtue ethics and knowledge in Islam 71
4.3.2. The place of virtue ethics and knowledge in Christianity 72
4.3.3. The place of virtue in the perennial tradition of
   education 72
4.3.4. Virtues as determinants of happiness in
   contemporary positive psychology 73
4.3.5. The place of honesty and integrity in Plato's
   philosophy of education 75

Chapter 5 Concepts of Academic Integrity, Dishonesty,
and Plagiarism 81

5.1. The rift between theory and practice in education............ 81
5.2. Plagiarism: an academic offence and indicator of
dishonesty 83
5.2.1. What constitutes plagiarism? 84
5.2.2. Degrees of unintentional plagiarism 86
5.2.3. The extent of academic dishonesty in higher education .. 86
5.2.4. Academic dishonesty correlates to future
dishonesty in the workplace................................... 87
5.2.5. How to avoid plagiarism: the need for ethics in
education... 88
5.3. To the nitty-gritty of how to avoid plagiarism.................. 90
5.4. Documenting, summarizing, paraphrasing, and quoting... 90
5.4.1. Documenting and synthesizing................................ 90
5.4.2. Documentation and citation of sources...................... 91
5.4.3. In-text citations and referencing.............................. 92
5.4.4. Summarizing... 93
5.4.4.1. Techniques for writing a good summary................. 94
5.4.4.2. Characteristics of a good summary 95
5.4.5. Paraphrasing.. 95
5.4.5.1. Elements of an effective paraphrase...................... 97
5.4.5.2. Techniques for paraphrasing 97
5.4.6. Quoting... 98
5.4.6.1. Short quotations 99
5.4.6.2. Long Quotations... 100
5.4.6.3. Punctuating Quotations.................................... 101
5.4.6.4. General hints on quotations............................... 105
5.5. Careful planning and safe practices to avoid plagiarism... 105

THE WRITING STAGE

Chapter 6 Writing the Introduction and the Main Body 113

6.1. Standard structure of the academic essay...................... 113
6.2. Writing the introduction 115

6.2.1. Parts of the Introduction:..115
6.2.2. Writing the thesis statement 116
6.2.3. Strategies for writing effective introductions 117
6.3. Writing the main body 118
6.3.1. Paragraph structure 118
6.3.2. The topic sentence in a paragraph 119
6.3.3. The Body of the Paragraph....................................120
6.3.4. Paragraph unity and coherence 121
6.3.5. Cohesive devices and examples 122
6.3.6. Paragraph development...124
6.3.6.1. Induction..124
6.3.6.2. Deduction..125
6.4. Methods of development of academic essays.................127
6.4.1. Definition essay 128
6.4.2. Descriptive essay 129
6.4.3. Narrative essay..130
6.4.4. Comparison and contrast.......................................130
6.4.5. Cause-and-effect essay 132
6.4.6. Classification and partition 133
6.4.7. Process essay...133
6.4.8. Opinion, or argument, essay..................................134

Chapter 7 Writing the Literature Review, Abstract, and
Case Study...139

7.1. Sections of the main body...139
7.1.1. Writing a literature review.....................................140
7.1.1.1. Giving your audience a general overview of the
sources of information 142
7.1.1.2 Identifying gaps and demonstrating the
contribution of your research to knowledge 142
7.1.2. Purpose (research problem) and contributions
(significance) of research 146
7.1.3. Writing an abstract..147
7.1.4. Writing a case study 149
7.2. Graphics and visual illustrations 151
7.2.1. Types and uses of graphics....................................151

Chapter 8 Writing the Conclusion 159

8.1. Conclusion techniques 161
8.1.1. Echo (refer back to the introduction and thesis
statement) 161
8.1.2. Summarize main points 162
8.1.3. Offer solutions to problems 163
8.1.4. Give warning 164
8.1.5. Address negative and positive consequences 165
8.1.6. Look to the future 165
8.1.7. Give opinion or speculation based on evidence 166
8.1.8. Recommend action 167
8.1.9. Give Advice 168
8.1.10. Answer the questions raised in the introduction 169
8.1.11. Ask questions 170
8.1.12. Make a prediction 171
8.1.13. Discuss Future Developments 172
8.1.14. Point out limitations and implications for
further study 172
8.2. What not to include in conclusions 173

Chapter 9 Writing in-Text Citations and Lists of References
in APA Style 176

9.1. Documentation and in-text citations 177
9.1.1. In-text citations 178
9.1.2. List of references at the end 178
9.2. Parenthetical referencing: an overview 180
9.3. The APA (American Psychological Association)
referencing and citation style 180
9.3.1. In-text citations in APA style 181
9.3.2. Writing the list of references in APA style 186

Chapter 10 Writing In-text Citations and the List of
References in Harvard Style 193

10.1. Introduction to the Harvard style of referencing
and citations 193
10.2. In-text citations in Harvard style 195

10.3. Writing the List of References in Harvard Style........... 205

Chapter 11 Writing In-text Citations and a Works Cited List in MLA Style.. 216

11.1. The history and evolution of MLA style...................... 216
11.2. The eighth edition of the MLA handbook.................. 217
11.3. MLA's list of core elements...................................... 218
11.4. The new concept of containers 221

Chapter 12 The Language of Academic Writing...................... 231

12.1. Types of sentences in English.................................. 232
12.1.1. The simple sentence: 233
12.1.2. The compound sentence 234
12.2. Basic English tenses and forms............................... 236
12.3. Basic English tense forms....................................... 237
12.4. Subjects and Verbs in Sentences 238
12.5. Tense and voice.. 239
12.6. Active and passive verbs 241
12.6.2. Passive verbs 241
12.6.2.1. Common errors of usage with the passive form 242
12.6.2.2. The passive voice is used in certain contexts........... 243
12.7. Phrases: types and uses.. 245
12.7.1. Prepositional phrases 245
12.7.2. Noun phrases 246
12.7.3. Gerund phrases.. 247
12.7.4. Infinitive phrases... 248
12.7.5. Verb phrases 249
12.7.6. Phrasal verbs... 249
12.8. Articles 251
12.8.1. The definite article "the" 251
12.8.2. The indefinite articles "a" and "an" 252

Chapter 13 Clauses, Adjectives, Adverbs, and Punctuation 254

13.1. Dependent Clauses and Types 255
13.1.1. Noun clause 255
13.1.2. Adjective clause... 256

13.1.3. Adverbial clause 256
13.2. Combining dependent and independent clauses 256
13.2.1. Combine by coordinating conjunctions 257
13.2.2. Combine by Subordinating Conjunctions 258
13.2.3. Combining by Relative Pronouns: 259
13.3 Common errors to avoid when writing clauses 261
12.3.1 Sentence fragments 261
13.3.2. Comma splices 261
13.3.3. Run-on (fused) sentences 262
13.4. Adjectives 263
13.4.1. Adjectives formed from verbs 263
13.4.2. Order of adjectives 265
13.4.3. Adjective endings 265
13.5. Adverbs 266
13.6. Punctuation 267
13.6.1. Comma 268
13.6.2. Full Stop (British English) / Period (American
English) 273
13.6.3. The colon 274
13.6.4. The semicolon 275
13.6.5. Quotation marks (American English) / inverted
commas (British English 276
13.6.6. Parentheses and brackets 277
13.6.7. The Hyphen 279

Chapter 14 The Style of Academic Writing 286

14.1. Academic style 287
14.2. Features of academic writing style 287
14.2.1. The overall picture 287
14.2.2. The tone of academic writing 288
14.2.3. The diction of academic writing 288
14.2.4. Language clarity and organizational structure 288
14.2.5. Adherence to academic conventions 289
11.2.6. Verifiability of evidence and strength of argument 289
14.2.7. Thesis formula 290
14.2.8. Complexity and higher-order thinking (HOT) 290
14.2.9. Formality of style 291
14.2.10. Objectivity, neutrality, and impartiality 291

14.3. Conciseness and how to achieve it 293

14.3.1. Use the active voice 294

14. 3.2. Put statements in positive form 295

14.3.3. Omit needless words 296

14.3.4. Avoid a succession of loose sentences 296

14.3.5. Combine sentences for conciseness, variety, and clarity 297

14.3.6. Combine sentences of equal weight 299

14. 3.7. Combine sentences of unequal weight 301

14.3.8. Reduce redundancy and wordiness 302

14. 3.8.1. Vary sentence length 303

14. 3.8.2. Vary rhythm by alternating short and long sentences 303

14.3.8.3. Vary sentence openings 304

14.4. General guidelines on style 305

14.5. Diction 306

14.5.1. Connotations 307

14.5.2. Types of bad diction to avoid 308

14.5.2.1. Clichés or triteness 308

14.5.2.2. Vagueness 308

14.5.2.3. Wordiness 309

14.6. Word choice: slang vs. formal language 309

14.7. Tone and voice 310

Chapter 15 Common Language and Style Errors 314

15.1. Sentence fragments 315

15.1.1. Common causes of sentence fragments 316

15.1.1.1. The present participle of verbs ("-ing") 316

15.1.1.2. Infinitives of verbs 317

15.1.1.3. Confusing the dependent clause and the main clause 318

15.1.1.4. Explanatory phrases 318

15.1.2. Types of sentence fragments 319

15.1.2.1. No main verb 320

15.1.2.2. No subject 320

15.2. Common types of sentence fragments 321

15.2.1. Run-on sentences 321

15.2.2. Comma splices 321

15.2.3. Fused sentences...322
15.2.4. Dangling modifiers 324
15.2.5. Misplaced modifiers 325
15.2.6. Parallel structures 326
15.3. Confusing words of quantity expression....................327
15.4. Confusing and commonly misspelt words.................329
15.4.1. Confusing pairs of words......................................330
15.4.2. Confusing and commonly misspelt words 330
15.5. Common style errors..331
15.5.1. Wordiness 331
15.5.1.1. Use of the passive voice 332
15.5.1.2. Nominalization...332
15.5.1.3. Padding: empty words and phrases 333
15.5.2. Patterns of wordiness and how to correct them..........333
15.5.3. Repetition 335

EDITING, PROOFREADING, FORMATTING, AND SUBMISSION

Chapter 16 Editing and Proofreading 341

16.1. Editing...342
16.1.1. Editing for content..342
16.1.2. Editing for clarity...342
16.1.3. Editing for paragraph unity and coherence 343
16.1.4. Editing for overall organizational structure 343
16.1.5. Editing for style 344
16.1.6. Editing for gender-sensitive language......................345
16.1.7. Editing for references and in-text citations...............346
16.2. Proofreading 346
16.2.1. An effective proofreading strategy...........................347
16.2.2. Checking for errors 349
16.2.2.1. Language errors...349
16.2.2.2. Checking for punctuation errors: comma errors 352
16.2.2.3. Checking for style, diction, and vocabulary errors...352
16.3. Strategies for editing and revising by computer 354

16.3.1. Using the computer to check spelling 355
16.3.2. Using the computer to check grammar 357
16.3.3. Criticism levelled against grammar checkers 357
16.3.4. Using the search-and-replace computer facility...... 359

Chapter 17 Formatting and Submission 364

17.1. General checklist of paper sections 365
17.2. General notes on formatting a research paper 366
17.3. General formatting guidelines for APA style 366
17.4. General formatting guidelines for Harvard style...... 370
17.5. General formatting guidelines for MLA style 374
17.6. Final draft...... 379
17.7. Final copy for binding and submission 379

Chapter 18 Samples and Illustrations 382

Sample Descriptive Essay 382
Sample Definition Essay 384
Sample Classification / Partition Essay 387
Sample Cause-and-Effect Essay 389
Sample Comparison/ Contrast Essay 392
Sample Process Essay 394
Sample Opinion / Argument Essay...... 397
Sample Survey Form...... 399
Sample Reference Page in APA Style 402
Sample Reference Page in Harvard Style...... 403
Sample list of works cited in MLA Style 405
Samples of Graphics and Visuals 406

Appendix I   List of Commonly Misused English Words 415
Appendix II List of Common Misspellings...... 423
Bibliography...... 425
Index...... 451

LIST OF FIGURES

Figure 1: Example Cartographic Presentation of Data.................. 57
(Source: https://en.wikipedia.org/wiki/OPEC)
Figure 2: Example Line Graph 156
(Global Mean Sea Surface Temperature 1880–2000)
Figure 3: Example Pie Chart 156
(Internet Users in Different Continents)
Figure 4: Example bar chart...157
(Contributors to Global Greenhouse Gas
Emissions in the Past 100–150 Years)

LIST OF TABLES

Table 1: Nominal and Ordinal Value Distribution 60
Table (2) How to Insert in-Text Citations in MLA Style
and Examples 223

CHAPTER 1

Introduction

Writing in general is a solitary activity; and academic research writing is more solitary, arduous, and rigorous. Dedication to a profession that demands seclusion, ardour, and rigour is perhaps what distinguishes academic professionals from ordinary people and accords them that deserved aura of respect and reverence; of being regarded as somewhat unworldly. This work, *Academic Research Writing*, highlights those features of academic writing as being rigorous, complex, original, and documented. Academic research demands a daunting amount of requirements that must be met, methods that must be strictly followed, values to be observed, and conventions to be adhered to for it to deserve the title "good academic work". Academic research is perhaps one of the most challenging tasks that can ever be undertaken. This is because researchers have to grapple not only with the complexities of academic subjects but also with a concomitant multitude of requirements pertaining to academic conventions, accuracy in language use, appropriacy of style, correctness of methods, reliability of information, and validity of results. It is precisely because of the complexity characteristic of research that it is rarely possible to find a book that covers all pertinent issues at one time. The norm is that many writings on research focus on a particular aspect within this many-faceted subject.

Available literature on academic research generally falls under one of three strands: (1) those that emphasize the technical aspects of research, such as methodologies, procedures, requirements, data, and analyses; (2) those that deal with the language and style of writing; and (3) those that focus on the type of audience. Researchers need all three, and this book gives them just that. It explains the methodological requirements and conceptual framework of conducting good academic research and gives a strong grounding in accurate language use and appropriate style required in academic writing. It also gives researchers guidance on how to avoid the most common language and style errors that usually vex writers. Additionally, this book is meant to address the research needs of a much wider audience than just college students. It targets various audiences, including graduate and graduating students, beginning as well as seasoned researchers, research institutions, college libraries, college writing teachers, and research supervisors. It blends the different approaches in one coherent sequential order, guiding the researcher step-by-step from a starting preparation stage to a finishing submission stage.

Academic Research Writing follows a certain structural order comprising three main consecutive stages: (1) a preparation stage, (2) a writing stage, and (3) a final editing and submission stage.

The preparation stage starts with an idea or question that the researcher wants to investigate, driven by various reasons, paramount of which is the quest to find answers to questions of academic, professional, or public concern. The idea usually starts in broad general lines which the researcher needs to narrow down to a more manageable scope that is researchable. Then a thesis is formulated to capture the specific aspects the researcher wants to focus on. The next step is to look for relevant sources of information to develop the thesis. Good and reliable sources of information need to be dug out from libraries, books, journals, encyclopedias, electronic online materials, databases, e-journals, and books. Care must be exercised to select the right sources by applying measures of selectivity and evaluation of the various sources. Also at this stage, the researcher needs to be familiar with important academic concepts, ethics, and conventions so that he or she follows appropriate academic practice, such as documentation, referencing, citation, and acknowledgement of the original sources used. After having found the suitable sources and having become familiar with requisite academic conventions, the researcher then sketches out an outline or a plan of the work in bare skeletal structure to form the basis for the next stage—the writing stage.

Second is the writing stage, which is when the researcher embarks on the actual writing process of the academic work. The writing process involves two elements: (1) the components of research and (2) the language and style of writing. The components include the various elements to be found in an academic work, such as table of contents, introduction, abstract, literature review, case study, methodology, data collection and analysis, discussion, and findings. The language of writing discusses the appropriate language to be used in academic discourse, the characteristics of academic language, linguistic accuracy, and proper diction. Another important aspect is style. Appropriate style is a key to distinguishing good academic work from a layman's. Objectivity, neutrality, impartiality, brevity, and conciseness are key characteristics in academic discourse. The researcher needs to be assisted on how to avoid the most common errors, and good lists of the most common language, style, and spelling errors are included to help writers avoid them. The writing process also includes guidelines on how to write good introductions, body paragraphs, and conclusions. The various conclusion techniques commonly used in academic essays are presented, with examples.

Third is the editing and submission stage, which starts from the point of compiling the first draft. The first draft is a rough work that needs revision, editing, and proofreading; it is to be edited first for major corrections, additions, omissions, and organization to smooth out the paper. After the first editing, the work is in the form of the second draft, which also needs thorough proofreading to correct minor errors in language, grammar, spelling, and punctuation. After everything has been done and the paper is completed in its "final draft", some final elements of formatting are necessary before submission. These include changes to the general layout, cover page, acknowledgements, page numbering, table of contents, lists of tables, font size, margins, graphic labelling, appendices, and indices to be written in proper format.

A general outline encompassing the three stages for writing research typically follows the steps shown below, and this book is carefully structured to follow them closely. At each step, researchers are guided on what to do and how to do it, with explanations of the methods and illustrations by way of examples.

The preparation stage comprises the following:

1. Choosing an idea or topic for research
2. Narrowing the topic and formulating a thesis
3. Preliminary reading to find suitable sources
4. Evaluating sources (print and electronic) for reliability
5. In-depth reading and note-taking
6. Preparing an outline
7. Learning the ethics of the academic community and the concepts of integrity and plagiarism
8. Learning how to avoid plagiarism by summarizing, paraphrasing, and quoting
9. Learning how to insert in-text citations properly in the body of a document
10. Establishing a methodology of research
11. Learning about data types and methods of collection

The writing stage comprises the following:

1. Writing the introduction
2. Writing the main body
3. Gaining an understanding of the language of academic writing
4. Applying the appropriate style
5. Learning about common language and style errors to avoid
6. Writing the literature review
7. Writing a case study
8. Writing an abstract
9. Writing the conclusion
10. Writing the list of references
11. Learning about three referencing styles: APA, Harvard and MLA
12. Writing tables, graphics, and charts

The editing, proofreading, and submission stage comprises the following:

1. Preparing the first draft
2. Editing the first draft for major changes
3. Proofreading for language errors
4. Proofreading for style errors
5. Preparing the final draft
6. Checking the format
7. Formatting in APA Style
8. Formatting in Harvard Style
9. Formatting in MLA Style
10. Reviewing the submission checklist

Closely following the sequence of steps shown above for conducting research, this book is carefully structured to guide researchers at each step in sequential order. The purpose of this unique organizational structure is to help researchers carry out their research effectively and smoothly in clear successive stages. This is meant to guard researchers against feelings of dismay, leading to falling morale, which usually happens when researchers discover at some point that they have to make changes—sometimes major changes—in earlier sections upon realizing that what was written earlier was not correct in light of what they learned later in the course of writing. This situation of retracking and rewriting has often been a major problem with research, entailing the waste of valuable time, increased effort, frustration, and loss of morale. Bearing this in mind, and to avoid such frustrating situations, this book is organized to correspond closely to the steps in actual research, and it is therefore organized as outlined below.

Organization of the Book

The book falls in three main parts and eighteen chapters, with appendices and an index.

Part I, "The Preparation Stage", consists of four chapters, starting from chapter 2 (chapter 1 being the introduction).

Chapter 2 focuses on the preliminary stages of how to choose a topic suitable for research and how to focus it to a manageable scope. The chapter stresses the importance of using effective strategies of reading as a necessary step to good writing. Related to reading is the importance of evaluating sources of information, and guidance is given on how to evaluate both print and internet sources, annotate sources, and take effective notes. The chapter ends with recommendations on writing an outline to sketch out the main sections and subsections that will form the main body of the research; an example outline is provided.

Chapter 3 deals with the methodology of research. It explains the main methods—namely the qualitative and quantitative methods— and notes that a combined method is generally preferred. It also covers the types of data obtained from primary and secondary sources. The chapter provides detailed coverage of the methods of data collection and treatment. It discusses four common methods of primary data collection—namely interviews, observations, surveys, and questionnaires, explaining their differences and highlighting the merits and limitations of each. The chapter ends with a summary on the treatment, processing, analysis, and presentation of data.

Chapter 4 alerts researchers in the academic field to the important aspect of academic ethics, values, and conventions generally observed by academic professionals. Essentially, the ethical values of integrity, honesty, and impartiality constitute the dividing line between true academic spirit dedicated to the pursuit of knowledge and ordinary people's pursuits. The chapter advocates that researchers should adhere faithfully to the ethics of the academic community and shun practices that violate them, such as plagiarism and other types of academic misconduct. The imperative for good ethical conduct is enshrined in religion, philosophy, and psychology.

Chapter 5 deals with plagiarism as a form of academic misconduct that is in breach of academic ethics regarding honesty and integrity. It gives an account of what constitutes plagiarism, its degrees, and its extent among university students. The chapter highlights the important research findings that relate academic dishonesty at college to future dishonesty in the workplace. The chapter concludes with recommendations on how to avoid plagiarism by educating students on ethical conduct and by proper instruction on the best strategies to use in order to avoid it, such as summarizing, paraphrasing, quotation, proper documentation, and acknowledgement of sources.

By the end of the preparation stage, the researcher has done the necessary readings, evaluated sources, selected relevant ones, taken accurate notes to use in the research, and drawn an outline sketching out the main sections and subsections of her or his research. The researcher has also gained clear understanding of the methods of research, data types, and methods on how to collect and analyse data. Before the researcher actually starts writing, he or she also needs to be aware of ethical values so crucial in the academic world—especially the importance of observing the ethics of honesty and integrity, and shunning dishonest practices, such as plagiarism. Equipped with this essential pre-writing knowledge, the researcher is now ready to go into the writing stage proper.

Part II, "The Writing Stage", consists of ten chapters, starting from chapter 6.

Chapter 6 starts the writing process, beginning with writing the introduction and the main body of research. It shows how to open one's work by writing an attractive introduction that captures the reader's attention and sets the boundaries of the work. The introduction also includes a thesis statement that focuses the work and indicates the issues that will be discussed in the main body. The main body consists of the paragraphs that develop and support the thesis stated at the end of the introduction. This chapter gives guidance on how to write good paragraphs, starting with an opening topic sentence followed by the development of the main idea through different methods of development. Paragraphs are unified and linked together by cohesive devices to lend logic and flow to the argument. Chapter 7 is closely linked to chapter 6; it continues with items related to composing the main body, including writing the abstract, literary review, contributions of research, and case studies as essential parts in longer pieces of research. The chapter explains these sections and what to include in them, and it provides examples for each. Chapter 8 continues in the same vein of the writing process; it deals with the writing of the conclusion. This chapter provides a summary of the various conclusion techniques (fifteen of them) commonly used in academic papers. It also includes some suggestions on what not to include in conclusions.

Chapter 9 deals with the important and thorny subject of writing citations and references. The chapter starts with an introduction on the concepts of documentation, in-text citations, and referencing as essential requirements in academic writings. It explains how to carry out the processes of citing and referencing properly, in three of the most widely used referencing styles—namely, the American Psychological Association (APA) style, the Harvard style, and the Modern Language Association (MLA) style. Each of the three styles is discussed in a separate chapter; chapter 9 explains how to write in-text citations and lists of references in APA style, chapter 10 is devoted to Harvard style, and Chapter 11 to MLA style.

Chapter 12 gauges the various aspects of the language used in academic writing. Essentially, this chapter deals with the use of accurate language in terms of correct grammar, sentence structure, subject and verb agreement, and the correct use of phrases and articles. The chapter provides a concise summary of the basic grammatical rules which writers need to know in order to write accurately in a way that makes their meanings easy to follow and clear to understand (as accurate language is necessary for the purposes of readability and clarity). Chapter 13 continues with language issues, focusing on accuracy of usage, such as the proper uses of clauses, adjectives, and adverbs. This chapter explains some problematic issues related to clauses and adjectives, seeks to dispel the confusion they create, and gives suggestions on how to correct common errors that are likely to occur in writing them. The chapter concludes with a summary on the right use of punctuation: the comma, full stop, semicolon, quotation marks, etc.

Chapter 14 is devoted to the style of academic writing. It provides an explanation of style, as well as the features of academic style and what distinguishes it from other styles of writing. It highlights important features of academic style, such as objectivity, impartiality, formality, and documentation of sources. A distinctive feature of academic style is conciseness, and a detailed discussion is given on how to achieve conciseness in writing. Diction and word choice are two important features too.

Chapter 15 is the last chapter related to the writing stage. It alerts writers to the common language and style errors that writers are likely to make. Common language errors include sentence fragments, run-on or fused sentences, dangling and misplaced modifiers, and parallel structures. Another area of concern is the confusion associated with the use of quantity expressions, such as *some, much, many, a lot, a little, a few*, etc. Common spelling errors are a major concern for writers at all levels, and an understanding of the most vexing spelling issues in English will help writers reduce spelling errors to a minimum. This chapter provides writers with lists of the confusing and most commonly misspelt words in English. Common errors of style include patterns of wordiness, redundancy, and repetition.

Part III, "The Editing, Proofreading, Formatting, and Submission Stage", is the final part, and it consists of two chapters.

Chapter 16 discusses editing, proofreading, and editing by computer. Editing has to be carried out on multiple levels relating to content, clarity, citations, references, organizational structure, and coherence. This chapter suggests formulating an effective proofreading strategy to meticulously check the minute errors in language, style, spelling, and punctuation. The computer can be a useful tool in detecting and correcting errors; however, the computer should be used sparingly and in conjunction with editing by a human.

Chapter 17 is devoted to giving guidance on the last stages of formatting and submitting research. It provides a general checklist of elements that have to be included. Formatting the final draft requires careful attention to the many requirements demanded by various formatting styles. The chapter highlights the guidelines required for formatting research papers according to APA, Harvard, and MLA styles, with examples and illustrations of how to make changes properly. Finally, some suggestions are given on preparing the final copy for binding and submission.

Chapter 18, "Samples and Illustrations", is intended as an additional chapter to enable research writers to see concrete examples of elements of research of which they may have only an unclear idea. The chapter aims to give them a clearer picture by providing visual illustrations of them. Samples are given of essays of various types, such as narrative, descriptive, opinion, and comparison and contrast, which would not have been possible to include in the main body of the book. Graphics and visual illustrations are another area in which there is special need among researchers to see concrete examples of the various types and uses of visuals and graphics, such as charts, tables, graphs, etc.

The appendices include three lists. Appendix 1 is a list of commonly misused words, appendix 2 gives a list of commonly misspelt words, and appendix 3 gives examples of dangling and misplaced modifiers.

The index lists the main entries of the most salient themes, terms, words, and concepts alluded to in the book, with page numbers.

PART I
The Preparation Stage

CHAPTER 2

Reading and Evaluating Sources, Data Types, and Treatment

Abstract: The onset of the preparation stage occurs with the researcher's choice of topic. Carefully choosing a "researchable" topic that is of interest to the researcher and focusing it are key to a successful project. After having a clear idea about the topic, the researcher turns to collecting primary information required to formulate a work plan, roughly outlining the main sections and chapters of the research. The outline directs the researcher to see what information he or she needs to look for in available literature and other sources. That leads the researcher to read relevant sources and employ various reading strategies to get the required information. More important, one needs to evaluate the worth and relevance of information in the sources. Evaluating sources is necessary, considering the vast volume of information available in this digital age. The researcher needs to take extra care to ascertain that the sources from which information is obtained are reliable and trustworthy—especially internet sources. After finding the right information, the researcher annotates it, highlighting main ideas and important details, raising questions, writing comments, and making notes. At the end of this stage, the researcher prepares an outline or plan to guide him or her through the work.

Keywords: focusing the topic, evaluating print and electronic sources, evaluating URLs, reading strategies, note-taking, outlining, methodology, data types, interviews, observations, surveys, questionnaires, data treatment

2.1. Choosing and focusing the topic

It is important for the researcher to choose a topic that interests him or her. Interest will maintain the momentum, especially at times of uncertainty, fluctuating morale, and mood swings typical of research life. But interest alone is not enough. It is equally important to choose a topic that is researchable—that is, one that has sufficient and varied sources of information, is manageable to the researcher within the scope of his or her field of knowledge, lends itself to elaboration and development, and can yield verifiable results. Experience shows that many students start research once they have decided on a topic that has captured their imagination, only to discover later, after having wasted valuable time; that they have found few or no reliable sources for their topic of choice. Again, some students are captivated with a certain topic, later to discover that it is too complex, too difficult, or unfamiliar to them, and that they are poorly equipped to deal with complexities posed by the topic. In choosing a topic of research, the researcher needs also to consider ways to elaborate on and develop the thesis of the research. Not all topics are amenable to elaboration, and the student may choose a topic but find it cannot be pushed beyond a limited boundary. In those cases, the final product is a thin piece of work that looks much like an immature newborn. Choosing a topic for research, then, has to meet at least two conditions:

1. It is interesting.
2. Is researchable; that is,

   a. it has sufficient sources of information,
   b. it relates to a subject familiar to the researcher,
   c. it can be elaborated on and developed, and
   d. it is apt to yield results.

Focusing the topic

After the researcher feels comfortable with the chosen topic, he or she needs to focus the topic. Focusing the topic is a delicate matter that needs close and careful attention. It is worthwhile to take time focusing the topic, as this will save valuable time and effort later. Usually, students choose broad areas or subjects for research, which may prove impractical within the constraints of time and resources. Therefore, it is necessary to narrow the scope of research to a manageable proportion. This can be conveniently reflected in the title of the research to capture both the general area of the subject matter and its specific focus. The two parts of the title are referred to as the *main title* and the *subtitle*.

To illustrate the above, a student of mechanical engineering may want to do research on the combustion engine. The combustion engine is a broad area of research. The student may want to focus on any of a number of possible foci or angles: main types of combustion engines, how the combustion engine works, the parts and the function of each of those parts, uses of the combustion engine, advantages of the combustion engine compared to other types of engines, disadvantages of the combustion engine, and so on. An indication of the relationship of the general topic to the specific focus is usually reflected in the title, which captures both the general area and the specific focus of the research, and it should be expressed clearly in the thesis statement. Table 1 illustrates how a general topic can be focused to address different angles.

General Topics and Specific Focuses for Common Subjects of Research

General Topic	Specific Focuses (for Thesis Statement)
Endangered Animals	Examples of endangered animals: the case of the Panda The ivory trade endangering the African elephant The white tiger as an example of endangered animals
Global Warming	Causes and effects of global warming Global warming: the need for substantial reductions in CO_2 emissions Fossil fuels: culprit of global warming
The Turbocharged Engine	Uses and operation of the turbocharged engine; How the turbocharged engine works
The Internet	How the internet affects our lives in positive and negative ways History of the development of the computer industry and the internet; How the internet affects our lives Effects of internet on business efficiency
Smartphones	Main types and differences of smartphones Effects of smartphones on classroom teaching environments Features of smartphones Software downloading in smartphones
Traffic Congestion	Effects of traffic congestion in city centres Effects of traffic congestion on business productivity Traffic congestion and road rage Traffic congestion and urban pollution

Domestic Violence	Effects of domestic violence on children Main causes of domestic violence Types of domestic violence Bad workplace environments as possible causes of domestic violence
Small Businesses	Financing small businesses Small businesses as family enterprises in Saudi Arabia Small businesses and the conglomerate threat Small businesses as a mechanism of wealth distribution
Solar Energy	Advantages and disadvantages of solar energy Cost-effectiveness of solar energy A comparison between solar energy and fossil fuels Solar energy and sustainability
Recycling	The environmental benefits of recycling Paper recycling and the positive impact for forest regeneration Incentives to encourage a culture of recycling Some success stories of waste recycling
Space Exploration	NASA's visits to Mars Possibilities for the colonization of Mars Costs and benefits of exploring space The role of space exploration in advancing science
Seawater Desalination Plants	Desalination plants with reference to Saudi Arabia's experience Costs of providing clean water in arid lands Desalination plants and the future water shortage

After choosing and focusing the topic, the next step is to look for and read the sources of information that the researcher will need to fall back on in developing the research thesis.

2.2. Reading as a necessary first step to writing

Research writers need to appreciate that reading is the first step necessary to writing good research. On the strong connection between reading and writing, Wyrick observes that it is not surprising that "good readers become good writers themselves" by emulating examples of the good writing they read. Like any other craftspeople, they acquire good skills from following the good examples of other experts in the trade, such as singers listening to good vocalists, tennis players watching championship matches, and medical students observing famous surgeons, ultimately "all with an eye to improving their own craft" (Wyrick 2014, p. 178). Exposure to a wide range of good examples of prose written by lucid writers is a key to developing a good mastery of writing by following examples. Developing good reading skills and observing how other writers present, organize, and communicate meanings help writers gain useful insights to follow in their writings. Reading, therefore, involves a number of important exercises necessary for writing.

- using different reading skills to look for various types of information
- identifying main ideas, details, examples, and other smaller details
- dealing with different levels of text complexity
- identifying and evaluating good reading materials
- reading from books, journals, encyclopedias, and other printed sources
- reading from the internet, websites, and other electronic sources
- finding and evaluating academic sources—especially internet ones
- developing effective reading to easily find the needed information from a source
- gaining exposure to good examples of academic discourse, style, and form

2.2.1. Preliminary overview reading to select suitable sources

The explosion of information in today's world, mediated through information technology, poses both opportunities and challenges to researchers. The massive increase in the volume of information gives researchers an abundance of data. At the same time, researchers are overwhelmed by the sheer amount of information and have to make strategic decisions about what types and amounts of information to select, and what to leave out. This is not an easy task as it appears; it takes time and effort to sift through the mass of information to select just what is needed. The researcher first makes the visit to the library to look for basic sources of information on the chosen research topic. The researcher needs to establish whether relevant and varied sources on the topic can be found, and on what basis to determine whether to carry on with the topic or drop it. Then the researcher selects from the vast array of sources—made abundantly available by today's technology—the ones that are especially relevant to his or her focus.

Selecting the right sources is not an easy task. The mass of information demands a careful evaluation of the various sources, both print and electronic. Researchers have to make decisions not only about the material itself but also about the author, his or her affiliations with institutions, and, possibly, the website, to ensure that the author is trustworthy and the material reliable. It is important, therefore, that researchers consider the following points when evaluating their sources of information.

2.2.2. Evaluating print and electronic sources

It is necessary to carry out a careful evaluation of both print and electronic sources to decide on their relevance and reliability. Generally, print sources are more reliable than internet sources. This is because print sources usually come from publishing companies which take utmost care to produce publications of high quality to meet the standards required by customers. Therefore, print sources go through a rigorous and lengthy process of editing, reviewing, checking, formatting, and proofreading. Publishing houses have professional reviewers, checkers, and proofreaders as part of their staff. Additionally, publishers seek established authors, academics, and researchers affiliated with known research institutions, universities, and organizations to ensure high quality and credibility.

Print sources, though highly valuable and reliable, are not as easy to get as electronic sources; they can involve costs of subscription or purchase, though they may also be obtained through loan from university or public libraries. Internet sources, on the other hand, largely lack the important checks that print sources have; and any person with a penchant for writing can write and post material on websites and blogs. Such material may be lacking in important features of credibility and reliability required in academic discourse. Most documents found on websites do not have editors, fact-checkers, or other types of reviewers and, as a result, are often strewn with language, spelling, punctuation, and factual errors. Some internet sources, though, may contain brilliant ideas and valuable content; and together with the abundance of information and ease of access, such sources make compensating factors that can offset the loss of the more reliable, yet costly, print sources. It is important to note that some sources, such as journal or newspaper articles, can be found in both print and electronic form.

2.2.2.1. *Evaluating internet sources*

When evaluating internet sources, there are several important criteria you need to consider when ascertaining the reliability of the sources. The first and most obvious is the website address, which is usually contained in the uniform resource locator (URL). These web addresses enable users to send and receive a wide range of information. Understanding how URLs work is necessary to help internet users know about the people or organizations they communicate with.

2.2.2.2. *Evaluating URLs before reading*

URLs contain four main sections, denoted as follows:

1. Type of transfer
2. Server name, or domain name
3. Directory/subdirectory
4. Filename / file type

Every URL has information directly before and after the //, but the last two elements may or may not be present. The first two (type of transfer://server name or domain name) are essential to ascertain the reliability of the site. The part of the URL that relates to the type of transfer indicates the type of information being transferred. The server name, or domain name, on the other hand, tells you about the location of the website. The URL will tell you a number of important issues about the nature of the site, its creators, their purpose behind creating it, and the type of audience it targets. The URL also tells you if the sponsoring organization is a company, an academic institution, or a for-profit or non-profit-making entity. These are contained in the domain name. The domain name comes after the World Wide Web (www) designation and usually gives the name and nature of the sponsoring organization; for example, the domain name *www.jic. edu.sa* refers to Jubail Industrial College on the World Wide Web as an educational institution in the country of Saudi Arabia. Domain names are styled in suffixes such as *.com*, *.net*, *.gov*, and *.org*.

.com refers to a commercial site. The information provided by commercial interests is generally going to shed a positive light on the products it promotes. While the information gleaned from such a website might not necessarily be false, you might be getting only part of the picture.

.edu refers to an educational institution. Sites using this domain name are schools ranging from kindergarten to higher education. If it

is from a department or research centre at an educational institution, it can generally be taken as credible.

.gov refers to a governmental site. Such sites give information such as census statistics, parliamentary hearings, and supreme court rulings. The information is considered to be from a credible source.

.org traditionally refers to a non-profit-making organization. Generally, the information in these types of sites is credible and unbiased.

.mil refers to a military website used by the armed forces.

.net refers to *network*. Any kind of site can use this domain suffix. Information from these sites should be given careful scrutiny.

(University of South Carolina, 2017)

2.2.2.3. *Criteria to evaluate URL sources*

It is important that researchers are able to judge the worth of website sources. This is for the sake of getting trustworthy, reliable information and saving time. There are five criteria on which URL source reliability can be judged, as outlined below.

Stance

Stance refers to the point of view the website adopts. To judge the information provided, ask the legitimate question, what is the stance or point of view the website upholds? Try to find answers to questions about whether the view presented is biased or neutral. What is the purpose of the page? Is the purpose stated or not, and if stated, does it spell out clearly the intention: to inform, teach, entertain, sell, or explain? Finding answers to such questions will give you a clear indication as to whether the information you obtain from URLs is reliable and trustworthy or whether it is biased and unreliable.

Currency

Currency refers to whether the information is up to date or dated. It is also important to see whether the information is updated on a regular basis or not, and how frequently the updates or revisions occur. Regular updates, revisions, and additions indicate that the page is popular.

Accuracy

Accuracy refers to the reliability, credibility, and truthfulness of the information obtained from a website. Determine whether the information includes documentation of sources, references, and in-text citations crediting original authors. Sources that are documented and credited are more reliable than those that are not. Also look for language errors relating to grammar, spelling, and punctuation. Such errors indicate that the material was written hastily and carelessly and is lacking academic rigour, indicating that it may be unreliable.

Relevance

Relevance refers to the content of information posted on the website and its relevance to the topic under investigation. Ask questions about whether the information is directly relevant and pertinent to your topic of research. Ask questions such as these: Is the topic covered adequately and in depth? Is it relevant to your research? Does it give you new insights and a fresh understanding of the topic? Is the material written in accurate language and presented in an acceptable format that complies with observed academic conventions?

Authority

Authority basically refers to the authority associated with the website or its management. In evaluating authority, ask questions such as these: Who manages the website? Do they have the right qualifications to run the page? Are they well known in the field?

Are they affiliated with reputed institutions or organizations, such as universities, research institutions, or international organizations? What is the entity of the organization managing the website— is it a government, an academic institution, a business, a private individual, or a company? More importantly, look at the domain; is it .com .edu .gov .org, or .net? Such information gives you a clear indication about the authority of the source.

Some general questions you might want to ask about an author and website are as follows:

- Is the name of the author given? Is he or she a well-known author?
- Is the language written in a good academic style?
- Are there mistakes in grammar, spelling, or sentences? If you find mistakes, this means it was written carelessly and cannot be reliable.
- Is it a reputable website? Is it academic?
- Is the site educational, with *.edu* in the URL?
- Is the author a well-known professional in the given field?
- If the author is not well-known, is the site run by an established authority on the subject?
- Has the author been widely quoted or referred to by reputed authorities in the field?
- Does the author include a contact address so that he or she can be contacted?
- Is she or he biased or impartial?
- Is the website administered by an individual, or is it administered by an organization, academic institution, or other group?
- Is a date given for publication or revision?
- Does it cover the subject matter adequately and in depth?

For accuracy and reliability of information, see if the source includes references to other sources or authors, bibliographies or citations, and URLs.

2.2.3. Developing an effective reading strategy

Once you have decided on what material to read, you need to develop an effective reading strategy to get the most out of your sources in the most economical amount of time. Here is a three-pronged reading strategy:

1. Read quickly as an overview to get the gist and decide on the relevance of material
2. Use close reading to get specific relevant information.
3. Use critical reading to evaluate the reliability of information as you read.

2.2.3.1. *Reading for overview:*

Look to the title (and subtitle) and decide whether they are relevant to your purpose. The title gives the broad subject area (e.g., building materials); while the subtitle gives the specific focus (the use of glass as a building material in tall buildings). Both the title and subtitle give you a condensed summary of what the paper is about.

Read the table of contents and see whether there are sections relevant to you. The table of contents is a detailed listing of the chapters, sections, and subsections included inside the body of the research, together with their page numbers. The table of contents gives you an overview of the topics in broad sections or headings. It helps you to see whether there are sections or topics that are relevant to your research purpose.

Read the index. The index is a detailed listing of all the topics covered in the book source, usually appearing at the end of the text. It shows you in alphabetical order the topics that are discussed and gives you the page numbers on which a certain topic has been mentioned in the various sections throughout the book. Topics are listed alphabetically in the index and are called entries. Each entry of a topic is shown with some additional phrases as it appears in the different pages in the work.

Encyclopedia indexes are extremely useful for finding the right sources for rich materials; however, they are a little more complicated than book indexes. Encyclopedias come in volumes. Each volume covers articles under one letter of the alphabet; for example, volume M contains articles on subjects beginning with the letter M (e.g., *magnetic field*). Sometimes topics may not be easily included in certain lettered volumes. In this case, you may look up the topic in the index, where you may find information on the volume, page number, and quartile. The index will help you find the topics that are relevant to your purposes; at the same time, it gives you the page numbers on which you can read more in depth to decide how relevant the information is to your research.

Read the abstract (if there is one) and part of the introduction and conclusion The abstract is a brief half-page summary of the whole work. It succinctly presents the topic, the purpose, the method, and the main findings of the research. Spending only two minutes reading an abstract saves you much time. From the abstract, you can decide whether the source is relevant to you and determine whether to go on and read further or not.

If you feel that the source is good, you may go on to read some paragraphs, or to read only topic sentences from some paragraphs. These simple steps will save you the time and effort that can be wasted in embarking on reading a source, only to discover after reading it that it is not relevant.

2.2.3.2. *Critical reading and source annotation*

After you feel satisfied that the sources you have evaluated are suitable and relevant to your research, go on to read in depth those that you have evaluated and selected. Evaluate in depth the information contained in those sources you have chosen. Ask questions about the reliability of material, the trustworthiness of the author, the date of the information, the language and style, the objectivity or bias, and the documentation and references. Write the source details down (author, title, date, and publication details) for reference.

One of the most useful reading strategies is annotating your sources while reading them. Annotation means marking the source by highlighting main ideas and important details by asking questions, by scribbling notes in the margins to record your impressions and evaluations about the source, and by writing comments and making notes. This process is sometimes called critical reading. When reading critically, you don't read passively but become fully engaged in what you read by imputing your own ideas, making the source your own. When annotating, consider asking questions about the material and the language.

Critically evaluate the material and the language

Critically evaluating the material and the language in which it is written gives you important clues on the reliability of the source. See whether the content gives facts or opinions, or whether it tries to promote products and services. If it gives facts, are these backed up by evidence, with the original sources acknowledged? It is also important to check the accuracy and validity of the information given. For the language, assess the style of writing and look for any errors in spelling, grammar, structure, or punctuation. If you spot slang words, language errors, and improper punctuation, this is a clear indication that the source was carelessly written and therefore cannot be reliable.

2.2.3.3. *In-depth reading and note-taking:*

At this stage, you have identified the sources that are relevant to your topic and have annotated specific sections you feel are of special value. You will need to read these sections in depth to find main ideas and the most important details to note down for later use in your research. Then you take notes of this useful information for inclusion in your research. Note-taking involves recording specific details of information from sources. Notes are condensed pieces of information that may include facts, statistics, tables, dates, figures, graphics, and quotations. Notes have to be concise, brief, and accurate because they will make up important parts of the main body of your research. Taking notes ensures that you won't need to go back to again dig information out from the original sources.

Effective note-taking requires that you condense the information in brief points by omitting unnecessary words, such as verbs, prepositions, and articles. Notes are short, simple phrases, not sentences. Summarize the main points from the original text and paraphrase ideas in your own words. Notes require skill in identifying main ideas and important details in a text. Effective notes make good use of symbols (e.g., $\neq$, $\geq$, $\frac{2}{3}$, $=$ $\uparrow$) and abbreviations (e.g., *e.g.*, *etc.*). The most important thing about notes is that they should be clear enough that you understand them when you need to use them later on. Therefore, you need to develop your own style and determine how to interpret your notes when you need them later.

Notes can be recorded on note cards or written down in note files on your computer. The salient pieces of information to include are

- a topic heading (the main idea of the note);
- the source and the date of source (including website addresses, URLs, and DOIs);
- a few points relevant to the topic, bulleted or numbered;
- chapter, section, or page numbers, especially in the case of quotations; and
- card numbers (for ordering according to themes or sections).

2.3. Preparing an outline

The next step after finding suitable sources of information and evaluating them is planning how you are going to organize your work before you actually start writing. It is important to start your organization plan by drawing an outline sketching out the main sections and subsections of your research, and the ideas you will include in each section. The various sections and subsections, headings and subheadings, should be arranged in a consistent manner that reflects the logical flow of ideas in your argument. A plan is important and helps you focus your topic, see the logical connections between ideas, and see gaps in information, and it guides you through to a successful completion of your paper. Your outline, therefore, should be a logical description of your work. A good outline states the main points and minor points, and gives a true summary of contents of a paper, clearly showing its pattern of organization and logical flow.

An outline follows a certain organizational structure, stating main headings, subheadings, and minor points in a hierarchical order according to levels of importance. Each lower level of importance is listed one level to the right, labelled by a letter or number. Points of equal importance are listed flush with other points at that level.

Following is an example of an outline:

Organizational Structure of a College

Outline

Introduction

Main Body

1. Administration
    1.1.   College management
    1.2.   The Finance Department

1.3.	The Personnel Department
1.4.	The Students Affairs Department
1.4.1.	Student registration
1.4.2.	Student accommodation
1.5.	The Logistics and Procurement Department

2. Academics

2.1.	Academic departments
2.1.1.	Engineering Department
2.1.2.	Technical Department
2.1.3.	Chemistry Department
2.1.4.	Management Department
2.1.5.	IT Department
2.1.6.	The English Language Institute
2.2.	Academic staff
2.3.	Facilities
2.3.1.	Library
2.3.2.	Computer labs
2.3.3.	Physics labs
1.1.4	Chemistry labs
1.1.5	Language labs

3. Students

3.1.	Prep-year students
3.2.	Student majors
3.3.	Students' assessment and attendance

Conclusion

Drawing an outline is important for the successful execution of your research. It helps in the following ways:

- gives you a clear picture of the sections of research in which to look for relevant information

- helps you decide on what information to include and what information not to include
- guides you through the research to a successful and convenient completion
- gives you clarity about what to write in the introduction and body
- organizes your research in sections and subsections, topic headings and subheadings
- organizes your ideas logically so you can see the connections between them clearly
- sets a frame of reference so you don't stray or lose sight
- enables you to see which sections have been covered and which have not
- helps you to identify gaps where information is needed
- helps you to divide your work into manageable target tasks and to manage your time accordingly to achieve targets

After having found suitable sources of information, evaluated them, and drawn an outline for your research, the next step is to deal with issues of methodology. You also need to choose the appropriate methods to collect the data you will need to answer the questions raised in the research thesis. It should be stated that good research requires both primary and secondary data.

Chapter References

Driscoll, Dana Lynn, and Allen Brizee (February 2013). "Evaluating Sources: Overview". The Writing Lab and the OWL at Purdue and Purdue University. Accessed 19 November 2016.

University of South Carolina (2017). "Evaluating Information - STAAR Method: URL and What It Can Tell You". University of Carolina Upstate Library Guides. Last updated 15 March 2017. Accessed 27 March 2017. http://uscupstate.libguides.com/STAAR_Web_Evaluation.

Wyrick, Jean (2014). Steps to Writing Well. 12th ed. Wadsworth Cengage Learning: Boston, Massachusetts. ISBA-13: 978-1-133-31131-7.

CHAPTER 3

Methodology and Data Types

Abstract: Methodology is perhaps the most prominent feature that distinguishes academic research from other types of writing, and it distinguishes sound academic research from weak academic research. Adhering to rigorous methodological measurements lends reliability, validity, and originality to the research results. This chapter gives the researcher a concise summary of the commonly used methods of research—namely, qualitative and quantitative research—in addition to a synopsis of the two main types of data: secondary sources and primary sources. A detailed description is then given of four commonly used methods of collecting primary data—interviews, observations, surveys, and questionnaires—with details about how to properly conduct these types of research, and how to maintain objectivity and avoid bias. The uses, merits, and limitations of each research type are explained as well.

Keywords: primary sources, secondary sources, data collection, interviews, observations, questionnaires, surveys, data treatment

3.1. Methodology

Methodology is an important requirement of good research. Researchers should state clearly the methods they intend to use in carrying out their research. Methodology remains an essential requirement of academic research, since the results of the research will need to be evaluated and judged for validity, and the only way to do this is by testing results against the hypotheses and the methodology that has been used to collect the data, and analysing them and the results obtained accordingly. Methodology provides the surest yardstick against which to verify the validity of the research results.

Different types of research methods are used, or a combination of them. Generally, there are three major methods:

1. The quantitative method (based on empirical evidence)
2. The qualitative method (based on causality and the inductive and deductive methods)
3. A combination of the two methods mentioned above

3.1.1. A Combined Qualitative and Quantitative Approach

In this method, data collection and analysis methods are combined to complement each other. Since each method has merits and limitations, researchers are advised to combine the two. Adopting a combined approach improves the overall quality of research by ensuring that the limitations of one type of data are offset by the strengths of the other. However, this combined method requires careful planning on how the two types of data can be balanced to achieve the best results. The researcher can choose the best way to collect data from among a number of possible options:

- parallel data gathering—gathering qualitative and quantitative data at the same time
- sequential data gathering—collecting one type of data first and then using it to inform the collection of the other type, in a sequential order

She or he then can decide on the type of design to follow:

a. A component design, in which the researcher collects sets of quantitative and qualitative data independently and then combines them at the end for interpretation and conclusions

or

b. An integrated design, in which the researcher combines different options during the evaluation process to lend better understanding and evaluation.

3.1.2. Merits of a combined qualitative and quantitative approach:

Combining a qualitative and quantitative method has a several advantages. Doing so is

- enriching, in that qualitative data is used to identify required data not obtained through qualitative methods;
- examining, in that it raises issues and questions from one method to be tested by the other method,
- explanatory, in that it uses qualitative data to understand unanticipated results from quantitative data, and
- triangulating (confirming, reinforcing, and rejecting), in that it verifies or rejects results from quantitative data using qualitative data (or vice versa)

(BetterEvaluation 2017)

3.2. Data Types

Data appear in print and electronic forms and are collected from major sources, such as encyclopedias, journals, holy books, classics, main references, and textbooks. These constitute the main pillars in any research, since they give the foundational dimensions of the field of research and help researchers form ideas and sharpen their focus of inquiry. Researchers need to be familiar with three major schools of thought that underpin current research paradigms—the Western, the socialist, and the Islamic approaches to knowledge— noting variations in interpretations that exist within each of the three paradigms (Mohammed 2008). Generally, there are two main types of data:

1. Secondary sources (published materials)
2. Primary sources (raw data collected first-hand)

3.2.1. Secondary sources of data

Secondary sources comprise existing literature written on the subject by other writers. The information obtained from such sources makes up the initial background upon which the researcher builds important subsequent decisions on the chosen topic of research, its scope, and its viability as a researchable topic. These sources enable the researcher to see what has already been written, in order to identify possible gaps in the available literature and to determine whether or not the chosen topic adds to existing knowledge. Secondary sources are economical, time-saving, and helpful in the overall understanding of the problem under investigation. Additionally, existing literature helps the researcher to narrow down the scope of research and sharpen its focus to a manageable proportion. Secondary sources of data include

- encyclopedia articles,
- book sources,
- periodical articles,
- publications of public libraries,
- databases,
- internet (electronic) sources, and
- newspaper articles.

Encyclopedia articles are useful starting points, since they provide general introductions on almost any subject, and that gives researchers a convenient start to gauge the topic and form a good first understanding of its nature and scope. Relevant books on the subject of inquiry also provide solid background—especially those written by experts in a given field. Books give both classic and current views on subjects, depending on whether the publication is dated or new.

Periodical articles are essential requirements in any serious research, since they provide current information on almost every specialized discipline and are written by renowned experts and professionals in accordance with high academic standards. Researchers may fall back on information obtained from periodicals at the stage of writing the main body of research where specific data and minute details are required to support the research argument.

Secondary sources are now available in both print and electronic forms. The internet provides researchers with a vast volume of information through which they have to sift to find suitable and relevant information. This is not as easy a task as it sounds. Internet sources need careful evaluation. (For specifics, see "Evaluating internet sources and URLs" above.)

Evaluating secondary sources of data

Secondary sources of data should be evaluated to get the best from them according to the principles of availability, relevance, accuracy, and sufficiency.

Availability

Availability is to determine whether the required data is available in sufficient quantity and good quality for use. If it is not, a researcher will need to either look for alternative sources or change the topic of research.

Relevance

Relevance is the degree to which the information relates to the specific requirements of the research. Relevance also entails depth, coverage, and currency of information.

Accuracy

Accuracy demands that the information obtained be specific, trusted, and methodologically reliable and verifiable.

Sufficiency

Sufficiency means that there should be adequate information available to cover the range of topics to be dealt with in the research.

Researchers should always remember that information borrowed from secondary sources must be meticulously acknowledged and credited to its original authors. This is a fundamental requirement in academic research; otherwise, a researcher runs the risk of plagiarizing, which is a serious violation of academic integrity.

3.2.2. Primary sources of data

Primary data include information that the researcher obtains first-hand from primary sources using his or her own design and effort. They are of two types—qualitative and quantitative—and include information obtained through interviews, questionnaires, discussions, observations, surveys, field data, case studies, and archives. Good research employs both qualitative and quantitative data. Collecting primary research data enables the researcher to produce original work. However, collection of such data also entails adherence to ethics of confidentiality, sensitivity, and courtesy to participants. The researcher also has to be clear about

    a.   methods of data collection,
    b.   treatment of data, and
    c.   data analysis and interpretation

3.3. Methods of data collection

Researchers use different methods of data collection depending on the nature of research under investigation and the discipline of study. The most commonly used methods are interviews, observations, questionnaires, and surveys. These are discussed in the paragraphs that follow.

3.3.1. Interviews

Interviews are some of the most effective and widely used methods of qualitative research. Interviews are used mainly to elicit both factual and conceptual information from respondents, although obtaining conceptual meanings is usually more difficult than getting factual data relating to the respondent's day-to-day life experiences.

3.3.1.1. *Types of interviews*

Structured interviews are of two types:

a. Open-ended interviews are interviews in which respondents answer the same set of open-ended questions in the same order. There are no preset answers provided by the interviewer for the interviewee to choose from.

b. Closed-ended interviews are structured interviews in which respondents answer the same set of closed-ended questions. Here the interviewer provides the interviewee with a limited number of predetermined optional answers to choose from. The interviewee's responses, therefore, are restricted to only those answers already provided. This type of interviewing allows for a quick and easy way of collecting and analysing data.

Unstructured or informal interviews are interviews in which the questions are not determined prior to the time of interviewing but are presented to the interviewee there and then in an ad hoc and informal manner. This type of interview is the easiest and most convenient, since it allows respondents to answer questions in an informal, natural conversational setting. It also gives the added benefit of enabling the interviewer to adapt the questions to the answers received, allowing for further probing and investigation. However, unstructured interviews are considered to yield the least reliable results. This is primarily because they are prone to bias far more than other methods.

Semi-structured interviews are those that contain elements of both structured and unstructured interviews. Here the interviewer prepares a set of the same questions (structured as open-ended or closed-ended) to be answered by all respondents. In addition, other questions may be asked in an informal ad hoc manner during the interview as the interviewer deems necessary to probe for further answers in follow-up to new issues arising from the responses given.

3.3.1.2. *Types of ambiguous questions to avoid*

One of the most important aspects of primary data collection is the creation of good interview questions. When creating questions, avoid the following five ambiguous types.

Biased (leading) questions

Biased questions are questions which are worded in such a way that makes the respondent answer the question in a certain way. These are sometimes called leading questions, implying that the researcher leads the respondent to an implicitly suggested answer.

Example:

Don't you agree that teachers should be given the highest salaries, considering the work they do in educating the young?

- ○ Strongly agree
- ○ Agree
- ○ Neutral
- ○ Disagree

Double-barred questions

A double-barreled question is a fallacious question which asks for consideration of multiple items that are usually joined together by conjunctions such as *and* but that allows for only one answer. The result is that the respondent answers one part, but not the other parts imbedded in the question.

Example:

What's the best time to have your English and maths classes?

- ○ Early morning
- ○ Midday
- ○ Afternoon
- ○ Evening

The question in fact asks about two different subjects—English and maths—but allows for only one answer for both.

Double-negative questions

A double-negative question may occur when respondents are asked about their opinions regarding a certain situation. If the premise of the question involves a negative statement with which they disagree, then a double negative occurs.

Example:

Do you agree or disagree that students should not be allowed to use mobile phones in classrooms?
There are two answers to this question:

    a.   Yes, I agree that students should not be allowed to use mobile phones in classrooms.
    b.   No, I disagree that students should not be allowed to use mobile phones in classrooms.

Answer b is a double negative implying agreement that mobile phone should not be allowed to be used in classrooms, which is not the respondent's intended answer.

Questions that assume the answer

These types of questions presuppose the answer they ask. They are another type of fallacious question. Sometimes also called circular reasoning.

Example:

Lord of the Rings is real. Do you agree or disagree?

The answer is already suggested in the first part, assuming the respondent to agree. To correct the question, it must be reworded:
Do you agree or disagree that *Lord of the Rings* is real?

3.3.1.3. *Requirements and ethical considerations for conducting interviews*

For interviews to yield the desired results, it is important that they meet the following requirements and ethical considerations:

- The interviewer should be well trained about what to do and what not to do. This is because the role of the interviewer is crucial to the overall outcome of the study and can influence the success of the project under investigation.
- She or he should be knowledgeable about the topic she or he is investigating.
- She or he should know about the pitfalls of bias and how to avoid them.
- She or he should exert time and effort to ensure well-prepared and clear sets of questions.
- She or he needs to clearly explain the purpose of the interview.
- She or he should prepare carefully for the time, duration, and setting of the interview to take place, and for the equipment needed to record data.
- More importantly, she or he has to be sensitive to respondents' concerns and should exercise courtesy, tolerance, and patience in attending to respondents worries.
- She or he should take utmost care to address issues of confidentiality and anonymity of respondents' identities.

3.3.1.4. *Advantages and disadvantages of interviews*

As a method of primary data collection, interviews have a number of advantages. Through interviews, one can obtain both factual and conceptual information. Interviews allow for obtaining in-depth information on a topic. More importantly, they enable the interviewer to engage in follow-up investigation. The interviewer thus has the opportunity to probe further with questions on new issues that arise as a session progresses. Interviews are generally easier and more convenient for interviewees when personal opinions are sought. However, interviews also have disadvantages. Most notably, they involve costs and are time-consuming. They also require that they be conducted with great care to guard against interviewer biases and prejudices, since it is not possible for interviewers to completely rid themselves of their own feelings and perceptions. Therefore, careful training on how to properly conduct interviews is required (Kvale, S. 1996).

3.3.2. Observations

Observation is another commonly used method of primary data collection that depends mainly on the observer spending time watching and observing different phenomena that she or he wants to investigate. Observations can be conducted individually or by a group of observing experts. In either case, observations do not yield reliable results unless they satisfy certain requirements. Observations are used extensively in the sciences to observe natural and biological phenomena to provide information for scientific inquiry. On the individual level, observations are commonly used by anthropologists to study life in certain communities by observing daily social and working life, ceremonies, rituals, and customs. Observations are also used in the social sciences. A good example of observation may be seen in what is called the rapid rural appraisal (RRA) method, in which a team of specialists visits a rural area and starts observing different phenomena, each from his or her own angle of expertise. Ultimately, the specialists compile a joint report explaining the phenomenon under study from different perspectives (Mohammed 2008).

3.3.2.1. *Observations: definition*

Observation is defined as the "systematic description of events, behaviors, and artifacts in the social setting chosen for study" (Marshall and Rossman 1989, p.79). Observations in general, and participant observations in particular, are some of the common and widely used methods in both quantitative and qualitative research. They provide a particularly useful research tool in socio-cultural and anthropological studies to describe the behaviour, attitudes, ceremonies, economic activities, and social interactions of rural communities, in what is generally termed *ethnographic studies*. Observation of community activities is carried out mainly through active fieldwork engagement with the observed community members, where the observer watches, interviews, records, and scribbles down her or his interpretations and impressions about what goes on in front of her or him.

3.3.2.2. *Uses of observation*

Observations provide the researcher with an effective method of interaction with community members, where she or he can closely examine nonverbal expressions of feelings, observe interpersonal interactions between members, gauge how participants communicate with each other, and measure how much time is spent on various activities. A number of reasons have been identified for using participant observation as a method of primary research. Schensul et al. (1999) have identified the following reasons for using participant observation in research:

- to identify and guide relationships with informants
- to help the researcher get a feel for how things are organized and prioritized, how people interrelate, and what are the cultural parameters

- to show the researcher what the cultural members deem to be important in manners, leadership, politics, social interaction, and taboos
- to help the researcher become known to the cultural members, thereby easing facilitation of the research process
- to provide the researcher with a source of questions to be addressed with participants (Schensul et al. 1999: 91)

3.3.2.3. *The role of the observer*

It is possible to identify four different roles—or stances, as Gold (1958) called them. The observer may take any of four roles, ranging from an extreme stance of *complete participant*, to another extreme of *complete observer*. The four stances can be summarized as follows:

1. The role of *complete participant*, in which the researcher is a full and complete member of the community under study but conceals his or her researcher identity in order to guarantee normal interaction with the study group
2. The role of *participant as observer*, in which the researcher is a full and complete member of the community under study and reveals his or her researcher identity to the group; in this role, the researcher's main interest is to observe rather than participate
3. The role of *observer as participant*, in which the researcher participates fully in the group's activities as an active participant but his or her main role remains one of observation—collecting information and recording his or her interpretations about the group's activities—with the group members being aware of his or her identity as a researcher
4. The role of *complete observer*, in which the researcher carries on his or her research activities openly and publicly while his or her true identity as a researcher is completely concealed from the group

Each one of the observer roles mentioned above has strengths and limitations. The different stances the observer takes can have a decisive impact on the overall results of the study. Observing is a skill which can be developed by continuous practice. That means that paying attention to minute details and recording them is a key to a successful observation. It is also important to focus on a predetermined range of important issues that need to be evaluated, since it is not possible to observe everything. When observing, observers should detach themselves emotionally from the phenomenon being observed; that is, they should not allow their feelings and prejudices to interfere with their objective judgement of the situation under investigation. For example:

Observation: The she-goat stays beside the newborn kid all afternoon.

Interpretation: Innate motherly care and affection is obviously the chief drive.

3.3.2.4. *Advantages and disadvantages of observation*

As a method of primary data, observation has merits and demerits.

- Observation affords the researcher the ability to gain depth of insight on the inner culture of the community.
- It allows for a wealth of vast and detailed description of the community culture.
- It raises new questions and opens new areas for further research to be pursued accordingly.
- It enhances the quality of the data collected.
- It lends more validity to the study's results.

However, observations have limitations, too.

- Participant observation is ridden with researcher bias, since the researcher serves as the main director of the flow of information.
- The researcher's identity, gender, background, and social class can influence the type of information she or he accesses, hence affecting the outcome of the study as a whole.
- Male and female researchers can have access to different sets of knowledge, since they engage with different informants in different settings and have access to different sets of information.
- As a human, researchers cannot rid themselves completely of their own world view—a view that shapes the way they look at, understand, and interpret external phenomena.

It is not easy for a researcher to maintain a balanced stance between a neutral detachment and a positive rapport; thus he or she will be divided between two conflicting emotional states.

3.3.3. Surveys

Surveying is a useful method of collecting primary data through questioning a sample of respondents on a particular issue and then studying and analysing their answers. Surveys are an effective method of qualitative data, especially when the objective of research is to gauge public opinion on a particular issue or to measure the response of a large segment of society or organization on a wide range of issues. In social studies, surveys are used mainly to study social attitudes, to test concepts, or to study market behaviour. Specifically, surveys are used to (a) study popular opinion on certain aspects of day-to-day life, and (b) test hypotheses or assumptions pertaining to specific social contexts. Surveying can be conducted following one of three methods: (1) by person, (2) via internet mail, or (3) by telephone (Jackson 2011).

Consider the following questions when conducting surveys:

Whom are you planning to survey? Decide what group or groups you are going to focus on, based on who you have access to and what your research focus is.

How many people do you plan to survey? Choose a reasonable target number of surveys to conduct—not too few, because you won't have enough answers to support generalizations or findings, and not too many lest you be overwhelmed with too much data to analyse.

How are you going to survey people? You may choose to conduct your survey in person, on paper, or via the internet. The survey method should be chosen based on the length of your survey and types of questions.

How long is your survey going to be? This will depend on what information you aim for and how much information you want. It is better to keep your questions short and simple.

What type of questions are you going to ask? You can choose between open-ended questions or closed-ended questions. Open-ended questions allow participants any type of response (e.g., "How do you feel today?"). A closed-ended question is one with a set of possible responses or yes/no responses (e.g., "Do you feel that the new campus regulations about parking are fair?"). Closed-ended questions are much easier to analyse, but they do not provide the rich responses you may get with open-ended questions. Ultimately, the type of question you should ask depends on what you want to discover.

3.3.4. Questionnaires

Questionnaires, a variant of surveying methods, are another very useful tool widely used to collect data from participants through sets of predesigned questions intended to gauge public or group opinions on various issues. Questionnaires provide a convenient tool to collect a wide array of information through which the researcher can tailor in advance the type of data she or he needs to obtain in order to answer specific questions in the research. Questionnaires are used as both qualitative and quantitative methods. Where questionnaires are designed as open-ended questions, a qualitative method of data treatment is used; and where questions are closed-ended, a quantitative approach is adopted for analysing data.

3.3.4.1. Requirements for good questionnaires

Although questionnaires are useful and widely used in data collection, there are a number of important criteria they should satisfy if they are to yield reliable information. Mohammed (2008) identifies six such requirements for a questionnaire to be a valid and reliable tool for collecting data.

First, the researcher needs to decide on the size of the sample to be targeted by the questionnaire. Is it the whole population, or only a sample of it? It is often the case that only a sample is used, in which case the researcher also needs to decide whether the sample is random or non-random and explain the reason for the choice between the two. Also, is it a simple, stratified, systematic, or cluster sample, or is it a combination of these?

Second, questionnaire questions have to be tailored in such a way as to accord with the specific research design, taking into account whether the research follows a cross-sectional design or is to be combined with other types of design, such as pretest, post-test, controlled group, experimental group, etc.

Third, the researcher should also be clear about the content she or he wants to obtain from the questions and is advised to categorize questions to obtain factual information, emotional or judgmental information, or opinions. And of these, she or he also needs to identify which among them constitute dependent variables, and which are independent variables.

Fourth, the level of education of a sample population and the language in which the questions are cast are important in determining whether the information eventually obtained will be very reliable or less reliable. The more the sample of respondents is reasonably educated to answer the questions, the more likely it is that the researcher will obtain reliable data. And the more technical and specialist the language is, the more likely it is that the researcher will obtain less-reliable data, since many of the respondents may not understand the meanings of the jargon and technical terms used.

Fifth, questions are of two types: open-ended and closed-ended. The researcher should plan in advance which of the two she or he is going to use, basing her or his preferences on the type of information she or he wants to obtain. Each of the two has advantages and disadvantages. Closed-ended questions, for example, are more flexible, less time-consuming, and easier to code electronically than open-ended questions, but they are restrictive in that they do not allow respondents to add further information which might be valuable for the research.

Sixth, the researcher will be advised to fashion questions in a way that moves from easier and simpler to more difficult and complex. Start with simple, so-called ice-breaking questions, and move on to more difficult, personal, and sensitive ones. It is also advisable that the researcher be sensitive to respondents' feelings and time, and design a questionnaire that is not too long.

3.3.4. 2. *Merits and limitations of questionnaires*

- Questionnaires enable gathering a large amount of data in a short period of time.
- Questionnaires involve much lower costs than most other methods of data collection.
- Questionnaires have the benefit of keeping anonymous the identities of respondents in the sample group.
- One of the great advantages of questionnaires is that the researcher need not be present with the respondents, but he or she can send the questions to them.
- Questionnaires are an economical and convenient tool in saving valuable time.
- However, not being present may also be a disadvantage, since the researcher will not be in a position to respond in a timely way to respondents to clarify what the questions actually mean.
- There are concerns that information obtained through questionnaires can lack sufficient depth and rigour.
- There are concerns that respondents are biased to select the first choice from among the answers, thus raising concerns about reliability of the data obtained.

3.4. Data Quality

Researchers will need to ensure good-quality data are collected by carefully developing effective methods for collecting, recording, processing, and interpreting information. Good data quality has to meet the following criteria:

- *Validity*: Data measure what they are intended to measure.

- *Reliability*: Data are gathered consistently according to the stated terms, definitions, and methodologies, and the process yields the same results when replicated.
- *Completeness*: All data elements are included according to the specified definitions and methodologies adopted.
- *Precision*: Data have accurate and sufficient detail.
- *Integrity*: Data are obtained in an impartial, neutral, and objective manner, free of bias and subjective judgement.
- *Currency*: Data are current and up to date.

3.5. Data Treatment

Primary data obtained firsthand through observations, interviews, surveys, or questionnaires will have to be treated electronically and analysed to arrive at the desired statistical information that is necessary both for valuation and validation of results. Raw data is first fed into the computer to convert it into computational units, which are then passed through a frequency distribution to get the results either on the screen or in printout form. Here the researcher gets computerized feedback from which she or he can detect inconsistencies or errors that might have occurred during the process of data entry; which she or he can then correct. Treatment of data involves three interrelated stages:

1. Processing
2. Presentation
3. Analysis or interpretation

3.5.1. Processing

Raw data collected directly from the field contains impurities and inconsistencies which need to be corrected before presenting and analysing it. The first step in data processing is to edit the raw gathered matter. Editing can be done in the field at the time of collecting the data. Editing can also be carried out in a post-field stage, when fieldwork has been completed and all the reports have been collated. In post-field editing, a comprehensive and thorough revision of the collected data is necessary. The second step is the coding of data, in which alphabetical or numerical symbols, or both, are assigned to the raw data. Then the data is organized in charts and tables, in ascending or descending order, arrayed in sets and fields. Finally, there is the classification of data, in which the gathered raw material is grouped into categories of similar detail, classified on the basis of certain characteristics. Generally, data are classified on the following bases: (1) according to numerical characteristics; (2) according to attributes; (3) according to descriptive characteristics (e.g., caste, sex, age); (4) according to time-, situation-, or area-specific characteristics; and (5) according to the nature of data as continuous or discrete. Classification helps in the making of comparisons between the various categories (data collection, processing, and analysis).

3.5.2. Presentation

After being processed, data are presented in various appropriate forms—mainly in three common forms: tabular, statistical, and cartographic. Tabular presentation is used to summarize data in its micro form. It helps in the analysis of trends, relationships, and other characteristics. There is simple tabulation, used to answer questions related to one characteristic, whereas complex tabulation is used to present several interrelated characteristics. Statistical presentation is used to process data statistically for precisely explaining the results. It is often necessary to work out a single representative value for the whole data set. The representative value is obtained through statistical measures known as central tendency, which denotes the central value points, distance, and occurrence in a distribution. Three commonly used measures of central tendency are arithmetic mean or average, median, and mode. The third form is cartographic presentation of data, in which primary data are presented cartographically in visual form of time, space, or both. The cartographic presentation refers to the display of data by constructing graphs, diagrams, or charts for the purposes of illustration and better clarification of ideas. Below is an example of a cartographic presentation displaying a line graph illustrating oil production for Saudi Arabia and the United States between 1975 and 1990 (in millions of barrels per day).

Oil Production for Saudi Arabia and the United States between 1975 and 1990 (In Millions of Barrels Per Day)

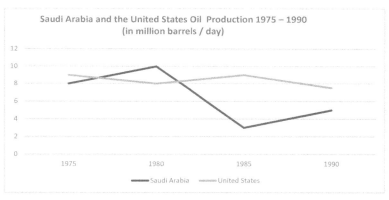

Figure 1: Example Cartographic Presentation of Data
(Source: https://en.wikipedia.org/wiki/OPEC)

3.5.3. Data Analysis and Interpretation

The final stage of data treatment is to analyse the data to find patterns of consistency and variance, and to look for patterns of convergence and divergence from which data can be synthesized. There are several analytical techniques in common use which fall under two groupings: numeric and textual analysis techniques.

3.5.3.1. *Numeric Analysis*

Numeric analysis is used to analyse numeric data, such as cost, frequency, or physical characteristics. Options include the following:

- *correlation:* a statistical technique used to determine how strongly two or more variables are related
- *cross-tabulation:* obtaining an indication of the frequency of two variables (e.g., gender and frequency of school attendance) occurring at the same time
- *data and text mining:* computer-driven automated techniques that run through large amounts of text or data to find new patterns and information
- *exploratory techniques:* taking a "first look" at a data set by summarizing its main characteristics, often through the use of visual methods
- *frequency tables:* arranging collected data values in ascending order of magnitude, along with their corresponding frequencies, to ensure a clearer picture of a data set
- *measures of central tendency:* a summary measure that attempts to describe a whole set of data with a single value that represents the middle or centre of its distribution
- *measures of dispersion:* a summary measure that describes how values are distributed around the centre
- *multivariate descriptive analysis:* providing simple summaries of (large amounts of) information (or data) with two or more related variables
- *non-parametric inferential analysis:* analysis of data that are flexible and do not follow a normal distribution
- *parametric inferential analysis:* analysis carried out on data that follow certain parameters, in which the data are normal
- *summary statistics:* a quick summary of data, which is particularly useful for comparing one project to another before and afterwards
- *time series analysis:* observation of well-defined data items obtained through repeated measurements over time

3.5.3.2. *Textual Analysis*

Textual analysis includes analysing written or spoken words obtained through respondents' answers to questions in interviews, questionnaires, observations, or surveys. Types of textual analysis include the following:

- *content analysis:* used to reduce large amounts of unstructured textual content into a manageable form that is relevant to the research questions
- *thematic coding:* the grouping together of textual data according to shared themes or concepts
- *narratives:* used to construct a coherent series of events (in narrative form) occurring in a community's, an individual's, or a locality's life
- *timelines:* a list of key events, ordered chronologically. (Peersman and Greet [n.d.])

The next step is to analyse the processed data. For social science research, methods of social statistics are used, which generally fall under one or the other of two methods: (1) descriptive statistics, and (2) inferential statistics (Mohammed 2008). The first analyses data on a univariate level (analyses variables each one at a time), while the other is multivariate (analyses a number of variables at a time). The researcher needs to identify different types of variables as nominal, ordinal, or interval. Each type of variable is used to measure specific values.

- Nominal variables divide values into categories (e.g., male or female; red, yellow, or blue; yes or no).
- Ordinal variables put values in sequential order (e.g., students' grades can be ranked as *excellent, very good, pass,* or *fail*).
- Interval (also called "ratio" or "scale") variables measure ratios and can range from zero to infinity (e.g., distances, heights, and sizes).

Here is an example showing nominal and ordinal variables in tabular display:

Table 1: Nominal and Ordinal Value Distribution

Grade	Frequency	Percentage
Excellent	10	11
Very Good	25	28
Good	20	22
Pass	30	13
Failure	05	06
Total	90	100

(Source: Mohammed 2008, p. 45)

Before embarking on the actual writing of the research paper, it is necessary to observe important academic concepts, conventions, and values required to produce research that is deserving of the title "good academic work".

Chapter References

BetterEvaluation. "Analyse Data" (online document n.d). http://betterevaluation.org/plan/describe/look_for_patterns. Accessed 7 December 2017.

BetterEvaluation "Combine Qualitative and Quantitative Data" (online document n.d). http://www.betterevaluation.org/en/plan/describe/combining_qualitative_and_quantitative_data. Accessed 7 December 2017.

Denzin, Norman K., and Yvonna S. Lincoln, eds. (1994). *Handbook of Qualitative Research.* 2nd ed. Thousand Oaks, California: Sage, 673–702.

Driscoll, Dana L., and Allen Brizee (2010). "What is Primary Research and How Do I Get Started?" The Writing Lab & the OWL at Purdue and Purdue University. Last updated on 17 April, 2010. Accessed 18 November 2016.

Geography Notes "Data Collection, Processing, and Analysis (online document n.d). Local Area Planning: Geography Notes. http://www.nios.ac.in/media/documents/316courseE/E-JHA-31-10A.pdf. Accessed 7 December 2017.

Gold, Raymond L. (1958). "Roles in Sociological Field Observations". *Social Forces* vol. 36, 217–23.

Jackson, S. (2011). *Research Methods and Statistics: A Critical Approach.* 4th ed. Cengage Learning. (online textbook).

Kawulich, Barbara B. (2005). "Participant Observation as a Data Collection Method". *Forum Qualitative Sozialforschung / Forum: Qualitative Social Research* vol. 6, no. 2. http://nbn-resolving.de/urn:nbn:de:0114-fqs0502430.

Kvale, Steinar (1996). "Interviews: An Introduction to Qualitative Research Interviewing". Sage Publications.

Marshall, Catherine, and Gretchen B. Rossman (1989). *Designing Qualitative Research.* Newbury Park, California: Sage.

Mohammad, Adam Azzain (2008). *Scientific Research Methods in Social Sciences.* Khartoum: Public Administration and Federalism Studies Institute, University of Khartoum.

Peersman, Greet. *Methodological Briefs Impact Evaluation No. 10, Overview: Data Collection and Analysis Methods in Impact Evaluation.* UNICEF Office of Research–Innicenti. https://www.unicef-irc. org/publications/pdf/brief_10_data_collection_analysis_eng.pdf. Accessed 7 December 2017.

Schensul, Stephen L., Schensul, Jean J., and Le Compte, Margaret D. (1999). *Essential Ethnographic Methods: Observations, Interviews, and Questionnaires.* Book 2 in Ethnographer's Toolkit. Walnut Creek, California: Alta Mira Press.

CHAPTER 4

Ethics of the Academic Community

Abstract: Researchers have responsibilities and obligations to the academic research community, to the general public, and to humanity at large, and it is important that they are sensitive to the ethical, religious and philosophical underpinnings of academic research. The academic community embraces values of integrity, honesty, and the pursuit of knowledge to advance societies and to champion humanity to happiness. Academic researchers belong to that breed of intellectually inclined people who, through the ages, have devoted their minds to finding answers to riddling questions in the quest for reaching the essence of things. Researchers, therefore, need to know not only *how* to conduct research, but more importantly *why* research must be conducted. Learning from the accumulated wisdom that has been passed down through generations of wisdom seekers, and adding their own contributions, researchers should do all this in the spirit of integrity and trust. Virtue ethics of integrity and honesty are cardinal pillars in academic research and should be carefully nurtured in students in higher education to prepare them to be ushered into the research community to become good citizens and good leaders.

Keywords: academic community, academic integrity, virtue ethics in religion, in the perennial tradition, Plato's philosophy of education, positive psychology, virtues and happiness

Higher education institutions have a responsibility towards society to create good citizens and good leaders. A recurrent dictum found in the vision and mission statements of a majority of universities worldwide is a commitment to creating good leadership. Whether the espoused commitment is followed or not is another question, but it remains a commitment that should be honoured dutifully. Teachers, students, and professionals in higher education need to be aware of their identity as part of an academic community whose role is to advance knowledge and produce graduates equipped with knowledge and moral fortitude who are able to lead society to a state of happiness for both individuals and communities. As part of an academic community, they need to be aware not only of *how* to carry out their teaching, learning, and research tasks but also of *why* they should do so—the conceptual and philosophical underpinnings of the educational roles and tasks they routinely perform. This chapter deals with these issues. It delineates the conceptual and philosophical contexts in which the educational operation should be placed. It starts with an appraisal of what constitutes an academic community: its values, its lineage to ancient wisdom, its responsibilities in advancing knowledge, and its role in leading societies to happiness. Specifically, it emphasizes the role of virtue ethics as a necessary imperative to be nurtured in college students through an initiatory process to integrate them into the academic community. Ultimately, the goal is to prepare them to assume future leadership roles as good, responsible citizens dedicated to serve the common good and the well-being of society.

4.1. Initiation into the Academic Community

Students, researchers, and professionals in the academic field belong to an academic community that is different from the community of ordinary people. The "academic world" and the "real world" are not the same, and researchers and students need to know the differences between the two. (Levin 2004) The academic community demands that its members adhere strictly to its traditions, conventions, and values. The real world is where we attend to our daily pursuits of living with family, working, socializing, and playing games. The academic world, on the other hand, is one of theories, ideas, abstraction, critiques, and questioning. The inquisitive academic mind entertains abstract notions and novel ideas, questions phenomena, and seeks to unravel the truth through exercising methods of meditation, contemplation, and investigation. In its quest for reaching to the truth about things, it is not enough for the inquisitive academic mind to rely solely on intellectual rigour. To reach to the realms of reality, intellectual exercise will have to be aided by ancient wisdom passed down through generations of wisdom seekers: messengers, philosophers, sages, seers, scholars, saints, thinkers, poets, and many other lovers of knowledge. Specifically, the academically inclined mind will need to know what others have already contributed to solving riddling issues and vexing questions. Academic enterprise then builds on the knowledge that already exists, learns from it, benefits from it, and adds to it. This is precisely the work of the academia. Yet the role of the academic community also involves responsibilities, sacrifices, and rewards. Responsibilities of the academic community entail ethical commitment to demands of integrity and honesty to faithfully relate what others have said, what one has learned from them, and what one has added to the accumulated wisdom, ultimately to contribute towards advancing human knowledge in the quest for the truth. Reaching to the bottom of things and revealing truth, however, can bring with it costs and sacrifices. History, ancient and contemporary, is replete with examples of wise men and women who suffered just in trying to reveal the truth. Consequently, academic enterprise and the academic community continue to sacrifice their own happiness for the happiness of others, yet they suffer in carrying out this noble mission. The rewards are being faithful to one's ideals and values, and remaining true to one's inner self as a human being seeking to bring happiness and well-being to other humans. The moral reward obtained from sacrificial self-satisfaction is valued by academics more than other material or social rewards. And the feeling of living a worthwhile life and doing good for humanity is even more rewarding. This is the ultimate goal of education—to enable people live a happy, worthy human life.

Boston University, commending its doctoral program on education, stressed the crucial role of education as the most important human endeavour, with the ultimate goal of enabling people to lead a "good life", stating that the role of educational institutions is to prepare people from an early age to be able to lead a good and worthy life. Unfortunately, however, this noble mission of education has often been neglected. The renowned historian Arthur Bestor observed that educators began to undermine the great traditions of liberal education and to substitute for them lesser aims, confused aims, or no aims at all. He lamented the current "preoccupation with the learning process" (i.e., the routine teaching practice), stating that it has grown so intense that "educationists lost sight of ultimate educational purposes" (Lawrence and Joshua 2006, p. 87).

The role of university teachers supervising students' research, therefore, should be to guide those students to understand the ethical principles of the academic profession. They need to be initiated carefully into this community, and to know that to become members of this community, they have to be committed to the ethical principles of integrity and dedication to the pursuit of knowledge to advance human welfare and happiness. The role of university teachers should be to "socialize" students into the academic community; students need to know that when they write research theses, they write them not for the world outside but for other members of academia. When students are socialized into the community's discursive practices, they learn about the community's expectations, ethics, values, and beliefs; the ultimate purpose of disciplinary knowledge; and student roles in the community. Such an initiation demands adherence to community values, traditions, and expectations. (Basturkme et al. 2014, p. 433)

Some people, however, chide academics for exactly the reasons they should be praised. Toor (2012), for example, quotes both Richard Hugo, the poet, and William Cronon, president of the American Historical Association, to corroborate her reproof of academics. For Hugo, she narrates a story he told about an academic colleague who, when asked if he liked a film he had just seen, said, "I don't know. I have to go home and think about it." For Cronon, she points to his essay titled *Professional Boredom*, in which he criticizes academics for carrying to the extreme the values of good academic practice—of being "rigorous, complex, and nuanced"—warning that pushing such good values to the extreme can make the discipline (in this case, history) accessible to only a small group.

Toor, in fact, brought the examples to back up her stance in reproof of academics for adopting what she believes to be a debilitating adherence to meticulousness and accuracy. She states that academics are "accustomed to having to justify and support every thought, back up every assertion, and hedge every idea", to such an extent that they "distrust their guts" (Toor and Rachel 2012, p. 1). Academics should not be chided; instead, they should be praised for being so thoroughly meticulous about what they say and write. Academia is not so much about "guts" as it is about intellects, and there is a big difference between the two—between feeling, the domain of creative writing, and reasoning, the domain of academic discourse. In the first, writers can write declarative statements adorned in bright colours and beautiful feathers without fear of being "irrefutably right". In the second, writers write tentative statements, afraid of passing absolute judgments until confirmed beyond doubt that what they write is irrefutably right.

The truth is that the nature of academics is indeed selective, accessible only to small groups of intellectually inclined people. In *The Republic*, Plato postulates that the best to rule are those endowed with strong philosophical minds and virtuous souls, guided by the twin virtues of wisdom and the exercise of intellectual contemplation that transcends the physical word to ascend to the realms of light— the immutable forms or absolute knowledge. He explains that the role of education is to prepare the best and the naturally inclined citizens to be the guardians (i.e., leaders) of the state and says, "Then there must be a selection." (Plato 2016 p. 106) Again, Holowchak (2013) points to that altruistic and sacrificial nature of true intellectually minded people, placing this quality in the Platonic virtue of wisdom and intellectual exercise aimed to bring happiness to the society. The nature of people endowed with wisdom and virtue is that they are least motivated to seek power and authority but find satisfaction in the pursuit of knowledge and intellectual contemplation; complete happiness, as they perceive it, "comprises solitary study of things unchanging". However, because they also recognize that they have a duty to the state and the people, they have to "compromise their happiness for the wellbeing of their polis and of the people in it". In *The Republic*, Plato argues that the solution is for the *"aristoi* [the best in society, noble, wise, and virtuous] would merely to recognize their duty to sacrifice personal happiness for the happiness of the polis". Academics belong to that breed of people who sacrifice their own happiness for the happiness of others, dedicating their life, in solitary seclusion, to the study and pursuit of knowledge, to arrive at those "things unchanging"—the forms. This is a lofty pursuit attainable only by people with compassionate hearts, great minds, and exceptional natures.

Additionally, scholarly academic writing is the medium through which academics communicate the wisdom and knowledge they attain through intellectual exercise in order to impart happiness to others. As such, the purpose of academic writing is not to entertain and please; it is to present solid facts and back up arguments with rigorous reasoning. It might not be sweet, buoyant, or pleasurable, but is essential; like water, academics may be colourless, odourless, and tasteless, yet they represent the surest path to humanity's happiness and well-being.

The lineage of academic communities reaches back to ancient Greece—specifically to the time when Plato established his famous academy, whose primary mission was the quest for knowledge with the aim of revealing the truth, through the practice of dialogue for both teacher and student. This notion has recently received a renewed resurrection. In the United States, for example, the Boyer Commission (1999) argued for a reconceptualization of undergraduate education to initiate students into an academic community in which every member is seen as a scholar moving between teaching, learning, and researching activities. A study in Australia has shown the strong connection between research and teaching, and has called for strengthening this relationship through building inclusive scholarly knowledge communities involving both staff and students (Brew, 2006, p. 137).

Higher education institutions are regarded as learning organizations with their own established and observed values and codes of ethics. They form special communities of academic professionals where people continually expand their capacity to create new patterns of thinking. College students and researchers need to be aware of these notions and to know the differences between the academic world and the real world. Such knowledge is crucial for the promotion of awareness that they are ushering into a new milieu of the academic community, with all that entails regarding responsibilities, sacrifices, and rewards.

4.2. Academic integrity rationale: education for good citizenship

Academic integrity is one of the fundamental requirements in the academic world. Students and researchers have to observe the rules of integrity and avoid practices that violate them. In particular, academic research demands accurate citations, proper referencing, and acknowledgement of information borrowed from other authors. Moreover, ways to avoid plagiarism are key to maintaining academic integrity. Unfortunately, awareness of the importance of integrity in academic practice has not been paid the attention it deserves either in day-to-day teaching or in assessment criteria in schools and universities. Commitment to academic integrity is crucial if universities are to prepare graduates for future leadership roles that necessarily require ethics and morality. Integrity as a means of virtue ethics needs to be inculcated in the young to prepare them to become good citizens and good leaders of the future. Therefore, academic achievement and professional competence alone are not enough to guarantee good leadership unless coupled with ethical values of integrity, honesty, justice, fairness, and responsibility. In religion, philosophy in the perennial tradition, and contemporary positive psychology theory, integrity has been very highly regarded as a necessary virtue of good leadership and good citizenship for the creation of a happy society.

4.3. The place of virtue ethics in religion, philosophy, and psychology

Virtue ethics is an essential requirement for good leadership which needs to be nurtured in the young. The important role of schools is precisely to initiate wise people whose role is to "use their abilities for a common good as determined by positive ethical values" (Sternberg 2009, p. 121). Ethical values are perennially enshrined in religious, philosophical, and sophist teachings that elevate the human soul to realms of metaphysical knowledge attainable to those with the right gift to receive it, such as prophets, philosophers, saints, and wise men and women through the ages. The Islamic, Christian, Platonic, and perennial traditions are replete with references to the importance of virtue in establishing harmony in society. Leaders are to be virtuous, wise, and just, and are to rule to enforce virtuous ethical conduct for lasting happiness among individuals and in society.

Wilson (2014), in his discussion on authentic leadership, refers to what he calls "moral and intellectual virtues" as necessary qualities for good leadership. He explains that since leaders are entrusted with power, trust brings with it social responsibilities and moral obligations for the people who have put trust in the leadership. He quotes Bill George (2003) in stating that "Authentic leaders genuinely desire to serve others through their leadership"—that they are not interested in gaining personal rewards, such as power, money, or prestige, but are "more interested in empowering the people they lead to make a difference". They are "guided by qualities of the heart, by passion and compassion, as they are by qualities of the mind" (Wilson, 2014, p. 12).

Preparation of future leaders is the exclusive responsibility of education in schools and colleges, and as such, educational institutions have a responsibility to create good, virtuous leaders for the benefit of society. These notions of virtue ethics as essential traits of good leadership date back to ancient Greece, and in particular to Platonic and Aristotelian philosophy. Wilson (2014) suggests that Greek virtue philosophy—in particular the neo-Aristotelian virtue ethics—can be adopted as a useful paradigm for a comprehensive theoretical model of authentic leadership studies (pp. 482–83). The role of virtue as both individual and societal imperative is necessary for the regulation of societies in the just dispensation of responsibilities, rights, and obligations. For these reasons, the call for virtue has always been a fundamental commandment in all major religions.

4.3.1. The place of virtue ethics and knowledge in Islam

In Islam, the *Ulama* (scholars)—those with learning and knowledge—are highly regarded as "heirs of the prophets"; in that they are gifted with virtuous qualities second only to those of the prophets in terms of justice, wisdom, temperance, compassion, honesty, integrity, humility, and love for humanity, which drive them to guide mankind to the path of happiness in life and in the afterlife. Indeed, the very first verse in the Koran speaks commandingly of knowledge: "Read. Read in the Name of your Lord who created; Created man from a clot. Read; and your Lord is the Most Generous; He who taught by the pen; Taught man what he never knew" (the Koran, Surah al-Alaq [the Clot] 96, 1–5). Islam accords knowledge and the knowledgeable a very high standing in social and religious hierarchy. Indeed, the Prophet Muhammad (may Allah bless him and grant him peace) stated unequivocally that his holy mission was to complement the best of virtues—an affirmation that the mission of Islam is to teach people how to lead a virtuous life, to reinstate those good virtues that were already extant, and to eradicate those that were vice in the era of ignorance in pre-Islamic Arabia, and to carry this universal mission to all humanity.

Ibn Rajab al-Hanbali (736–795), a famous Muslim scholar, wrote a small book explaining the Hadith that "the scholars are heirs of the prophets", in which he brings out the essentially Islamic concept of what knowledge is. He enlists the merits and distinctions of the learned and knowledgeable. He explained that Allah has praised the scholars in numerous verses in the Koran. One verse informs us that "Indeed, among His servants, it is but the learned who fear Allah most" (Koran 35:28). Ibn Abbas, commenting on this verse says that God's good servants to whom truthful knowledge has been revealed comprehend Allah's majesty, grandeur, and sublimity, which leads them to know Him and fear Him. In the Islamic traditions of both the Koran and the Hadith, the knowledgeable and the learned are highly reverenced as the elite of mankind—the best of humanity second in rank only to the prophets and messengers (al-Hanbali, *Scholars are Heirs of the Prophets*).

4.3.2. The place of virtue ethics and knowledge in Christianity

In the Christian tradition, learning to know the truth is associated with knowledge of God. In an interview, William C. Ringenberg (2016) states that love of learning and wisdom is rooted in Christian virtues of honesty, humility, and love, and adds that "for Christians, seeking truth is closely related to seeking God. The Bible tells us that God is light—a classic synonym for truth" (p. 74).

4.3.3. The place of virtue in the perennial tradition of education

The collective human heritage of wisdom and knowledge for the quest of ultimate truth has been passed down through generations of wisdom seekers in what has generically been termed *the perennial tradition*. One of the famous proponents of the perennial tradition is the famous traditional spiritual leader, metaphysician, and poet Frithjof Schuon (1907–1998) (Algis Uzdavinys 2003, p. 139). Frithjof Schuon was the leading protagonist of the perennial tradition and philosophy in the second half of the twentieth century. His writings bear affinities to neo-Platonic philosophy. In the perennial tradition, knowledge and the pursuit of truth are of a universal metaphysical nature and are viewed as (1) a perennial message immanent to the reality itself, (2) a sort of self-centred mysticism, and (3) a thorough explanation of the origin, present condition, and final goal of humanity" (ibid). The perennial tradition champions the eternal pursuit of wisdom and truth through the ages. It carries that stream of light which has been transmitted through all the world's major mystical and spiritual systems (Walbridge 1999).

Contemporary notions of virtue ethics have recently stressed the importance of cultivating virtues through education in the souls of the young as necessary imperatives for the creation of virtuous, good leaders who can lead societies to happiness. This is what ancient wisdom has been telling us for thousands of years—that living a virtuous life is synonymous with living a happy life.

4.3.4. Virtues as determinants of happiness in contemporary positive psychology

Empirical research has recently established that virtues are indeed necessary for the happiness of individuals and societies. Research findings in the contemporary field of positive psychology, especially that pioneered by Martin Seligman, Csikszentmihalyi, and Peterson, corroborate the ancient wisdom that virtues are essential to live a worthy, happy life. Living a virtuous life of goodness, wisdom, compassion, justice, integrity, and temperance can guarantee lasting happiness for individuals and social groups. In his groundbreaking work *Authentic Happiness*, Seligman (2002) shows that happiness is possible and indeed practically accessible through focusing on one's virtues and strengths to attain a higher order of emotional uplifting, psychological balance, and well-being.

Peterson and Seligman (2004) identified a set of core virtues which they called virtues in action (VIA). It is a model originally used in psychological treatment to create a state of balance and well-being called *human flourishing*. According to the VIA model, virtues are considered to be commonly shared acceptable social and individual values that are cherished by humans across cultures and through the ages; these include wisdom, courage, humanity, justice, temperance, and transcendence. (Shryack et al. 2010). Seligman, for example, demonstrates that the virtues of gratitude and forgiveness are important to mental health and personal happiness. Indeed, the insights gained from research in positive psychology corroborate the truth enshrined in religious beliefs and ancient philosophy that virtues are essential determinants in living a worthy and happy life. Ultimately, virtue ethics can be understood to have a practical or utilitarian function—what Plato in *The Republic* calls "excellence or good". The basic rule is that each and every thing has a good function, which is its excellence (or *utility*, in the language of economics). "The art of the ruler, considered as ruler, whether in a state or in private life, could only regard the good of his flock or subjects. And each art gives us a particular good and not merely a general one—medicine, for example, gives us health; navigation, safety at sea, and so on?" (Plato 2016). And the good or practical utility function of virtue is that it gives us happiness. Plato identified the virtues of wisdom, justice, courage, temperance, honesty, integrity, love of knowledge, perseverance, and moral fortitude. Seligman's concept of VIA as essential determinants to happiness, in fact, has very close affinities to the Platonic concept in the close association between virtue and happiness; both emphasize that virtues have an objective utilitarian function in human life, which is the attainment of happiness.

It can be seen from the above that contemporary notions of virtue ethics have their lineage in Platonic and Aristotelian philosophy. It is therefore worthwhile to consider a reorientation of education towards its perennial sources. Below is an appraisal of the salient features of Plato's philosophy of education, from which most contemporary educational paradigms draw fundamental principles.

4.3.5. The place of honesty and integrity in Plato's philosophy of education

In *The Republic*, Plato viewed education as the nexus where the acquisition of knowledge and the inculcation of virtue in the young prepares a successful elect to be philosopher kings endowed with the twin virtues of wisdom and rule. Through a rigorous educational regime, those with the true intellect and grit will endure to acquire the requisite spiritual and physical strength necessary to assume leadership. He believes that the role of education is to prepare the best and the naturally inclined citizens to be the guardians of the state, and he says: "then there must be a selection. Let us note among the guardians those who in their whole life show the greatest eagerness to do what is for the good of their country, and the greatest repugnance to do what is against her interests" (Plato 2016, p. 106).

Honesty and integrity, cultivated through a rigorous education regime, remain central focal concepts in Plato's philosophy of education for the creation of what he calls the "happy Polis [state]". Those with the right calibre should be subjected to rigorous testing to ascertain their true mettle: to ensure that they are incorruptible and insusceptible to the forces of deception, forgetfulness, or temptation—virtues that are to be cultivated through education. They have to go through a lengthy, tough educational regime to test their emotional strength and select from among them those with the hardest grit, fortitude, and immutable morality. He says

> ... that we may discover whether they are armed against all enchantments, and of a noble bearing always, good guardians of themselves and of the state ... and retaining under all circumstances a rhythmical and harmonious nature, such as will be most serviceable to the individual and to the State. And he who at every age, as boy and youth and in mature life, has come out of the trial victorious and pure, shall be appointed a ruler and guardian of

the State; he shall be honoured in life and death, and shall receive sepulture and other memorials of honour. (Plato 2016, p. 106)

These are the philosophical bases of Plato's concept of an education aimed at producing virtuous good citizens and good leaders actively engaged in the pursuit of a worthy and happy life. Plato's concepts of education have been passed down via contemporary educational thought and are especially pronounced in the perennial tradition of education.

Following is a summary of Plato's philosophy of education:

- The purpose of education is the development of virtuous, good citizens into philosopher kings.
- Education is the breeding ground for enlightened leadership.
- The ultimate goal of education is the attainment of happiness for both individuals and society.
- Education is where citizens' roles are charted, based on individual aptitudes (a yardstick for division of labour).
- Hierarchical division of individuals' statuses in society accords naturally with their intellectual aptitudes and moral inclinations.
- There are those fit to do crafts (inclined for money and desires), those fit for power (inclined for honour and glory), and those fit for rational, moral, and intellectual reasoning (inclined for knowledge and wisdom).
- Rulers (philosopher kings) are chosen from the latter category.
- Education is meant not as an amassment of information but as a system of exercise and training intended to uplift and purify the soul to allow one to reach higher realms of rational knowledge. It is a path that can allow individuals to transcend the limitations of illusory human perceptual reality and attain of the knowledge of truth (the forms).

- As such, Plato views academic subjects such as maths, the arts, and music as means not just for acquiring knowledge but also of continuous training to elevate the soul in the quest for ascendancy towards a higher philosophical understanding of reality.

Viewed from a Platonic perspective, the pandemic of dishonest academic practices among university students is an alienation from the basic tenets of education. Dishonest practices, such as plagiarism, indeed go in exactly the opposite direction of true education. The alienated status of contemporary education calls on those concerned to take action if societies are to be blessed with virtuous, good leaders whose main interest is to serve and lead society to happiness.

The purpose of the above advocacy for virtue ethics as both religious and social imperative is to call attention that there is a pressing need in higher educational institutions to integrate ethics as a fundamental part of curricula and in assessment practices. Current educational practice lays heavy emphasis on *how* to attain proficiency in academic achievement, neglecting *why* the ultimate goal of education is a means to create capable ethical leaders who will be entrusted with the fulfilment of the public good. In this context, virtues of integrity, honesty, truth, justice, studiousness, and fairness should be given prominence in assessing students' moral character, emotional fortitude, and preparedness to assume future leadership roles.

Chapter References

Algis, Uzdavinys (2003). "Approach to Philosophy, Theology and Metaphysics: Frithjof Schuon and Neo-Platonic Tradition". *Dialogue and Universalism* vol. 1, no. 2, 139–47.

Basturkme, Helen, Martin East, and John Bitchener (2014). "Supervisors' on-Script Feedback Comments on Drafts of Dissertations: Socializing Students into the Academic Discourse Community". *Teaching in Higher Education* vol. 19, no. 4, 43–45. http://dx.doi.org/10.1080/13562517.2012.752728, Routledge, Francis and Taylor Group.

Brew, Angela (2006). *Research and Teaching: Beyond the Divide*, Palgrave Publishing.

George, Bill (2003). *Authentic Leadership: Rediscovering the Secrets to Creating Lasting Value*. John Wiley & Sons.

Hanbali, Ibn Rajab al- (2006). *The Scholars are Heirs of the Prophets*. State University of New York Press, Albany. */ReligionKnolwledgeScienceFiles/ ScholarsareHeirsofProphets2061252.pdf.*

Holowchak, M. (2013). "The Paradox of Public Service: Jefferson, Education, and the Problem of Plato's Cave". *Studies in Philosophy and Education* vol. 32, no. 1, 73–86.

Johns, Beverley H., Mary Z. McGrath, and Sarup R. Mathur (2008), *Ethical Dilemmas in Education: Standing up for Honesty and Integrity*. Lanham, Maryland: Rowman & Littlefield.

Lawrence, Joshua (2006), "Perennial Themes in Education". *Journal of Education* vol. 186, no. 1, 87–95.

Levin, Peter (2004). *Academic Essay Writing.* Booklet sponsored by the Australian Centre for Indigenous Knowledge and Education, Charles Darwin University.

Oliveira, Renato José de. "Plato and Philosophy of Education", in *Encyclopaedia of Philosophy of Education*, Universidade Federal deRio de Janeiro.

Plato, *The Republic.* Translated by Benjamin Jowett. Internet Classics Archive. *http://classics.mit.edu//Plato/republic.html.*

Ringenberg, William C. (2016). "Academic Freedom: An Interview". Christianity Today.com, September 2016, 74–5.

Schuon, Frithjof (1953). *The Transcendent Unity of Religions.* Translated by P. Townsend. London: Faber and Faber.

Seligman, Martin E. P. (2002). *Authentic Happiness: Using the New Positive Psychology to Realize Your Potential for Lasting Fulfillment.* New York: Free Press.

Senge, P. M. (1990). *The Fifth Discipline: The Art and Practice of the Learning Organization.* New York: Currency Doubleday.

Shryack, Jessica, Michael F. Steger, Robert F. Krueger, and Christopher S. Kallie (2010). "The Structure of Virtue: An Empirical Investigation of the Dimensionality of the Virtues in Action Inventory of Strengths". *Personality and Individual Differences* vol. 48, 714–19. Available at *ScienceDirect/ journal homepage: www.elsevier.com/locate/paid.*

Smith, Pete, and Chris Rust (2011). "The Potential of Research-Based Learning for the Creation of Truly Inclusive Academic Communities of Practice". *Innovations in Education and Teaching International* vol. 48, no. 2, May 2011, 115–25.

Sternberg, Robert J. (2009). "Ethics and Giftedness". *High Ability Studies* vol. 20, no. 2, December 2009, 121–30.

The Boyer Commission Report (1998). *Reinventing Undergraduate Education: A Blueprint for America's Research Universities*. Sponsored by the Carnegie Foundation for the Advancement of Teaching, Princeton, New Jersey.

Toor, Rachel (2012). "Becoming a 'Stylish' Writer". *Chronicle of Higher Education* vol. 58, no. 40. http://search.ebscohost.com/?authtype=cookie,ip,uid. Last revised July 2015.

Walbridge, John (1999). *The Leaven of the Ancients: Suhrawardi and the Heritage of the Greeks*. SUNY Series in Islam. New York: State University of New York Press.

Wilson, Michael (2014). "Critical Reflection on Authentic Leadership and School Leader Development from a Virtue Ethical Perspective". *Educational Review* vol. 66, no. 4, 482–96. http://dx.doi.org/10.108 0/00131911.2013.812062.

CHAPTER 5

Concepts of Academic Integrity, Dishonesty, and Plagiarism

Abstract: Plagiarism is a serious academic offence that violates the good values of education and undermines academic principles. Educational institutions are social organizations responsible for the preparation of responsible future leaders. Because of this crucial role of education, dishonest practices, such as plagiarism and other forms of academic misconduct, must not be tolerated. More importantly, students should be enlightened on the rationale for penalizing dishonest academic practices. As a first step, students need to know the boundaries between plagiarism and legitimate writing. They should then be instructed on the best practices on how to avoid plagiarism and other forms of academic misconduct. This chapter gauges the extent of plagiarism and its far-reaching social and political consequences as it is found to correlate strongly with future dishonest practices in professional life. The chapter then defines plagiarism, charts out its boundaries, and gives the best practices on how to avoid it. Specifically, it stresses the need for students to acquire the requisite skills of summarizing, paraphrasing, quoting, and providing proper documentation of sources as the best techniques to avoid plagiarism.

Keywords: academic integrity, dishonesty, plagiarism, synthesizing, summarizing, paraphrasing, quotations, citations, referencing

5.1. The rift between theory and practice in education

Current academic practice assesses academic competence and neglects academic integrity, focusing on the *how* and neglecting the *why*. The logical corollary is that such emphasis on competencies and neglect of ethics produces skilled graduates competent in their specialties but possibly lacking in the ethical virtues so vitally important for persons whose future roles are predetermined as ones of social responsibility and leadership. Graduates of such an educational practice will have blurred vision, regarding education as a means of personal utility with benefits to be reaped for themselves. As such, they may engage in dishonest and unethical practices in the workplace specifically to further their own interests in line with their perceived self-centred vision of the education they have received. That is the education they know—one that is devoid of instruction on ethics, social responsibility, and good citizenship roles; and one that has no provision for virtue ethics or the values which are so crucial in building students' characters to assume future leadership roles. The consequences of such flaws in current educational practice can be—indeed, are—tectonic, permeating institutions, businesses, and societies, with deep societal and political ramifications.

Students need to be reminded that as members of the academia, they belong to a long and age-old tradition of wisdom lovers in pursuit of knowledge for the happiness of humanity. They have a lineage to those who continue to champion humanity's march for ascendancy towards the realms of enlightenment, justice, beauty, and happiness. Students need to be reminded that they are crossing the threshold of becoming members of an international academic community with its long established traditions and its own conventions, values, ethics, and codes of conduct that reach deep in human history and are markedly different from ordinary people's lives.

Integrity as a virtue has to be inculcated and continually nurtured in students at schools and colleges. Educators should explore possibilities of incorporating integrity as part of assessment in higher education, alongside exams, coursework, and other forms of assessment. Higher education institutions should aim not only to produce graduates who are academically outstanding and professionally proficient but also to produce graduates who are morally responsible, honest, fair, and ethically committed to performing their future leadership roles most dutifully, justly, and conscientiously.

Teachers have a duty towards their students to elucidate the concepts of academic integrity, academic dishonesty, and plagiarism at an early stage at university. This should be an integral part of university curricula. Addressing the eighth International Management Conference, Rujuoiu and Rujuoiu (2014) emphasized that "promoting academic honesty and integrity must be one of the objectives of any university" (p. 46). This is because an awareness of what constitutes academic honesty and dishonesty involves moral implications that reach beyond the confines of individual interests to wider social obligations and institutional responsibilities at the workplace. It has been observed that the rate of cheating incidences drops when students are sensitized to the ethical dimensions of academic dishonesty. It has been noted that when expectations have been clarified, it becomes more difficult for students to rationalize cheating. Students may also value the trust and related privileges attached to the codes of ethics more than what they gain from cheating.

A number of studies have indeed established a strong correlation between dishonesty at college and dishonesty at the workplace after graduation. It has been established that students who engaged in unethical behaviour at college are more likely to behave unethically in the workplace. The long-term consequences of academic dishonesty at college impact negatively on future professional life, with serious implications for institutions and for society at large. This situation calls on teachers and educators to take necessary action to address issues of academic dishonesty, such as plagiarism, with the ultimate aim of producing more ethically inclined future leaders and professionals.

5.2. Plagiarism: an academic offence and indicator of dishonesty

Plagiarism is derived from the Latin words *"plagiarius"*, and *"plagiary"* (pl. *"plagiaries"*), the latter of which means "plunderer" (*Webster's New Collegiate Dictionary* 1985, p. 898). As a term, it refers to the practice of making use of other people's ideas, words, or information without acknowledging or properly crediting the original authors, implying that the writer assumes ownership of the borrowed material. Plagiarism is a serious academic offence, entailing moral, ethical, and legal implications. Plagiarism should be put in its proper context as an instance of academic dishonesty, an indicator of a lack of integrity, and a predictor of dishonesty in future professional life. However, for the sake of fairness and good judgement, care should be exercised to define what, in fact, constitutes plagiarism.

5.2.1. What constitutes plagiarism?

It is important to ask some legitimate questions about whether students plagiarize wilfully and intentionally or whether plagiarism occurs because of inaccuracies in citations and source use.

- Do the majority of students choose wilfully to commit dishonest academic practices when they plagiarize?
- Are they tempted by some strong irresistible motive to do so?
- Are they aware or not that plagiarism is a serious offence?
- Are they simply ignorant about the rules governing the use of information borrowed from other sources?

As a general rule, plagiarism refers to the unacceptable act of a writer copying or using someone else's ideas or words without properly giving credit to the original author. As a form of academic dishonesty, plagiarism is also an indicator of lack of integrity. To rule out the unfair judgement that a student lacks integrity when plagiarizing, there is a need to make a careful distinction between students who plagiarize because of ignorance and those who do so because of will. If the student is aware that plagiarism is an offence and knows about the rules on how to avoid it yet commits it under the compulsion of influences she or he cannot resist, this is a clear instance of plagiarism. If, however, a student plagiarizes but does so because she or he is unaware that what she or he is doing is wrong, or because she or he has not been well informed about the rules on how to avoid it (by crediting, acknowledging, summarizing, paraphrasing, quoting, or referencing), the student may be pardoned and given the chance to correct himself or herself. The issue of plagiarism goes beyond the confines of college responsibilities and student performance; indeed, it is laden with ethical, moral, and social valuations. Therefore, it is necessary to make distinctions about what constitutes plagiarism and what does not.

In institutional settings, plagiarism has been identified to occur "when a writer deliberately uses someone else's language, ideas, or other original (not common-knowledge) material without acknowledging its source." (Council of Writing Program Administrators, CWPA", 2003, p. 1). CWPA distinguishes between intentional and unintentional or accidental plagiarism resulting from carelessness or ignorance of the rules. They point out that current discussions on plagiarism fail to make the distinction between intentional and unintentional plagiarism. They identify two distinct modes of plagiarism:

1. Using someone else's words or ideas without giving credit to the original author, attributing that to one's own effort
2. Inadvertently or improperly citing words and ideas borrowed from other sources

They conclude that such discussions confuse between plagiarism and the misuse of sources, and observe that "ethical writers make every effort to acknowledge sources fully and appropriately." However, students often lack the experience necessary to properly document the sources they use, and as a result, they fall into unintentional plagiarism. This occurs when students use specific citation formats incorrectly or fail to use quotation marks properly. This distinguishes between those who attempt to acknowledge sources of information but fail to cite the sources properly, in which case they have committed unintentional plagiarism (The Council of Writing Program Administrators 2003, p. 1).

5.2.2. Degrees of unintentional plagiarism

The general rule is that every information that is not your own or that is not general knowledge should be cited and credited to its source through summarizing, paraphrasing, and quoting. When paraphrasing, the resultant new text should be substantially different from the original in terms of language and style.

There are many slippery situations where writers may fall into plagiarism unintentionally or inavertently. Students and researchers need to be careful about such murky situations:

- o copying from a source but changing only a few words in attempting to summarize or paraphrase
- o summarizing or paraphrasing without acknowledging the source
- o borrowing information or ideas without crediting the author
- o not copying the exact words as they appear in the original text
- o writing the author's name but misspelling it
- o writing the wrong date of a source
- o writing the wrong page number of a quotation
- o writing a quotation but forgetting to put it within quotation marks
- o omitting words from a quotation without indicating the omission with ellipsis points
- o using your own previously published works without citing them

5.2.3. The extent of academic dishonesty in higher education

Plagiarism and other forms of academic misconduct are so prevalent that they have become issues of major concern for college administrations and professionals in higher education institutions worldwide. In one of the earliest surveys of its kind to measure the extent of academic dishonesty in US universities, Bowers (1964), surveyed more than five thousand students in a sample of ninety-nine US colleges and universities. Bowers's survey established that three-fourths of the respondents had engaged in one or more incidents of academic dishonesty. This study was replicated by McCabe and Treviño (1997) some thirty years later in nine US colleges. Although the latter study found a modest increase in cheating, it also established that academic dishonesty and cheating have been prevalent and on the rise. Another study discovered the alarming fact that one in ten PhD students reported that falsification and fabrication of data was acceptable (Hoffman 2010).

In an Australian setting, a research survey sample of 205 Australian university students (47 male, 158 female, ages eighteen to fifty-three) was conducted. A revised model accounted for a substantial 40.8 per cent of the variance in student engagement in research misconduct and questionable research practices (Rajah-Kanagasabai and Roberts 2015). More seriously, academic misconduct prevails even within teacher-training institutions intended for the training of teachers and students to become teachers responsible for the ethical conduct of their students (Gal 2015).

5.2.4. Academic dishonesty correlates to future dishonesty in the workplace

It has been found that there is a positive and significant correlation between unethical behaviour in the workplace and dishonest academic practices at college. It has been observed that those who lie at work also used to engage in frequent academic misconduct at college, such as plagiarism. In a wide investigation of this kind, authors examined a total of 1,051 students from six university campuses in the United Sates to determine whether a relationship exists between academic dishonesty at college and dishonesty in the workplace. The study addressed academic integrity in both the classroom and the work environment. The authors found that "students who engaged in dishonest acts in college classes were more likely to engage in dishonest acts in the workplace" (Nonis and Cathy 2001, p: 1).

The results of this and similar studies establish a positive and significant connection between dishonest academic practices at college and future dishonest practices in the workplace. This fact has far-reaching implications for individuals, businesses, and society at large. Some college graduates who take up jobs and assume responsibility after graduation will also be found to engage in different types of dishonest practices instead of conscientiously observing justice, fairness, and impartiality in carrying out their duties. But these are the type of students who used to engage in similar dishonest practices at college. The consequences of unethical behaviour can be serious, ranging from losses to businesses, losses of individuals rights, and the undermining of social cohesion and political stability.

There is a global concern at present for a reorientation towards ethics to be incorporated as an integral part of curricula, especially in business and management schools. This concern comes as a response to reported widespread unethical practices, especially among corporate and business leaders; such reports are replete with financial scandals, bribery scandals, and instances of fraud and unethical decision-making. The Madoff investment Ponzi scheme and the bribery scandals at Siemens Germany, Walmart Mexico, and Hewlett-Packard in the US are just a few examples to "illustrate the global nature of the problem. Corporate scandals across all major industries are now so pervasive that several organizations are dedicated to tracking and listing instances of unethical corporate behaviour" (Bagraim, Suki, and Stephanie 2014, p. 1).

5.2.5. How to avoid plagiarism: the need for ethics in education

Students should be educated in the rules of ethics and integrity and taught about the rules on how to avoid plagiarism. The first step is to educate students on good conduct and to refrain from dishonest academic practices. But such exhortation would be of little import unless the rationale behind it is explained to students. University and college students are grown up young men and women who want to be treated as responsible adults. They need to be reminded that they are going to assume leadership roles in society after graduation and that the university is keen to equip them not only with academic learning and practical training but also with high moral standards for themselves and for the good of the general public at large; therefore, they must strive to be good, honest people deserving of the trust that will be accorded to them as future leaders. Such education will receive keen listening ears, and hearts yearning for virtue and goodness. It is important, however, to avoid a "policing approach" to academic misconduct. A scrutinizing approach can only be educationally counterproductive. Instead students should be encouraged to emulate the best thinkers, at the same time maintaining their own originality. This is not easy if they are constantly being scrutinized for unintentional plagiarism (Martin 1992).

Guiding students through a rationalistic approach that explains the reasons behind penalizing plagiarizers is an important first step to preparing students to receive the rules which will enable them to avoid plagiarism and other forms of academic misconduct. In effect, they will realize that observing the rules fulfils their ambition for becoming good for themselves and good for their society. Students strive for success in school in order to be successful in life. They need to see the connections between success at school and success in life. Success in school does not necessarily mean success in life. Success in life requires further qualities than just academically excellence or professionally adeptness; it requires good moral standards of integrity, justice, honesty, fairness, and responsibility. Students will be more than eager to take in such moral exhortation as makes them good citizens—and successful people, too.

Such instruction to explain the rationale behind a stern commitment to academic values (i.e., integrity) is more apt to convince students to adhere to such rules out of proper understanding than if they were to receive them merely as red-tape instructions. At this stage, students will be ready and eager to learn the rules on how to avoid plagiarism (and indeed other dishonest practices), and to observe these rules out of conviction and good faith.

5.3. To the nitty-gritty of how to avoid plagiarism

To avoid plagiarism, writers have to properly credit the original authors from whom they borrow information or ideas. The name of author, the name of the original work, and the date of publication must be cited every time the writer employs one of the following methods of making use of the information from a source:

- o paraphrasing or summarizing someone else's ideas
- o copying another person's exact words (quoting)
- o presenting facts, statistics, charts, or diagrams developed by another author

It is important that people embarking on research are well informed about the various requirements of properly conducting research. Not knowing the rules is an unacceptable excuse. Writers doing research must know what is required and how to do it. They must know the rules pertaining to documentation, citation, synthesis, referencing, and other essential requirements.

5.4. Documenting, summarizing, paraphrasing, and quoting

5.4.1. Documenting and synthesizing

Synthesizing refers to the act of combining diverse information from various sources, weaving it seamlessly into the fabric of a piece of writing cast in a new form and style. This requires combining the original information obtained from various sources and moulding it anew to fit in with the demands of the new research. In synthesizing, the researcher identifies similarities, differences, contradictions, supporting evidence, examples, and ideas across the corpus of information from the various sources and groups them together, contrasts them, compares them, evaluates them, and casts them in a new form as fits the requirements of the new thesis she or he is developing.

Students need to understand that writing a research paper necessarily requires reading other sources and taking information from them. There is no harm in taking information and ideas from other writers, but this must be done in the proper manner prescribed by international academic practice, which involves crediting sources of information in order to avoid plagiarism. In fact, successful writers do this every time they write academic papers, without being accused of plagiarism. So how do successful writers do it? The secret is that they take information and new ideas and write them in their own language and style such that the borrowed information appears in a completely novel shape. But when they borrow information and ideas, they credit the original authors every time they do so. This is called documentation and citation.

5.4.2. Documentation and citation of sources

Documentation takes place on two levels with distinct terms:

1. *In-text citations*: These give credit to the author briefly in the body of text.
2. *References*: These appear as a complete listing at the end of the paper of all the sources cited in the body, giving full bibliographical details of each source.

Documentation and citation are carried out through the important anti-plagiarism trinity: summarizing, paraphrasing, and quoting. Students have to master these writing skills and apply them in their writings. A good grounding and drilling is necessary to acquire these writing skills, which are by no means easy. Teachers of composition writing need to spend time drilling students on these important skills, which then enable students to draft their research papers with ease, efficiency, and confidence.

5.4.3. In-text citations and referencing

In-text citations appear in the main body text of the research to acknowledge sources and to credit authors from whom a writer borrows information or ideas. Any source that is cited in the body of the research should also appear in full detail in the list of references at the end. So there is a close connection between citations and references. When citing a source, the researcher needs to record the source information in brief in the body of the text. Three essential elements need to be recorded for citations:

1. The author's family name
2. The date of publication
3. Page numbers (in the case of a quotation); for example: (Arthur 2009, 132).

However, the full source details *must* appear in the list of references at the end of the paper, in the following way:

> Arthur, B. (2009). "The Effects of Civil Wars in Central Africa on Children". *African Affairs* vol. 12, no. 3, pp. 128–42.

Students and new researchers often overlook the organic link between citations and referencing, and think that only citing the source is enough, forgetting or neglecting to include the full details in the list of references. Supervisors and assessors frequently move back and forth between citations and the list of references to make sure that cited information is properly referenced and to check the validity of the sources cited.

The three pieces of information needed for citations (author, date, and page number) and the full details for referencing come in different ways with regard to the place of full stops, brackets, commas, and quotation marks. These tiny details are used differently in different referencing systems. There is the Harvard referencing system, the APA (American Psychological Association) style, the MLA (Modern Language Association) system, and others. The basic rule here is that consistency matters. Be consistent with the use of tiny details.

The rationale behind documentation and citation

- o The reader may want to check that the information you cited is correct.
- o She or he may want to find out and read more about the topic
- o Citation and documentation show that you are not copying—plagiarizing.

What types of information need to be documented?

- o specific information and main ideas that you take from sources
- o new, unusual information and ideas
- o statistics, dates, numbers, etc.
- o illustrations, pictures, diagrams, graphics, tables, etc.
- o quotations and texts

5.4.4. Summarizing

Summarizing is the act of reducing the length of a text to a brief and concise form, while at the same time retaining the main ideas. Summarizing is a very useful and important technique that greatly helps researchers to condense large portions of information in a brief, concise form. It is also one of the key strategies to guard against plagiarism, together with paraphrasing and quoting. However, summarizing is not easy; it is a skill that requires much hard work and practice to master. It demands that the writer

- o be able to read carefully and understand what she or he reads;
- o be able to identify main ideas, key points, and important details;
- o be able to point out unimportant information and leave it out;

- ○ retain the main ideas and important information and express these in a new style and form, which requires the writer to
- ○ know how to express borrowed ideas in his or her own words and style; and
- ○ master the skill of paraphrasing as a first necessary step to writing good summaries

Summarizing is a difficult skill to master, especially with students having to grapple with diverse sources on difficult and sometimes unfamiliar topics. It is true that even professors who are expert writers experience difficulty when summarizing texts on unfamiliar topics. Summarizing and paraphrasing are some of the most difficult skills for students to master. Good teachers need to exert extra effort to teach their students how to do these things well, and they will therefore need to develop good teaching strategies to help students master these difficult skills. The best way is first to master the technique of paraphrasing. This is an important first step towards mastering summarizing. In both skills, it is important to be able to identify main ideas and keywords, and restate these in different words in the one's own style. Substituting words with synonyms alone does not make a good paraphrase. Other important actions involve changing the structure and organization of the original text to guarantee good paraphrasing. A good deal of practice on paraphrasing is a necessary step towards writing good summaries.

5.4.4.1. *Techniques for writing a good summary*

- Read the original text carefully and check new difficult words.
- Mark the key points by underling or highlighting while you read.
- Make notes of the key points, paraphrasing them in your own words.
- Write the summary from your notes
- Check the summary for ideas, brevity, and accuracy.

5.4.4.2. *Characteristics of a good summary*

A good summary is

- objective, meaning that it reports only the author's point of view;
- concise, meaning that it is complete and brief, containing all the main ideas but in few words;
- balanced, meaning that it gives equal weight to each of the ideas expressed by the author; and
- accurate, meaning that it gives the reader an exact picture of the ideas expressed in the original text.

5.4.5. Paraphrasing

Paraphrasing is the act of using one's own words to express ideas in an original text without changing the meaning. A paraphrase is a form of an indirect quotation. It states borrowed ideas in the writer's own words and style; therefore, it must be documented, giving credit to the original author. Paraphrases are a convenient way of expressing others' ideas, and at the same time, they are flexible enough to enable writers to include their own interpretations and thoughts about the issue at hand and fit them smoothly into the fabric of their work. However, note that changing only a few words from the original text of another author does not constitute a legitimate paraphrase.

Paraphrases take two distinct forms: plagiarized and legitimate. In a plagiarized, or literal, paraphrase, the writer uses synonyms to substitute words in the original text, but the overall structure of the original remains unchanged. In literal paraphrases, a writer may run the risk of plagiarism. Moreover, a sentence-by-sentence paraphrase makes the writing look as though it is patched up and unauthentic. In legitimate paraphrases, the writer not only substitutes original text words with synonyms but also undertakes a complete restructuring of the original, retaining only the main ideas and casting them in a new form and style. Free paraphrasing makes writing more authentic and natural.

Original text:

> William Hanson and colleagues (August 2016) conducted a wide research to test the Theory of Moral Development, especially of business students. They report that their research findings indicate that students are morally developed by the university system, showing ethical character outcomes. Implications suggest universities might maximize environmental artifacts and student-university relationships to develop students as effective moral agents in university, business, and community settings.

Plagiarized paraphrase:

> William Hanson and associates report about their research findings that students are morally developed at the university. They show moral characteristics. Implications suggest that universities can maximize environmental benefits and strengthen student–university relationships. This will develop students as effective, morally responsible agents in university, business, and community settings.

Legitimate paraphrase:

> In a study undertaken by William Hanson and colleagues (August 2016) on the moral development of business students, the researchers found that students indeed develop morally and gain positive ethical traits from the university environment. Universities can gain useful insights from these findings by working to maximize students' potentials through various programs to graduate

students who are morally responsible citizens, good for themselves and for society.

5.4.5.1. *Elements of an effective paraphrase*

An effective paraphrase

1. has a different structure to the original text,
2. has mainly different vocabulary,
3. keeps the same meaning, and
4. keeps some phrases from the original

5.4.5.2. *Techniques for paraphrasing*

1. Change vocabulary by using synonyms (for example, use *career* rather than *job*).
2. Change grammatical structure from verb to noun (for example, use *act* rather than *activity, action*, or *active*).
3. Change the order of information by shifting focus from that of the original (for example, you may bring a main point stated at the end in the original to the front of your work).

Whenever original information or ideas are paraphrased or summarized to be used in the document, the writer must credit the original author. This can be done simply by introducing the name of the author using words and phrases such as these:

- According to ...
- In the words of ...
- Huda observes that ...

Paraphrases and summaries should be accurate and faithful to the meaning of the original. If some key terms or unique ideas are copied exactly, either because of their originality or the difficulty of substituting them with synonyms, quotation marks must be used to indicate that these are quoted exactly from the original text.

Example

> In *The Republic*, Plato argues that the best guardians should be subjected to a rigorous educational regiment to test their abilities and emotional fortitude. He contends that they must be tried with "enchantments" to pass them through difficult trying times, then through pleasures to "*prove them more thoroughly than gold is proved in the furnace.*" (Plato 2016, p. 106)

When referring only to ideas borrowed from an original source, the name of the originator must be cited somewhere in the paragraph. It is useful here to refer readers to extra sources on the same idea. If the writer wants to retain any unique and distinctive expressions that the original author used to express original ideas, these must be clearly distinguished by enclosing them within quotation marks.

5.4.6. Quoting

"To quote" means "to use the exact words of", and "quotation" means "copying from the original text exactly word for word." Quotations are used to give support to an argument. They emphasize a certain point by enlisting what experts or other authorities in the field have said about a particular point. But quotations should not be overused, lest the paper come to look like a patched piece of odd fragments from diverse sources. Quotations in the body text must always be referenced with page numbers.

The citation of a quotation should include three elements put between round brackets:

1. the author's family name (not the first or middle names)
2. the year of publication (followed by a comma)
3. the page number, or a range of page numbers (e.g., "(Arthur 2009, 231)" for a single page, or "(Arthur 2009, 231–239)" for a range of pages.

Quotations use quotation marks to contain the original quoted words within them.

Example

> "Authentic leaders genuinely desire to serve others through their leadership" (Wilson, 2014, p. 12).

There are two types of quotations: (a) short quotations and (b) long quotations.

5.4.6.1. *Short quotations*

A short quotation has the following characteristics:

- It is less than three lines.
- It comes as part of the paragraph.
- It comes within quotation marks ("…").
- It is cited using a source and page number inside round brackets prior to a final full stop, question mark, exclamation mark, or an elipsis.
- Its line spacing is the same as that used in the running text.

Example

> Dewey, father of Progressive Education states that "this view of educators holds that education involves the rote memory of facts and formulas and that the goal of education is little more than training for the

professional and commercial activities of adult life"
(in Chambliss, J. J. 1996: p: 146).

5.4.6.2. *Long Quotations*

A long quotation has the following characteristics:

- It is more than three lines.
- It is set as a separate paragraph.
- No quotation marks are used in a long quotation.
- A cited source and page number for a long quotation appear in round brackets following a full stop, question mark, exclamation mark, or an elipsis.
- Line spacing is single (sometimes double depending on formatting style).
- Special indentation is used to highlight the quotation.

Example

> In *The Republic*, Plato believes that some people have an in-born desire for learning and love of knowledge. He says:

> ... anyone whose predilection tends strongly in a single direction has correspondingly less desire for other things, like a stream whose flow has been diverted into another channel ... So, when a person's desires are channelled towards learning and so on, that person is concerned with the pleasure the soul feels of its own accord, and has nothing to do with the pleasures which reach the soul through the agency of the body. (Plato 2016)

In both short and long quotations, ellipsis points are sometimes used to indicate that words are omitted from the original text:

> Western philosophical tradition began in ancient Greece, and philosophy of education began with it. The major historical figures developed philosophical views of education that were embedded in their broader metaphysical, epistemological, ethical and political theories ... the Socratic method of questioning ... began a tradition in which reasoning and the search for reasons that justify beliefs, judgments ... (Contributions of Greek Education to the Development of Modern Education 2011)

Quotations are one of the techniques used to avoid plagiarism. However, they should be used sparingly and properly, documenting such details as the author's name, date, and the page numbers of the original text, using quotations marks. In many situations, though, writers forget to include some of the small details when quoting, which may result in unintentional plagiarism.

5.4.6.3. *Punctuating Quotations*

Various types of punctuation are used to cite quotations properly. Punctuation marks used in quotations include of brackets, single quotation marks, full stops, commas, colons, semicolons, and ellipsis points. Below is a short summary of how punctuation is properly used in quotations and what positions that punctuation takes in relation to the quote.

The use of brackets in quotations

Quotation marks are used to enclose short quotations of less than three lines to be inserted as part of the running text. Sometimes, however, writers may want to add additional information of their own, for clarification or explanation. Such additional information should be enclosed within square brackets.

Example

"Clover asked Benjamin to read the Seven Commandments of Animal Farm, [as they finally changed]. Benjamin revealed that the Commandments now consisted entirely of the sole message 'All animals are equal, but some animals are more equal than others'" (Orwell 1954).

The use of single quotation marks

Single quotation marks are used to enclose a quotation within a quotation.

Example

The advertising industry believes that "H. G. Wells's famous statement that 'advertising is a legalized lying' is not true in modern times."

Block quotations

For quotations of more than three lines, no quotation marks are used, and the quote is set apart from the rest of the paragraph by indenting it differently, such that it stands out clearly as a separate block, sometimes called "*block quotation*", ending with a full stop, question mark, exclamation mark, or an elipsis, followed by the citation.

Example

The inexperienced in wisdom and virtue, ever occupied with feasting and such, are carried downward, and there, as is fitting, they wander their whole life long, neither ever looking upward to the truth above them nor rising toward it, nor tasting pure and lasting pleasures. Like cattle, always looking downward with their heads bent toward the ground and the banquet tables, they feed, fatten, and fornicate. In order to increase their possessions they kick and butt with horns and hoofs of steel and kill each other, insatiable as they are. (Plato 2016, 586a–b)

Use of commas and full stops in quotations:

The use of commas and full stops in quotations is determined by the presence and place of the parenthetical reference. They are placed inside the quotation when a parenthetical citation is not provided.

Example

"Notwithstanding the fact that you copied unauthorized material", the supervisor told the student, "I give you the benefit of the doubt. You need to rewrite this section of your paper."

The full stop is placed outside the quotation marks when the parenthetical reference is mentioned.

Example

"In order to defend Animal Farm, we must realize Old Major's dream of a life without humans. For that end, we must stir up rebellions in other farms throughout England" (Orwell 1954).

Use of the colon and semicolon

The colon and semicolon always fall outside the closing quotation marks.

Example

"Orwell's heroic characters included pigs": Old Major, Napoleon, Snowball, and Squealer.

"Squealer was a small, white, fat porker who served as Napoleon's second-in-command and minister of propaganda; he held a position similar to that of Vyacheslav Molotov in the USSR".

Use of ellipsis points in quotations

Ellipsis points— or three spaced dots (…) are included in a quotation to indicate that part of the original text is omitted. Ellipsis points are very useful and widely used in quotations for purposes of brevity and conciseness. They help writers to omit unnecessary details to focus only on important text and keywords that carry the strongest and most potent effect the writer wants to convey to his or her audience.

Example

Sammy was soft-spoken, but he believed strongly in "respect for women, love of country … and a bright, sunny day" (87).

When the omitted part is a whole page, a paragraph, or part of a poem, as a general rule, a single line of spaced dots as long as the preceding line is used.

> Of Man's First Disobedience, and the Fruit
> Of that Forbidden Tree, whose mortal taste
> Brought Death into the World, and all our woe,
> . . . .
> Who first seduc'd them to that foul revolt?
> Th' infernal Serpent; he it was, whose guile
> Stird up with Envy and Revenge, deceiv'd
> The Mother of Mankind, what time his Pride
> Had cast him out from Heav'n, with all his Host
> Of Rebel Angels,
> (Milton 1674)

5.4.6.4. *General hints on quotations*

- In quotations, the author's name must be kept adjacent to the quote in the same sentence.
- Short quotations should be included as part of the running text, contained within quotation marks.
- Long quotations should be marked off as a separate block, indented on both right and left, and single-spaced to set them clearly apart.
- If a quote is long and needs to be shortened, ellipsis points are used to indicate omitted words.
- Sometimes a writer may want to explain or contextualize a quote, or add extra information. In such cases, the new words should be contained within square brackets.

The writer must be careful not to alter the tenor of the original meaning, edit it, or make any additions that skew the original meaning of the quoted material.

Quotations are effective and useful, especially when strong, succinct language is used to give the strongest rhetorical and argumentative impact. However, they should not be overused lest the paper end up looking like it is an uneasy mix of patched materials of sorts.

5.5. Careful planning and safe practices to avoid plagiarism

As noted by the Council of Writing Program Administrators, students and writing professionals in general do not, in fact, intend to plagiarize, and when plagiarism does occur, it is more likely to be a result of misuse of sources or inaccurate citations, which often result from time pressure and inaccurate recording of source details. Most often, students realize that proper citations and documentation indeed help them build confidence and trust in their work. This, of course, does not rule out that there are some who do plagiarize deliberately. Below are some suggestions for good planning and safe practices that can help researchers avoid plagiarism and improve the efficiency and organization of research writing.

Some of the best safe practices to avoid plagiarism start from the early preparation stages of reading and note-taking. At this stage, the writer should take every care to record accurate bibliographic details of sources in order to avoid much agony later on if otherwise such information is inaccurately recorded or missing, in which case the writer will have to retrace the original sources, losing valuable time in the process, and perhaps becoming tempted to plagiarize. Simple steps can be of great value to safeguard against plagiarism. As you go through your readings and take notes, always mark off quotations in bold colours to set them distinctively apart from the rest of text. Record the complete bibliographical information of the sources from which you have taken notes. It is advisable to also distinguish between ideas which are your own and those which you borrow from others.

Chapter References

Adams, George (2008). *Plagiarism in Higher Education Institutions: a Study on Sudents' Ethical Behavior at College and Future Ethical Behavior in the Workplace.* Oxford: Oxford University Press.

Bagraim, Jeffrey, Suki Goodman, and Stephanie Pulker (2014). "Understanding Dishonest Academic Behavior amongst Business Students – the Business Leaders of the Future". *Industry & Higher Education* vol. 28, no. 5, October 2014, pp. 331–40. DOI: 10.5367/ihe.2014.0222.

Basturkme, Helen, Martin East, and John Bitchener (2014). "Supervisors' on-Script Feedback Comments on Drafts of Dissertations: Socializing Students into the Academic Discourse Community". *Teaching in Higher Education* vol. 19, no. 4, pp. 432–45. http://dx.doi.org/10.1080/13562517.2012.752728, Routledge, Francis and Taylor Group.

Bowers, W. J. (1964). *Student Dishonesty and Its Control in College.* New York: Bureau of Applied Social Research, Colombia University.

Chambliss, J. J., ed. (1996). *Philosophy of Education: an Encyclopedia.* Garland Press, 1996.

Council of Writing Program Administrators (2003). *Defining and Avoiding Plagiarism: the WPA Statement on Best Practices.* http://wpacouncil.org/files/wpa-plagiarism-statement.pdf.

Gal, Yoav (March 2015). "Knowledge Bias: Perceptions of Copying among Lecturers and Students of Education" (case study of a teaching college).

Hoffman, Rachel M. (2010). "Trustworthiness, Credibility, and Soundness: A Vision for Research". (Editorial). *Journal of Mental*

Health Counseling vol. 32, no. 4, October 2010, pp. 283–87. Files/ Editorial%20Paper%20Craedibilityl.pdf.

Howard, Rebecca Moore, and Laura J. Davies (2009). "Plagiarism in the Internet Age". *Literacy* vol. 66, no. 6, pp. 64–67.

Lourev, Jessica (2000). "Punctuating Quotations". Written for the Write Place, St. Cloud State University. http://leo.stcloudstate.edu/ research/puncquote.html.

Martin, Brian (1992). "Plagiarism by University Students: the Problem and Some Proposals". Published in *Tertangala* (a publication of the University of Wollongong Students' Representative Council), p. 20. DOI: I:\Philosophy of Education\Plagiarism by university students the problem and proposals.mht.

McCabe, D. L., and Trevino, L. K. (1993). "Academic Dishonesty, Honor Codes and Other Contextual Influences". *Journal of Higher Education* vol. 64, no. 5, pp. 520–38.

McCabe Donald L., and Linda K. Trevino (June 1997). "Individual and Contextual Influences on Academic Dishonesty: a Multi-campus Investigation". *Research in Higher Education* vol. 38, no. 3, pp. 379–96.

Nonis, Sarath A. and Cathy Owens Swift (2001). "An Examination of the Relationship between Academic Dishonesty and Workplace Dishonesty: A Multi-campus Investigation". *Journal of Education for Business* vol. 77, no. 2, 69–77, ResearchGate. Accessed 21 April. 2016. DOI: 10.1080/08832320109599052.

Plato, *The Republic*. Translated by Benjamin Jowett. Internet Classics Archive. http://classics.mit.edu//Plato/republic.html.

Rajah-Kanagasabai, Camilla, and Lynne D. Roberts (2015). "Predicting Self-reported Research Misconduct and Questionable

Research Practices in University Students Using an Augmented Theory of Planned Behavior". *Frontiers in Psychology* vol. 6, no. 535, May 2015.

Rujoiu, Octavian, and Valentina Rujoiu (2014). "Academic Dishonesty and Workplace Dishonesty: an Overview". *Proceedings of the 8th International Management Conference: "Management Challenges for Sustainable development"*, pp. 928–38. Accessed 16 August 2015.

Stolley, Karl, Allen Brizee, and Joshua M. Paiz (2013). "Best Practices for Research and Drafting", written for Purdue University Online Writing Lab. Last edited 2013-10-07. *https://owl.purdue.edu/*

The Boyer Commission Report (1998). *Reinventing Undergraduate Education: A Blueprint for America's Research Universities*. Sponsored by the Carnegie Foundation for the Advancement of Teaching, Princeton, New Jersey.

Westphal, Donella (2004). "Plagiarism". Created for St. Cloud State University. Last updated 26 May 2004. http://leo.stcloudstate.edu/research/plagiarism.html.

PART II
The Writing Stage

CHAPTER 6

Writing the Introduction and the Main Body

Abstract: This first chapter regarding the writing stage deals with elements of research that explain the organizational structure of writing, such as introduction, thesis statement, body paragraphs, and conclusion. Because this part makes up the core of research, writing a good introduction and good paragraphs is key to a successful paper, and a number of guidelines are suggested to write effective introductions, thesis statements, and bodies. The chapter provides the researcher with the best techniques on how to develop the thesis through coherent and logically connected paragraphs. Paragraphs are developed in the body through techniques of writing called "methods of development", each suited for a particular type of essay, such as description, narration, opinion, etc. This chapter elucidates these elements of research and gives examples for illustration.

Keywords: thesis statement, body paragraphs, paragraph unity and coherence, methods of development, cohesive devices

This section in the writing process discusses those elements concerned with the organizational structure of academic research writing, such as the introduction, thesis statement, topic sentences, body paragraphs, paragraph cohesion, and methods of development. Close attention to these elements ensures better readability and clarity of research.

6.1. Standard structure of the academic essay

The academic essay has three main parts: introduction, body, and conclusion. Each of the three parts includes features that meet specific requirements, which in totality add to the overall unity and coherence of the essay.

Introduction

A good introduction has

- ○ a hook (an opening that attracts the reader's attention),
- ○ background sentences to lay out the context of the topic, and
- ○ a thesis statement to give specific focus to the essay.

Body

- ○ The body includes a number of paragraphs to develop the thesis statement.
- ○ Each paragraph discusses one idea related to the main topic.
- ○ Each paragraph starts with a topic sentence that states the topic.
- ○ Each topic sentence is followed by sentences that provide details to support and develop the idea.
- ○ Examples, descriptions, evidence, and reasons are used to support and develop the topic.
- ○ A final sentence concludes and wraps up the paragraph.

Conclusion

- ○ The conclusion is a restatement of the main points discussed in the body.
- ○ The writer gives a final message based on the discussion in the body.
- ○ This final message may be an answer to question raised, a warning, a recommendation, a piece of advice, or a forecast relating to the future

Many academics write their introductions and conclusions last to reflect the information contained in the body. For beginner essay writers, it is advisable to write the introduction first to ensure that they answer the questions asked, but they should also check and revise if necessary when the body of the essay is completed.

6.2. Writing the introduction

The introduction states the subject of research, its purpose, its scope, and its organization. A good introduction includes some important elements that guide the reader easily through the research (i.e., the opening gives the main idea of the subject, followed by some background information that sets the stage for what is to follow in the main body). It should also state the purpose and the structure of the research, and explain how the various chapters, sections, and subsections are organized. Finally, the introduction closes with a thesis statement that clearly explains the specific focus of the research in precise, specific, and concise language.

6.2.1. Parts of the Introduction:

A good introduction should include three main parts:

1. A hook (an interesting opening to attract the reader's attention)
2. Sentences to give background information to help the reader understand the context
3. A thesis statement that gives the specific focus of the paper and guides the reader to follow the chain of argument in the body paragraphs that follow

It is advisable to follow a top-down method of writing, in which the writer moves from general to specific; starting with a general statement that attracts the reader's attention. This is called a *hook*. The hook is followed by a few more sentences to lay out the background and context of the subject matter, as well as its relevance and importance.

115

The introduction ends with a specific focus in which the writer states squarely what she or he is going to discuss in what follows in the body of the paper. This is called a *thesis statement*. A good introduction is key to a successful research paper. It sets the boundaries of what to include and what not to include. Although writing the introduction first could be useful, it is often true that many things may change in the course of writing, and modifications may be necessary later on. Therefore, it would be a good idea to write the introduction after completion of the whole work, whereupon the various sections to be included are clear and in their proper order, reflecting the main sections, subsections, and corresponding page numbers.

6.2.2. Writing the thesis statement

The thesis statement is the main claim expressed in a single sentence or a combination of sentences at the end of the introduction. In most short essays, a single sentence suffices for the thesis statement. However, in longer and more complex papers, the thesis statement may require a few sentences.

Following is an example introduction pargraph to an academic essay:

> Below, an appropriate introduction gives a definition of the main topic (cancer) and an attractive statement that hooks the reader into following the argument.

Cancer patients will be greatly relieved to know that their condition is not a result of malignant genes, but is one of metabolic malfunctioning, and there is a big difference between the two causal factors. The first presupposes a terminal condition associated with genetic mutations

> The background consists of a number of sentences that set the context and give background information to the reader to facilitate understanding of the subject.

which are difficult to alter, while the other implies impaired metabolism which could be corrected through medical intervention. The discovery was made in 1931 by Dr. Otto Warburg, who revealed for the first time that cancer is, in fact, the result of impaired cellular respiration, meaning that the diseased cells fail to utilize oxygen to burn sugar in order to generate energy. Under this condition, the impaired cells rely on a primitive form of energy production called *glycolysis* (from *glycose* and *-lysis* [meaning *degradation*]), a condition of oxygen-related metabolic anomaly in which cells do not use molecular oxygen. In order to adapt to the new conditions, certain genes called *oncogenes* are turned on, while others, called *tumour suppressor genes*, are turned off. **This important discovery paved the way for a new form of cancer treatment called the "Integrative Oncology Approach", in which medical intervention is used essentially to restore the cells' normal ability to utilize oxygen.**

> The thesis statement is one last sentence giving the specific focus and establishing what will be discussed in the body paragraphs that follow.

The thesis statement is the most important sentence in the introduction; it states the writer's specific focus, signals his position, and guides the reader to what she or he is going to say in the body. The reader will want to see how you are going to develop and support your thesis with sufficient reasons, examples, explanations, facts, and statistics. Some useful tips on how to support and develop your thesis are given below.

6.2.3. Strategies for writing effective introductions

An effective introduction may include some strategies that are often used to hook readers and attract their attention. One such strategy is to open with an interesting or surprising piece of information or statistic; an anecdote, story, narrative, or event that is relevant to the topic. It is possible to start with the definition of an unfamiliar term or concept, or to give a dictum from an expert or a famous authority. In longer academic papers, such as dissertations and theses, the introduction is much longer and includes several important sections; therefore, more than one paragraph may be necessary. Introductions to longer papers may include definitions of unfamiliar terms, background on a subject, the writer's stance about the subject, the methodology used, review of the literature, and the general organizational structure of the paper, outlining the sections and subsections of the main body. Introductions should be written with great care; they are the first part the audience reads, so it is important that they are vigorous, effective, and informative.

6.3. Writing the main body

The main body consists of a number of paragraphs. Each paragraph begins with a topic sentence that gives the main idea, followed by supporting sentences to develop the topic. Therefore, a paragraph is composed of a group of sentences centred on one idea (Bailey, 2015). Each body paragraph discusses one particular idea and starts with a topic sentence that captures the main idea and shows how it relates to other paragraphs and to the main topic contained in the thesis. The topic sentence is developed by giving reasons, examples, facts, explanations, statistics, and other details. The thesis usually contains a number of related ideas, which could not be adequately exhausted in a single paragraph, so a number of paragraphs are usually necessary.

6.3.1. Paragraph structure

- A paragraph usually starts with a topic sentence that is followed by supporting sentences.
- A paragraph should be neither too short (less than four or five sentences) nor too long.

- Linguistic devices (connectors, conjunctions, and transitional words) are used to link information within and between paragraphs.
- Examples of connective devices to achieve coherence include phrases such as *Going back to the previous point…, As mentioned earlier …, Turning to the issue of …, Notwithstanding the shortcomings mentioned above,* and *Finally …*
- The use of linguistic devices serves to maintain the flow and logical continuity of the argument for better clarity and readability.

6.3.2. The topic sentence in a paragraph

The topic sentence introduces the topic or main idea to be discussed in the paragraph. Consider the following points when writing the topic sentence:

- The topic sentence serves as a hook to catch the reader's attention; therefore, it should be interesting, attractive, novel, or unusual in order to engage the reader and get him or her to read what follows.
- An important characteristic of the topic sentence is that it should be neither too general (vague) nor too specific.

Example

Petrochemicals are produced from petrol. [This is too general.]
Ali and I had dinner yesterday at Al-Bukhari Restaurant. [This is too specific for a topic sentence.]

- A good topic sentence contains a controlling idea that indicates the direction in which the argument develops and guides the reader.

Example

Female students at JUC Female Campus are young ladies who come from different parts of Saudi Arabia.

This is a good topic sentence which can be developed on a number of possible angles:

1. That JUC has two campuses—one for females and one for males
2. The female student population (numbers, characteristics, age groups …)
3. The various localities or regions from which these students come (percentages, representation)
4. The state of female education in Saudi universities

The topic can be developed from various perspectives and elaborated on in a number of paragraphs; each point being discussed in a paragraph (four paragraphs in this case).

6.3.3. The Body of the Paragraph

The body of the paragraph follows the topic sentence and develops it. Essentially, the body paragraphs contain diverse information to support and elaborate on the topic. This is done variously by giving examples, definitions, explanations, illustrations, reasons, justifications, restatements, etc. Look at the development of the paragraph below.

> Following the recommendations, many governments encourage their citizens to own property. Some countries in the Middle East, such as Saudi Arabia and the United Arab Emirates, encourage families to own their homes by allowing them to pay in instalments over long periods of time—twenty or

thirty years. Families are even offered subsidies to buy land for building a house. These incentives are seen as part of a wider strategy to build stable, harmonious, and happy communities for whom services can be better provided. Such communities, with good education and health services, it is believed, will contribute to the social cohesion, economic prosperity, and political stability of the country as a whole.

The opening links this paragraph to the previous one through the use of a modifier ("following the recommendations"); it then introduces the topic ("governments encourage their citizens to own property"). Various development techniques are also used—for example, "such as Saudi Arabia and The United Arab Emirates". Reasons are given to explain why governments encourage families to own homes. Governments aim to achieve three goals: (1) social cohesion, (2) economic prosperity, and (3) political stability of the country as whole.

6.3.4. Paragraph unity and coherence

Good paragraph writing achieves unity and coherence to reflect the relationships between the ideas discussed. Unity in a paragraph means that all sentences are related to the main idea contained in the topic sentence. Sentences that don't add to the main controlling idea are irrelevant and should be crossed out. *Coherence,* on the other hand, refers to the logical flow of ideas as expressed in sentences; it is achieved when all sentences in the paragraph convey the relationships between ideas smoothly and logically. Unity and coherence make a clear connection and succession of ideas that the reader can easily follow.

How to achieve unity and coherence

Cohesion is the glue that holds together the elements in a piece of writing. Unity and coherence can be achieved by a variety of cohesive devices, including transitions, sequence words, repetition, reference words, and patterns of organization.

6.3.5. Cohesive devices and examples

○ Transitional words and phrases (e.g., *for example, in addition, however, therefore, furthermore*) clarify the relationships between ideas in a piece of writing so the reader can follow the logic of the argument.

○ Sequence words (e.g., *first, next, then*) guide the reader through a process, steps, or the order of events.

○ Repetition of keywords and phrases in a piece of writing emphasizes the importance of the recurring words and shows their relationships and their relevance to the main idea.

○ Reference words (e.g., *this, these, his, theirs, them, such, that*) are one of the effective cohesive devices that tie sentences and paragraphs to one another.

○ *Pattern of organization* refers to the way the information is ordered in the essay. Organization may follow a chronological order (the sequence of events in time) or a spatial order (in space or place), or it may follow an order of importance (from the most important to the least important, or vice versa). The way the information is organized in the essay makes it easier for the reader to follow the succession of ideas and logic of the argument.

○ Transitions are very useful in guiding the reader and in gluing the texture of writing, since they are essential to achieving unity and cohesion. They are also used for a wide range of thematic purposes, including listing items, giving examples, sequencing events in time, adding information, comparing, summarizing, and showing emphasis. You can use transition words for a variety of purposes aside from listing.

- listing items, events and ideas (e.g., *First ... Second ... Last ...*)
- to show examples (e.g., *for example, for instance*)
- to show sequence (e.g., *first, second, third, next, then, following this, finally, consequently, subsequently, thus, therefore, hence*)
- to add information (e.g., *and, again, then, besides, equally important, finally, further, furthermore, nor, too, next, lastly, what's more, moreover, in addition, first, second*)
- to compare (e.g., *but, yet, on the other hand, however, nevertheless, on the contrary, by comparison, whereas, compared to, although, in contrast, although ...*)
- to summarize or conclude (e.g., *in brief, summing up, to conclude, in conclusion, as I have shown, as I have said, hence, therefore, thus, consequently, overall, to sum up, in summary*)
- to emphasize (e.g., *definitely, extremely, obviously, in fact, indeed, absolutely, positively, naturally, surprisingly, always, forever, never, emphatically, unquestionably, without a doubt, certainly, undeniably*)
- to show time (e.g., *immediately, thereafter, soon, finally, then, later, previously, formerly, first, second, next*)

It is important that paragraphs have unity and coherence, and that all sentences are centred on the main topic expressed in the topic sentence. A good paragraph should have four main elements—a transition, a topic sentence, evidence, and support—and a final wrap-up sentence. Sentences in a paragraph must all follow each other logically by employing a variety of connectors, transitions, cohesive devices, and sequencing words. Paragraphs should also contain enough sentences to adequately give supporting evidence, with examples sufficient to develop the main idea given in the topic sentence. Generalizations (if any) should also be explained and clarified for the benefit of the reader.

6.3.6. Paragraph development

Paragraphs can be developed using a variety of details to support the argument. These include

- proper reasoning,
- good examples,
- descriptions,
- appropriate definitions,
- clear explanations,
- facts and statistics,
- convincing evidence, and
- supporting evidence arrived at through the methods of induction and deduction.

6.3.6.1. *Induction*

Induction is the type of reasoning that moves from specific facts to general conclusions. When engaging in deduction, you begin with some specific data and then work towards general conclusions that can logically be drawn from the data. In other words, you determine what theory or theories could explain the data. The writer first states the thesis of the argument, which is, in fact, the final end result to be arrived at; then she or he tries to support it by deploying a variety of reasons, facts, and other details to prove the validity of the evidence. What is important in inductive reasoning is that the theory does indeed offer a logical explanation of the data. The following is an example of inductive reasoning.

Facts:

The man was carried hastily to hospital in the early hours that day but died three hours later. The dead man was knocked down by a truck loaded with bricks. The truck was seen speeding down the road that night. The accident happened shortly after midnight on 12 August. Bloodstains were spotted on the right side of the truck. The truck driver was reported to have been working all day on the day of the accident.

The obvious conclusion:

The truck driver knocked the man down and caused the man's death; thus the inductive logic argument:

Conclusion: The truck driver knocked the man down and caused the man's death.

- ○ Evidence: The truck was seen down the road, bloodstains were found on the truck, and the truck driver worked all day that day, so he was obviously sleepy when he was driving.
- ○ Assumption: The facts represent a series of connected events that justify the conclusion.

6.3.6.2. *Deduction*

In the deductive method of reasoning, the argument moves from general premises to specific conclusions. It begins with some general statements, called *premises*, which are assumed to be true; then it is determined what else would follow as true if the premises were true. It can be assumed that if you think, then you must exist. As French philosopher René Descartes said, "cogito ergo sum", which roughly translates into English as "I think, therefore I exist." The premises themselves, however, may be unprovable. They must also be accepted on face value or by faith. For this reason, deduction (also called *syllogistic reasoning* or *syllogism*) can give you absolute proof of your conclusions, provided that your premises are correct. The deductive method follows a set pattern of reasoning premised on three logically connected steps.

1. Major premise
2. Minor premise
3. Conclusion

For a syllogistic argument to be correct, the first two premises must lead logically to the conclusion. Below is an example of deductive reasoning:

A. Major premise: All Muslims fast during the month of Ramadan.
B. Minor premise: Salman is a Muslim.
C. Conclusion: Salman fasts during the month of Ramadan.

This is a sound syllogism, since the first two premises are generally accepted as facts—that all Muslims fast and that Salman is a Muslim—leading to the logical conclusion that Salman will also fast, since he is a Muslim. Sometimes the relationship between the two major premises is not so clear, and this is where many arguments may be accepted as correct when in fact they are only fallacious and logically erroneous. Take the example below:

1. Major premise: All wild beasts prey on humans.
2. Minor premise: The African elephant is a wild beast.
3. Conclusion: African elephants prey on humans.

In form, the syllogism looks perfect, but when scrutinizing the major premises, it can be seen that they might not be accepted as true, since not all wild beasts do, in fact, prey on humans. This renders the argument invalid.

With a variety of techniques to develop body paragraphs through proper reasoning, good examples, appropriate definitions, facts and statistics, and convincing evidence through methods of induction and deduction, the researcher has the necessary tools to write the main body of the paper. The important outline, or plan, of the research comes in here. At this stage, the information is readily organized according to sections in the outline which show the connections between various sections and subsections. The outline provides a skeletal frame for the main body, and information on notecards—which the researcher has kept orderly and safe—from the various sources provides the flesh to fill in the frame. Each section in the main body starts with a main idea indicated in the outline according to its level of importance. Each idea is dealt with in a separate paragraph, and each paragraph starts with a topic sentence that introduces the main idea, followed by other sentences to support and develop the topic. The researcher may need to write a couple of paragraphs in order to deal with one particular topic exhaustively, and each paragraph discusses one idea, which in turn moves on to the next idea; the ideas are logically linked to each other within and between paragraphs through linguistic cohesive devices to maintain logical flow and consistency of the argument.

Here students and research writers need to know the different types of essay themes and how to develop them; such methods are called *methods of development.*

6.4. Methods of development of academic essays

Paragraphs are developed along various lines to achieve different thematic purposes of writing; for example, they may be used to describe an object or event, narrate an incident or story, or define a concept. Below is a list of the most common methods used to develop various genres of writing. More important than the technical structures of how to write the main body given above is coming to grips with the actual methods which the researcher needs to use to develop the argument of research. There are some common methods of development, each suited for a particular type of argument, and each has its distinct style and language. Here are some of these methods and specific types of language to use:

- definition
- description
- narrative
- comparison/contrast
- cause and effect
- classification and partition
- process
- opinion/argument

(For samples of different types of essays, refer to the chapter "Samples and Illustrations".)

Expository vs. argumentative writing

Methods of development can be subsumed under either *exposition* or *argumentation*. Expository writing is a type of writing which explains things and gives information. It uses methods of exposition to explain and inform the reader. Argumentative writing, on the other hand, seeks to convince the reader, using the language of evidence and persuasion. Accordingly, the first seven methods in the list above are examples of expository writing whose purpose is to explain and inform. The last one, "opinion/argument" refers to argumentative writing, the purpose of which is to persuade and convince.

6.4.1. Definition essay

"Definition" essentially means "the act of stating a precise meaning". Definitions are very useful and are frequently used in writing to give precise meanings—especially for explaining new concepts, unfamiliar terms, or a special meanings attached to common terms. Definitions can be used to give a short, precise meaning for a term (e.g., "stethoscope"), or they can be the subject of a whole piece of academic work (e.g., a whole essay devoted to comparing driving in Tokyo and driving in Cape Town).

Definitions are of two types:

1. short definition (consisting of a synonym, phrase, or sentence)
2. extended (or long) definition

A formal definition consists of three elements: term, class, and defining characteristics / specific features. For example, "A dentist is a doctor who specializes in the treatment of teeth."

An extended (or long) definition consists of one or more paragraphs that define a particular term. An extended definition usually has a formal definition (topic sentence) followed by extended support. Support can be provided by adding more information, such as examples, classification, comparison or contrast, and description. These methods of development can be used in combination to support and extend the definition. (For a sample definition essay, refer to chapter 18, "Samples and Illustrations".)

6.4.2. Descriptive essay

In descriptive essays, the writer gives details about the appearance, function, behaviour, or structure of an object. Descriptive essays follow certain patterns of organization to render the information accessible to the reader. Information may be organized in chronological order, in spatial order, or in order of importance. Chronological organization describes details according to time sequence—which happened earliest and which followed. Information organized in spatial order gives details about the locations of objects: in front, on top, or behind. In order of importance, the description moves from the most important to the least important, or vice-versa. (For a sample descriptive essay, refer to chapter 18, "Samples and Illustrations".)

6.4.3. Narrative essay

In narrative essays, the writer gives details of a narrative or story in a series of events that usually happened in the past. Narrative essays follow events as they happened in the past in chronological order, starting from the earliest, then moving to what followed and what happened last. Time words, such as "first", "next", "then", "afterwards", and "finally", are frequently used to show the order of events as they actually happened. Narrative essays, moreover, are seen to be formative experiences that teach us useful lessons and morals which shape our personalities and future vision on life.

6.4.4. Comparison and contrast

Comparison and contrast are useful and widely used methods of writing in which the writer depicts two or more items and notes their similarities or differences. The writer identifies a limited number of points on which to compare and contrast the objects. These are called "points of comparison" or "bases of comparison". For example, in an essay comparing Japanese cars and American cars, the writer may choose to carry out the comparison on the following points (or bases):

- price / cost
- dependability on the road
- fuel consumption
- availability of parts
- comfort
- engine horsepower
- interior space
- towing capacity

To write a paragraph or a multi-paragraph essay based on comparison and contrast, you need two subjects and at least one point of comparison or contrast. For example, one could compare petrol engines and diesel engines (two subjects), focusing on cost (one point of comparison). As another example, one could compare travelling by car and travelling by air, based on cost, convenience, and time (two subjects and three points of comparison).

How to organize comparison and contrast essays

There are two methods of organization.

1. Organization by subject—block organization

    When organizing by subject, focus first on one subject then move to the other. You may devote a whole paragraph to one subject and another paragraph to the other subject.

    o   In this method, both subjects should receive similar treatment.
    o   This method requires little or no comparison vocabulary, since each subject is discussed separately.

2. Point-by-point organization

    o   In this method, you take one point of comparison and describe the two subjects accordingly. For example, one could use the point of "convenience" for the subjects "travelling by car" and "travelling by air."
    o   This method is used when there are a number of specific similarities or differences to discuss.
    o   The points should receive equal treatment and order of organization
    o   In this method, vocabulary relating to comparison and contrast is needed and is more widely used.

In both methods of organization, a good introduction is necessary, in which a clear topic sentence sets the two subjects and their points of comparison and contrast. (For a sample comparison or contrast essay, refer to chapter 18, "Samples and Illustrations".)

6.4.5. Cause-and-effect essay

Cause-and-effect reasoning is a type of reasoning we normally use in many situations in our daily lives. For example, when we are confronted with problems, we want to understand the causes that underlie such problems or the effects that are likely to ensue. The focus of writing could be the investigation of causes leading to a situation, or it can focus on the effects that result from a situation, or it can focus on both the causes and effects. The relationship between the causes and effects in a given situation can be expressed in a variety of ways, called causal relationships. There are four main structures that can be used to explain causal relationships:

1. An effect leading to multiple causes
2. A cause leading to a number of effects
3. Causal chains, in which causes lead to effects, which themselves become causes leading to further effects, and so on
4. Causal circles, which are a variant of causal chains in which the ultimate effect is itself the cause of the primary cause, meaning that the causes feed into one another in a cause-and-effect circle

Cause-and-effect relationships are expressed in a distinct type of diction to capture the nature of the relationship. Common vocabulary used includes "result in", "lead to", "bring about", "contribute to", "as a result", "in consequence", "consequently", "in effect", "caused by" and "therefore".

Examples

City growth contributes to better chances of finding jobs.

Declining purchasing power is the main cause of hunger, not food availability decline (FAD).

Global warming brings about major changes in global climatic conditions, such as rising sea levels.

(For a sample cause-and-effect essay, refer to chapter 18, "Samples and Illustrations".)

6.4.6. Classification and partition

"Classification" means "the dividing of a number of items into a smaller number of groups". It is a convenient method used to analyse objects, events, and situations. For example: "There are two groups of students at university—graduate students and undergraduate students." "Partition", on the other hand, means "the taking of one item and dividing it into a number of parts." For example, "The eye consists of four parts: the pupil, the cornea, the retina, and the optic nerve."

6.4.7. Process essay

A process essay usually describes a series of actions that lead to a specific result or outcome at the end. For example, in an essay describing the process of refining crude oil in Saudi Arabian oil refineries, the writer starts with a description from the point at which crude oil is transported from the oil fields to the boiler tanks. Then follows the process in the boiler tanks, the heating stages, the different cooling stages, and the separation of various gases at different temperatures. (For a sample process essay, refer to chapter 18, "Samples and Illustrations".)

6.4.8. Opinion, or argument, essay

An opinion essay gives opposing views between two sides on a controversial issue on which there is disagreement; each side tries to "convince" others of its opinion by giving evidence and support. The goal of convincing is what makes an opinion essay different from other forms of expository writing, such as description, classification, definition, and comparison and contrast whose primary purposes are to inform.

Elements of an argument

There are three elements of an argument: thesis, reasons to support the thesis, and evidence to support the reasons.

1. Thesis: A thesis is basically an opinion, sometimes called a "claim" or "proposition". The thesis in opinion essays poses a controversial subject (e.g., "Space exploration is an expensive luxury").
2. Reasons: You must give reasons why you believe the thesis and why you want your audience to believe it too. But reasons alone are not enough. Reasons need to be supported by concrete evidence. (e.g., "Building a station in space costs hundreds of millions of dollars").
3. Evidence: Evidence is information that supports your reasons and gives them credibility. Strong evidence is a key to a good argument. (e.g., "If spent here on Earth, this money will improve the conditions of millions of people").

Rational or Emotional Appeal

"Rational appeal" refers to arguments which try to convince by appealing to the minds of the audience; emotional appeal, on the other hand, tries to convince by appealing to the feelings of the audience. Emotional appeal evokes feelings of fear, anger, pity, amusement, compassion, etc.

Dealing with Opponents

Your opponents will have a counter-argument with equally strong reasons and evidence; thus, the best ways to deal with your opponents are as follows:

- o Do not ignore your opponent's point of view; concede the strong points.
- o Include your opponent's position. This will give you honesty and credibility.
- o Including your opponent's view gives you the chance to refute your opponent's argument by exposing its weaknesses, at the same time showing the strengths of your own.

Organization of an opinion, or argument, essay

An opinion essay consists of three parts: introduction, body, and conclusion.

1. **Introduction**

   a. An attractive opening "hook" to set the stage of the controversial topic
   b. Background to give the context of the two opposing views
   c. A thesis statement that includes the opinion that you want the audience to accept

2. Body

    a. Consists of paragraphs which offer reasons and supporting evidence

    b. Includes your opponent's position

    c. Should be fair and avoid exaggeration

    d. Can be organized in two ways:

        i. Method 1: Opponent first
        - Discuss your opponent's view, followed by your own reasons.

        ii. Method 2: Opponent in the middle
        - Put your opponent's view in the middle, bracketed between your reasons.

3. Conclusion

The conclusion summarizes the main points of the argument and can end up with a prediction, warning, or advice based on the outcome of the argument.

The Language used in opinion, or argument, essays

Specific vocabulary choices are used to express ideas in opinion, or argument, essays. Typical diction used includes the following expressions: "it is proven", "science [or 'scientists'] have established that", "it is agreed that", "in my view", "think", "believe", "it supports", "it fosters", "adds to", "contributes positively [or 'negatively'] to", "encourage", and "discourage".

Examples

> Satellite technology supports many important applications used in our daily lives, such as communications.

> Cancer research has established that cancer is not the result of mutations in the genes but is a metabolic disease, meaning that it is the result of an altered metabolism.

(For a sample narrative essay, refer to chapter 18, "Samples and Illustrations".)

Chapter References

Bailey, Stephen (2015). *Academic Writing: a Handbook for International Students.* 4th ed. Oxford: Routledge.

Brizee, Allen (2013). "Body Paragraphs: Moving from General to Specific Information". The Purdue OWL, Purdue University Writing Lab. Last updated 25 February 2013, https://owl.english.purdue.edu/owl/resource/724/02/.

Gibaldi, Joseph (2003). Review of *MLA Handbook for Writers of Research Papers*, 6th ed. *Journal of Scholarly Publishing, pp. 179–83.*

Seyler, Dorothy U. (1994). *Understanding Argument: a Text with Readings.* McGraw-Hill College.

CHAPTER 7

Writing the Literature Review, Abstract, and Case Study

Abstract: This second chapter regarding the writing stage deals with those elements of research concerned with theoretical requirements, such as literature review, case study, and abstracts. These constitute essential requirements in good academic research. The purpose of these elements is to ensure academic credibility as regards the original contribution of the research, the authenticity and reliability of data, and the verifiability of results. The elements are explained, and supported by examples for illustration. Another essential part of good research is the presence of graphics and illustrations, and the proper use of the language of graphics. The chapter also gives detailed instructions on how to write the language of tables, charts, and graphs—how to write titles, numbers, captions, and sources relating to graphics.

Keywords: literature review, abstract, case study, contributions of research, graphics, illustrations, the language of graphics

This chapter on the writing process discusses those theoretical requirements essential in any research—namely, abstracts, literature reviews, case studies, graphics, and visual illustrations.

7.1. Sections of the main body

The main body of the research is the core part where the researcher presents his or her argument and develops it by providing evidence, support, examples, and illustrations to persuade the audience of its validity. The main body consists of different sections and subsections presented in headings and subheadings, each developed in a number of paragraphs; the various sections and subsections link to each other logically to develop a coherent persuasive argument. In academic research, the main body includes all or some the following sections, depending on the nature and scope of the subject matter under investigation.

- ○ literature review
- ○ purpose and contributions of the research
- ○ abstract
- ○ case study
- ○ methodology
- ○ data types and treatment
- ○ results and findings
- ○ illustrations, graphics, charts, and tables

7.1.1. Writing a literature review

A literature review is a comprehensive overview of what the researcher has read on existing literature written on the subject matter of the research. It summarizes, comments on, and critiques these writings. A literature review is not a mere summary of previous writings; indeed, it involves a lot more hard work of interpretation and critical evaluation of information to fit in with the direction of the research argument at hand. It requires the writer to do extensive research on existing published material in the field of research in order to justify why the work is important and how it contributes to the existing body of knowledge. A literature review has two main purposes: (1) to give your audience a general overview of the sources of information you have read and the views expressed by different authors, and (2) to demonstrate how your research fits into the larger field of study and advances knowledge by adding something new. The literature review is a singularly essential feature of academic writing, and it is one of the most difficult sections of research, requiring great care, effort, and skill. It is an integral part of the main body of the research.

The literature review is the first part of the main body that immediately follows the introduction. In it, the researcher reviews and summarizes relevant research previously carried out by other researchers on the topic. The purpose is to show that the researcher has exerted real effort to study in depth such previous research and is familiar with the subject matter, the current state of debate, the main arguments, and the different positions and views expressed by others on the topic. Three justifications can be identified for writing a literature review:

1. It justifies the undertaking of the research.
2. It provides the researcher with in-depth information on the topic.
3. It convinces the supervisor and examiners that the student not only knows about the topic but has also demonstrated the ability to analyse and synthesize information.

The extent and scope of the literature being reviewed gives the researcher confidence about what areas of the subject have or have not previously been researched so that she or he does not choose a topic that may have already been thoroughly investigated. This is to guard against possible duplication in research. A literature review is a tiresome and time-consuming task that demands much effort and attention. It is therefore advisable that researchers take care to do it more judiciously in the following ways:

○ It is not required to read all literature on a topic closely and in detail.
○ Read a source generally for overview, title, topic, results, and conclusion.
○ Read salient text features, such as table of contents, abstract, introduction, main arguments, and conclusion.

This will enable the researcher to identify gaps in previous research which she or he wants to fill and which make his or her particular area of inquiry distinctively different from others' work.

7.1.1.1. *Giving your audience a general overview of the sources of information*

In a literature review, the researcher summarizes, paraphrases, and quotes from original sources to show the various views expressed by other authors on the subject; comments on them and evaluates their views; and gives authors' names, titles of works, and sometimes page numbers if explicit material is quoted. This is called "in-text citation".

In longer theses, the literature review occupies an independent section. Because of the complexity of the literature review, it is advisable to organize it in a way that makes it easy for your audience to follow its logic. Two approaches are common in literature review organization: (1) chronological ordering, in which studies are reviewed from oldest to most recent, and (2) topical grouping, in which studies are reviewed by subject or theme. (Mike 2014) It is also useful when writing literature reviews to try to manoeuver your interpretations to fit within the direction of your argument. Use headings and summaries to guide readers to follow the chain of your argument.

The second main purpose of the literature review is to identify gaps in current research and show how your research contributes new knowledge to the field of inquiry.

7.1.1.2 *Identifying gaps and demonstrating the contribution of your research to knowledge*

- The researcher has to present a case to prove the importance of his or her work and show how it contributes new insights to existing knowledge.
- She or he has to point out where gaps exist in the current state of knowledge in the field.
- Specifically, the researcher must identify what has been lacking, overlooked, underinvestigated, or misinterpreted

in previous studies to justify the reasons for undertaking new research in a particular domain of academic inquiry.

In general, at the end of a literature review, it is advisable to ask questions such as those listed below to ascertain whether the important features of a good literature review are in place:

- Does the writer use any special methods to draw distinctions between groups of studies with similar or opposing views on the topic under investigation?
- How is the literature review organized? Is it grouped under sections, by headings, by similar or contrastive topics, or chronologically?
- What criteria do the writer use to group studies?
- Does the writer give explicit or indirect clues to which of the studies under review are most important?
- Does the writer give reasons why she or he has chosen particular groups of studies for review?
- Does the writer make frequent useful references to show connections to the research topic she or he is investigating?
- How does she or he transition from one group of studies to the next?
- Does the literature review give adequate coverage of key studies related to the topic under investigation?
- Does the literature review cast sufficient light to show gaps in the existing body of literature on the topic?
- Does the literature review show convincing reasons to justify the importance of undertaking the research?
- Does the writer explain the methods of research used?
- Does the writer identify any shortage in areas of research in this field that have been overlooked or not adequately investigated?

A sample literature review

The different theories and approaches discussed below reveal a considerable overlap between them, with the inevitable implication of giving different and sometimes conflicting interpretations of famine, as we will see later. The importance of theory to understand the phenomenon of famine stems from considerations for practical policy-making and vital issues which may mean life or death. This necessitates laying out a proper theoretical framework to understand and explain famine; on which understanding appropriate policies could be made. Five major approaches can be distinguished in the literature on famine. These are: (1) the naturalist thesis, (2) the population thesis, (3) the holistic or interactive approach, (4 & 5) the Entitlements Approach and the Food Availability Decline (FAD) Approach.

The Naturalist Thesis:

The naturalist thesis holds that "natural phenomena" are the prime causes of famine. Natural causes in fact are an amalgam of diverse natural phenomena, including aspects of the physical environment such as climate, drought, rainfall patterns, desertification, and soil erosion. According to the naturalist school, all or some of these aspects are responsible in varying degrees for the creation of famine.

Drought:

The intensity and frequency of the Sahelian drought has been a subject of controversy. Rasmusson (1987) points out that the extent of the mid-1980s drought has been exceptionally sweeping, and admits that "the coincidence of drought over such a vast region was the result of complex climatic processes which are inadequately measured, difficult to describe, and poorly understood" Rasmusson 1987: 3). It can be argued that the confusion surrounding the nature of the drought stems from the fact that the phenomenon has until recently sought purely "technical" climatological explanations offered by climatologist. It is only recently that the recognition of the anthropogenic social impact on the ecology and climate has gathered momentum (Recliff 1994, Sage 1994, Glantz 1978, 1987, Watts 1983, Nicholson 1986, Folland, Parker and Palmer 1985). Nicholson, for example, observes that the recent drought is particularly severe and prolonged. He observes that since the early 1960s a regular downward trend in rainfall over the Sahel is clearly the most severe of the twentieth century. ... Recently, attention has been drawn to an apparent relationship with global-scale changes in sea-surface temperatures (SST) (Folland, Parker and Palmer 1985) to be the determining force of climatic change and variability.

At a theoretical level, Shukla (1984) argues that climatic variations can be viewed as resulting from two mechanisms: (a) internal atmospheric dynamics and (b) boundary forcing. The first set comprises the internal structure of the atmosphere, i.e. wind, temperature, and moisture. The second set is associated with complex interactions between the atmosphere and the lower boundary and are influenced in the lower boundary by changes such as SST, snow, soil moisture, albedo (incoming and outgoing solar radiation) and vegetation cover as it affects the exchange of heat and moisture between the earth's surface and the atmosphere (Rasmusson 1987: 16).

In this complex interchange of processes the human social impact on the ecosystem is unmistakable. As social communities and their activities occupy the lower boundary, that can potentially upset the boundary forcing mechanisms. Excessive farming and deforestation can lead to loss of the vegetation cover, and consequently upset the balance of heat and moisture, and between the earth's surface and the atmosphere. Or again, excessive heating can upset albedo balance (the in-coming and reflective radiation) and can thus lead to the phenomenon of "global warming" and the problems of the "greenhouse effect". Many or any of the human practices can have strong impact on the ecosystem.

(Source: Hamid, Ahmed H. Fadlalla (1996), unpublished PhD thesis.)

7.1.2. Purpose (research problem) and contributions (significance) of research

In this section, the researcher presents his or her purpose for doing the research. Usually, she or he identifies a problem that requires research. The researcher sees a need to find an answer to a certain question or inquiry, or to explain a certain phenomenon which she or he thinks has not been adequately investigated. It is advisable that researchers identify their specific purpose for research and posit it in question form. They will formulate the research problem in a clear set of questions which they raise, and for which they try to find answers in the course of the research by providing sufficient support and evidence.

Closely linked to the purpose is the contribution which the researcher foresees to add to the general academic literature on the topic. The researcher may want to investigate a completely novel idea that has not been studied previously or may identify gaps in existing research that need further investigation; or she or he may want to present a new argument that challenges prevailing notions on a particular issue or contribute to solving problems of a societal, institutional, or theoretical nature. Contribution is an expediency that stems from the fact that academic research is a spearhead in the quest for accumulating human knowledge that is being continually expanded and enriched by ongoing additions contributed by individual researchers, institutions, and organizations for the benefit of mankind. The researcher should identify himself or herself with this milieu of an international academic community dedicated to the pursuit of knowledge for the advancement of humanity. There is vast literature made available by researchers in every field of knowledge, regulation for which demands that researchers have to specifically state their particular areas of work and the specific contributions that they want to make to the existing body of knowledge. This is what is generally referred to as "contributions" to research, or sometimes as "research significance".

When a researcher states the contributions and significance of research, these should be linked to the type of audience she or he targets to benefit from the findings—for example, he or she could note how society, decision-makers, or researchers can benefit from the research.

7.1.3. Writing an abstract

An abstract is a condensed version of a longer piece of writing that provides the main themes of the work and describes the content in a brief, concise form. An abstract also gives a brief note on the main findings of the research. Two types of abstracts are in common use: descriptive abstracts and informative abstracts. There is not much difference between the two. In general, an abstract should do the following:

- introduce the subject matter to the audience
- provide the scope, methods, and purpose of study
- provide a general idea about the outcome of the study
- provide a brief summary of the results, findings, or recommendations
- be short—a single paragraph or half a page

Abstracts are important to include in your research paper, especially now, in the new electronic age. Important information and keywords in abstracts, alongside titles, are stored electronically in databases for easy reference and retrieval for people who want to access them.

A sample abstract

The paper sets out to explore the views of a sample of Sudan public officials on job satisfaction. The study has two primary objectives. The first is examining how the public officials would fair in the measurement of job satisfaction. The second objective is what the public officials consider as prerequisites for promoting job satisfaction in their institutions. The sample included 337 participants, men and women, of varying age categories. Their views were solicited through a questionnaire that included dependent and independent variables. Descriptive statistics (mainly frequency distribution) and inferential statistics (correlation and cross tabulation) have been used to analyze data. Part of the research objectives is also to train participants on how to design and implement a quantitative research and how to write up a scientific report, guided by the principles of IMRAD. It has been eluded that the research is exploratory, aiming at laying the foundation for future rigorous investigation on job satisfaction in the Sudan. (Mohammed, 2008, p. 109)

7.1.4. Writing a case study

Case studies are widely used in research as both qualitative and quantitative methods of data. They are particularly useful in analysing issues in specific contexts, such as an organization, business, or social or political situation. They can be used to explain phenomena in real-life contexts. They can also be used to describe a series of past events to provide understanding of the key elements underpinning certain social or cultural phenomena. For example: "An examination of factors underlying widespread malnutrition among children in South East Asia: the Case of Bangladesh".

A case study is part of the main body of the research in which the researcher takes one example and studies it in detail with the purpose of generalizing the results of that particular case to other similar situations or replicating them. Usually, it is not possible in actual research to carry out an exhaustive study—say, of all the petrochemical companies operating in Saudi Arabia. A feasible approach would be to take one example, such as a particular company (e.g., SABIC [Saudi Arabian Bio-Industries Company]), as a case for study; show exactly what happens inside this particular company; and then generalize and replicate the results to other companies whilst taking into consideration minor idiosyncratic differences when generalizing the results.

A sample case study

Complying with Environmental Regulations

Case Study of Al-Noor Company

Complying with environmental regulations has become one of the important requirements for the proper and legal operation of companies and businesses. This is envisaged to protect people and the environment from harmful effects usually associated with companies' improper use of a wide array of noxious substances, chemicals, and wastes. According to the new environmental legislations, companies and businesses are liable if they violate environmental laws. Management boards of companies often seek ways to evade laws on the environment, or dodge them in some way. This paper presents a case that complying with environmental regulations guards companies from violating the law and paying liabilities. It is also good for business, as companies which comply with the laws get rewarded in many different ways, such as government subsidies and bank loans.

In this case, Al-Noor Company has to make the difficult decision to build an expensive technology to reduce the levels of chlorofluorocarbon (CFC) emissions to 0 per cent. Al-Noor is a company producing air conditioners and refrigerators, and it uses excessive amounts of cooling gases in its products. A considerable portion of gases leak out of the plant, negatively affecting the surrounding environment.

The company now is required by law to test the emissions from the plant and report on the health of the environment on a regular basis to ensure that emission levels are in line with the required safety standards. However, the company found that installing a new technology to eliminate CFC gas emissions is very costly and will negatively affect its operation and profitability. After careful consideration, the company's management decided to hold a meeting with the Environmental Protection Department (EPD) to discuss the matter. The company presented its view to the EPD that it would be financially unfeasible to install a very advanced purification system, but a moderate one would be good enough. Also, they wanted the EPD to help in obtaining government subsidies to purchase land on which to build showrooms for their products, thus helping in reducing marketing costs, getting access to markets and customers, and getting an edge over competitors.

7.2. Graphics and visual illustrations

Graphics and other visual illustrations, such as, charts, tables, diagrams, and maps come as part of the main body to provide further visual support to the argument. Visual information is an important part of good research. It helps present complex information in a concise form for good readability and visual balance. The researcher needs to provide a list of tables and figures at the beginning of the work, indicating numbers, titles, and the page numbers on which they appear in the body of the research. Students and researchers need to be familiar with how to present, label, and comment on the various types of visual information properly.

7.2.1. Types and uses of graphics

There are different types of graphics; each is suitable for use to display certain types of information. Below are some examples commonly in use:

Type of graphic	Common Use
Table	to compare and display information on various items
Diagram	to show the functions of different parts or areas
Pie chart	to display the proportions of elements in relation to a whole unit

151

Bar chart	to compare and display statistical information and to show relationships between groups
Line graph	to display changes in a situation across a specified time period
Map	to show locations

7.2.2. The language of visual illustrations

Specific vocabulary is used when converting graphic statistical data into written words. Describing a graph, chart, or table begins with a general statement on the topic of the graph, identifying the objects, the themes according to which the objects are to be considered, and the time period covered. The object may be one item or more (e.g., mobile phones), considered according to one or more themes (e.g., prices, unit sales, features) over a certain period of time (e.g., between 2008 and 2015). Usually, a general statement begins with the phrase "The graph [chart, table] shows [reveals, gives, illustrates] ...", followed by the themes to be considered (e.g., prices, unit sales), the objects (e.g., two types of mobile phones: the Galaxy Note and the iPhone), and then the period covered (e.g., between 2008 and 2015). Thus, the topic sentence would be "The graph shows the prices and unit sales of two types of mobile phones: the Galaxy Note and iPhone, between 2008 and 2015."

Then a description of the salient points in the movement of the graph is given, showing the upward, downward, or stable trends in the graph. Linguistic features are used, such as verb phrases, noun phrases, prepositions, and conjunctions. For example: "Prices of the iPhone *rose steadily* between 2008 and 2010 until they *peaked* at the end of 2010 at about $2,500; they then *dropped sharply* in 2011."

Or noun phrases may be used: "There was *a steady rise* in the prices of the iPhone between 2008 and 2010, until they reached *a peak* at the end of 2010 at about $2,500; then there was a *sharp drop* in 2011.

To describe the fluctuating or level movements of a graph, specific phrases are used:

Upward movement	Level	Downward movement
Rose slightly, a slight rise	Stayed the same	Dropped slightly, a slight drop
Rose considerably, a considerable rise	Remained the same	Decreased steadily, a steady decrease
Rose sharply, a sharp rise	No change	Fell dramatically, a dramatic fall
Increased steadily, a steady increase	levelled	Declined sharply, a sharp decline
Increased significantly, a significant increase	Plateaued (at a high)	Went down steeply, a steep drop
Went up gradually		Plummeted
Peaked, reached a peak		Dived, a dive
Reached a high, the highest		Trough

Usually the writer uses the verbs "show", "display", and "illustrate" to write a lead-in sentence to guide the reader follow the information displayed in table, chart, or graph. The description follows the graphic aid and is used to integrate the graphics into the text to lend supplementary factual support to the general argument. Descriptions should highlight only the salient features of the graph (e.g., the highest or lowest, peaks and troughs), leaving the rest to the reader to interpret the information before him or her. The description usually concludes with a forecast on what is likely to happen in the future, based on the understanding gained from the information displayed.

For example

The chart (below) illustrates the differences in life expectancy at birth between men and women in the EU-25 member states between 1980 and 2004. Life expectancy at 60 has increased by 18 per cent since the first half of the 1980s, from 16.7 to 19.7 years. The corresponding percentage for women is 13 per cent (i.e., from 21.1 to 23.9 years). Two things emerge. First, the increase in life expectancy at birth is for the major part due to lower mortality rates at older ages. Second, the more than 6 years difference in life expectancy at birth between males and females is reduced to 4 years at the age of 60. These trends are likely to continue in next ten to twenty years.

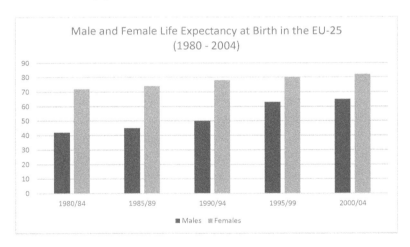

Visual illustrations should be labelled properly. Each graphic should be labelled in three areas; each is (1) given a number, (2) given a title, and (3) given source documentation. However, different graphics have different labelling formats for (a) tables and (b) other visuals, as follows:

a. Tables

Tables should be numbered and titled above, and cited underneath. Table number and title are centred above the table, separated by a single space. The table below is an example.

Table (1): Actual Development Expenditure
1970/71–1972/73 (in £S. Millions)

Sector	Allocation (1)	Actual Expend. (2)	(2) as % of (1)	Sector Exp.as % of Total Exp.	Sector Alloc. as % of Total Alloc.
Agriculture	62.9	29.9	47.5	34.1	36.3
Industrial	12.1	4.7	38.8	5.4	7.0
Transport, Power, and Communication	61.1	23.0	56.0	26.4	23.7
Services and Reserves	48.7	21.5	44.1	24.5	28.1
Technical Assistance	8.4	8.4	100.0	9.6	4.9
Total	173.2	87.5	50.6	100.0	100.0

(Source: Economic Survey, Sudan 1973: 113)

b. Other types of visuals

All other types of visuals (below) are given the same name, "Figure", which may be abbreviated as "Fig.". They are labelled, numbered, titled, and cited beneath. Figure number and title are placed in the same line underneath, separated by a colon and followed by the source on a separate line.

Samples of visual illustrations

Line graph

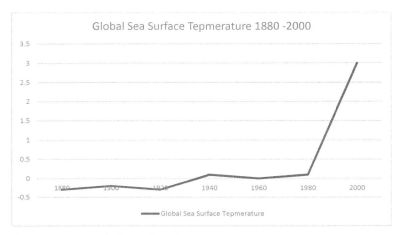

Figure 2: Example Line Graph
(Global Mean Sea Surface Temperature 1880–2000)

Pie Chart:

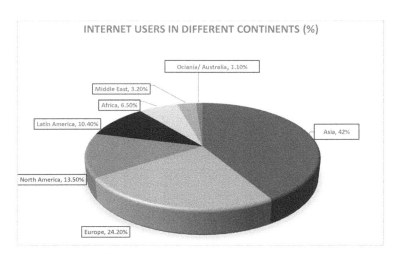

Figure 3: Example Pie Chart
(Internet Users in Different Continents)

Bar chart

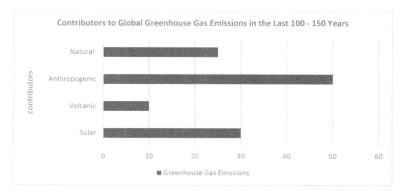

Figure 4: Example bar chart
(Contributors to Global Greenhouse Gas Emissions in the Past 100–150 Years)

(For more, see "Samples of Graphics and Visuals" in chapter 18, "Samples and Illustrations")

Chapter References

Hamid, Ahmed. H. Fadlalla (1996). *The Politics of Famine in Sudan: the Case of Dar Hamid and Dar Hamar.* Unpublished PhD thesis. University of Leeds, UK.

Kilborn, Judith (2004). "Writing Abstracts". Written for the Writing Lab at Purdue University; the Write Place, St. Cloud State University. *https://owl.purdue.edu/*

Mike, Gracemarie (2014). "Literature Reviews". The Writing Lab and the OWL at Purdue and Purdue University. Last updated June 2014. *https://owl.purdue.edu/*

Mohammad, Adam Azzain (2008). *Scientific Research Methods in Social Sciences.* Sudan: Public Administration and Federalism Studies Institute, University of Khartoum.

CHAPTER 8

Writing the Conclusion

Abstract: The conclusion is a necessary, integral part of research. It gives the final message of the argument succinctly and forcefully. Readers often go straight to the conclusion to get the final message. It is therefore important that researchers write it with utmost care to leave a lasting impression on the reader. Different techniques are used to write conclusions, depending on the type of argument presented in the main body. Conclusion techniques include echoing the ideas stated in the thesis statement, summarizing the main points discussed in the body, offering solutions to problems raised, giving warning, giving advice, forecasting the future, addressing consequences, calling for action, giving opinion, and speculating on future developments. A number of points have been suggested as guides to writing good conclusions. Most importantly, an effective conclusion should answer the big question, And so what?, which naturally arises in the reader's mind after finishing reading the research. Caution should also be taken to avoid some common errors in writing conclusions. Such errors to avoid include writing a vague conclusion or forgetting to write one, using trite and overused expressions, introducing new information, and cramming it with too many details.

Keywords: conclusion techniques, echo, summary of points, answer questions, warning, advice, prediction, recommendation, forecasting the future, opinion

Writing the conclusion

The conclusion wraps up the ideas discussed in the body. A conclusion should give the reader a sense of finality and completeness; she or he must feel satisfied that this is the end. The conclusion is an important part of academic research, and often readers go directly to the conclusion to gain a sense of what the final message and import might be. Bearing this in mind, a conclusion should be written with care to leave a lasting impression on the reader and to forcefully put the message across. In academic writing, a formal conclusion is an integral part of the work that is just as important as any other part. A successful conclusion brings the argument to a satisfactory close. The reader should feel satisfied that you have provided a logical answer to the lingering question: "Why is this argument important?"

When writing the conclusion, consider these points:

- After having finished with your research, ask the big, important question, And so what? Try to make your conclusion answer that big question.
- Your conclusion should give a gist of the ideas discussed in the main body, putting the main themes and important points in your own voice.
- Give your audience food for thought by leaving them with a lasting worthwhile issue or cause to think about.
- It is good to give yourself a sense of human worth that you would want to communicate through your academic work and share with others.
- Before closing your essay, always look back at your introduction to make sure that you have expressed the main idea contained in the introduction in a fresh form and style.
- Bear in mind that short conclusions are usually preferable to long ones.
- Try to add important insights to your conclusion—ideas which you want your audience to take home, and which you feel you have not expressed clearly enough.
- It is worth mentioning that there is no one sure method of writing a conclusion. One approach might work better in one paper than in another.
- Whenever you feel you have run out of ammunition to say something in conclusion, ask the stimulating question, And

so what? This question gives you momentum to rationalize your thesis in a brief and consistent manner as if you were explaining the tenor of your argument to your audience in a nutshell. You will be able to explain the importance of your argument, and point out some of the wider implications that go beyond the confines of the research paper.

8.1. Conclusion techniques

In writing conclusions, you can use one of the following techniques or a combination of them:

1. Echo—refer back to the introduction and thesis statement.
2. Summarize main points.
3. Offer solutions to problems.
4. Give warning.
5. Address negative and positive consequences.
6. Look to the future.
7. Give opinion based on evidence.
8. Recommend action.
9. Give a call for action.
10. Give advice.
11. Discuss future developments.
12. Answer the questions raised in the introduction.
13. Ask questions.
14. Make predictions and deductions.
15. Point out limitations and implications for further study.

8.1.1. Echo (refer back to the introduction and thesis statement)

Echoing is an effective concluding technique that connects the claim made in the thesis at the beginning to the final outcome at the end of the paper. If, for example, the thesis has raised a question, the conclusion should say something in answer to that questions. If the thesis states a specific view or opinion on a controversial issue, the conclusion should list briefly the points that support that view.

Example echo conclusion

In a narrative essay of a farm boy success story, focusing on the importance of hard work for success and achievement, the conclusion echoes the main stages of success that are already mentioned in the body of the narrative.

> Dammar's success story gives a good example to follow. We have seen that he has gone a long way in his turbulent and exciting journey to achieve all that amazing success. From his being a simple farm boy in rural Ethiopia to his becoming a university student in Addis Ababa, gaining a scholarship in England, and finally crowning his achievements with a ministerial portfolio in his own country at the age of thirty-five, his life story proves that success is inextricably bound with grit, perseverance, and hard work.

8.1.2. Summarize main points

The summary technique is a common simple way of concluding. In the absence of a more complex method of conveying your final message, the summary gives you an easy and convenient escape. However, avoid merely restating your main points. It is much better to synthesize the main points of your argument, weaving them into a fresh look to show your audience the logic behind them. Alternatively, you can just wrap up the main idea in different words.

Example summary closing

> Because of all the genuine and continued efforts since the 1970s by the Royal Family under the patronage of the King and the Prince of the Eastern Province of Saudi Arabia, and the dedication and hard work of the executive body of Jubail Industrial City, as represented by the Chief Executive Officer and staff of the Royal Commission, Jubail now is one of the most vibrant international industrial centres of innovative technologies in petrochemicals, steel, chemicals, fertilizers, and a host of related industries, making it a world industrial hub that draws partnerships of similar industries from around the world.

8.1.3. Offer solutions to problems

If you have raised a problem in your thesis statement, your conclusion should say something in the way of offering a solution to the problem raised.

Example

> People with special needs frequently complain that they are discriminated against, especially when they apply for jobs. This is no doubt a real problem that needs to be addressed, not only from a humanitarian perspective but also from a moral commitment to justice and fair opportunity. From the discussion that has been presented in this paper, businesses and companies have no excuse to discriminate against people with special needs. Personnel and human resource departments can think of many ways to accommodate these people

in their workforces. Some of these ways may include evaluating an applicant's strengths and weaknesses, and placing him or her in the right department. It is also a good way to evaluate the type of disability and place the applicant in the department where his or her disability will least interfere with him or her performing his or her responsibilities.

8.1.4. Give warning

Warn against possible consequences of action or inaction. You might point to possible negative consequences of lack of action (of what you have urged doing in your thesis).

Example

Thesis:

> Introduction: A global mean temperature rise of between 1.1 to 2.0 degrees is damaging to life on earth. Measurements of rising temperatures over the last hundred years have revealed a steady rise that threatens biotic life on land and sea. The main culprit is CO_2 concentrations in the atmosphere. CO_2 is emitted from the burning of fossil fuels, which is a shared responsibility involving individuals, societies, and governments worldwide. Combating global warming, therefore, requires concerted action on three levels: a global zero-carbon emissions strategy, official government policies, and a social individual level.

Conclusion giving warning:

> Grave inevitable consequences will ensue as a result of inaction on the part of the global community, governments, and societies and individuals in combating the underlying causes of global warming. Turbulent climatic aberrations will lead to catastrophic damage to coastal areas, farming communities, and urban centres. Low-lying lands will be submerged by rising sea levels as a result of melting glaciers in the arctic regions. Indeed, the livelihoods and future of whole communities hang in the balance between action and inaction on the challenge of global warming.

8.1.5. Address negative and positive consequences

Address the negative consequences by asking: What happens if we don't learn from the lesson of the experience? What has been (or what will be) the negative impact? For example, what might happen if children aren't taught the values of other cultures and religions?

Address the positive consequences by asking: What can we do to learn from the experience, and what positive results will be gained if we do employ it? For example, what can we do to share the many benefits gained from hiring more graduates in big business organizations?

8.1.6. Look to the future

Looking to future invites your audience to read your thesis in a new light, forecasting what likely developments of the situation could be in the future, possibly on a much wider scale.

Example

> It is estimated that at present over 60 per cent of the world's population use mobile phones. Satellite technology has made it possible for people to communicate across continents in seconds. The benefits of easy, sometimes free, communication are enormous, and such communication allows the reaching of simple people in remote and isolated communities. If current trends on mobile phone use continue, we can expect a complete transformation of traditional communities in terms of higher levels of literacy, improved health, and shared common values of freedom and knowledge in a globalized culture.

8.1.7. Give opinion or speculation based on evidence

After having discussed the subject of your thesis enlisting sufficient reasoning, it is a good and convenient method to conclude with an opinion based on the evidence already presented. Sometimes, when the evidence is invalid or inadequate to support the thesis, it is convenient to conclude with speculation or a question, such that the audience is left with an open-ended issue for contemplation and further thinking.

Example

> Current trends in global gas emissions reveal alarming facts about the accelerating deterioration of global environmental conditions. Erratic and dwindling rainfall patterns in much of the world, rising temperatures, melting ice caps, and rising sea levels are but a few examples of the many

devastating effects of increased CO_2 emissions associated with fossil fuel consumption. If current trends continue, we may witness catastrophic effects on whole communities in the foreseeable future.

8.1.8. Recommend action

Recommending or calling for action is another strong strategy for concluding your essay. Calling for action is especially useful in issues requiring social or ethical commitment that you want your audience to feel passionate about and take action on in support of a moral or humanitarian cause.

Example

Citizens in parts of the developed world have a moral duty towards people in developing countries. They must know about the dubious and corrupt practices of their home-based companies operating overseas. Much of the corruption and many wars perpetrated by notorious dictators in third-world countries are in some way fuelled through the interference of big multinational companies in local politics who secretly finance corrupt leaders in order to reap profits through illicit deals behind closed doors, as the examples in this study have revealed. Citizens in the developed world should know that part of their countries' prosperity in fact comes as a result of impoverishing people in third world. But they need not be accomplices in this crime; they should take action to expose those of their home-based companies engaging in corrupt practices overseas, check their trade records and deals, and publicize results. Such concerted action will make for strong checks against those companies and force them to operate fairly and ethically.

8.1.9. Give Advice

The *"Giving Advice"* technique is useful when you have evaluated a situation, carefully considering possibilities and pitfalls, such that you arrive at a clear vision on what the right course of action should be. You can then recommend action accordingly in the way of advising decision makers to take that course as the best possible option.

Example

> Saudi Arabia and the other Gulf Cooperation Council (GCC) states have accumulated huge money reserves from the oil boom over the past thirty years or so before the recent slump in oil prices. The oil slump has, in fact, done a good service to Middle Eastern economies in that it has alerted decision makers to the inherent vulnerability of their economies in their dependence on one strategic product as the backbone of their revenue generation. The reserves that have been accumulated could be depleted in a relatively short time in the absence of more permanent long-term plans for alternative sources of national income. As has been shown earlier in this study, for example, these countries together currently spend a staggering $35 billion on food imports annually, and this appears to be set to rise to $70 billion in two decades. Saudi Arabia and the other GCC member states are better placed if they can utilize their accumulated money surpluses in (1) diversifying their sources of revenue generation, and (2) setting up long-term food

security strategies in partnership with neighbouring countries that lack the financial resources to tap their agricultural potentials. This will reduce their food import bill substantially; at the same time, it will free them from the conditional strictures that are usually attached to food imports from major international exporters, such as the United States.

8.1.10. Answer the questions raised in the introduction

If you raised a question in your thesis, your conclusion should say something to answer that question.

Example

Introduction

The problem of global mass poverty in a world glutted with mountains of surplus money and surplus food is morally inexcusable. While half of the world dies "with a fork and knife", the other half dies of hunger and want. The real issue at stake here is the responsibility of the international economic system and key players who have systematically created the conditions that in the end led to this unjust distribution of international wealth at a time of global interdependence. The international economic and financial order should urgently turn to address this skewed situation not only because of moral responsibility but also for real pragmatic reasons. In the paragraphs that follow, we address the challenging question, What can the international financial system do to help poor people out of poverty?

Conclusion answering the question

Obviously, the international financial system bears the major blame in creating the conditions of poverty in many parts of the developing world and therefore has a moral responsibility to redress the problem. It has an obligation to remove the trade barriers that it created in the first place to discriminate against products of developing countries entering the international market. It should also legalize free movement of labour on a global scale; since trade markets are globalized, it is only fair to also globalize the labour movement. A third important measure is to reconsider international price and tariff systems to allow for fair pricing of commodities based on actual labour cost and the effort exerted in producing both primary and finished goods. These measures, if faithfully adopted, will certainly go a long way towards fighting poverty in many parts of the world.

8.1.11. Ask questions

By using the strategy of asking questions to write your conclusion, you pose an unexpected challenge to your audience to look again into your claim under a new perspective. It may alert them to consider other possibilities of addressing the issue, which they might not have considered previously. This strategy is also used when new insights develop and questions arise as the research progresses, and the arising new questions can provide a good way to conclude.

Example

> In the new IT age, people everywhere are now more attached to their mobile phones, laptops, and other devices than actual face-to-face interaction in the real world. Students are no exception to this rule. However, students' addictions to IT gadgets pose real questions to teachers and education professionals alike: Are we to strictly prohibit, say, mobile phone use in classrooms? Or are we to allow it to a certain degree? And what about exams? Are we to allow students to sit for exams using computers? Or are they to rely only on memory to answer exam questions? We need to address such questions pertaining to educational practices in the new IT age, and to find answers to such questions if we want the new generations to get the full advantages of the fruits of modern technology.

8.1.12. Make a prediction

The strategy of making a prediction is best used after carefully considering and evaluating the various angles of a situation to be able to predict with some degree of certainty the likely future developments of the subject under investigation. For example, the following conclusion on the melting ice caps in the arctic regions predicts what the negative consequences are likely to be.

> The ice caps in the Arctic and Antarctic regions remained intact for millions of years, maintaining the equilibrium of global environmental conditions. This balance has now been seriously upset as a result of melting ice caps in the Arctic and Antarctic regions caused by increased warming of the global

environment. The increased global warming is causing the ice sheets to melt, forming glaciers that move and crash into the sea. It is estimated that about twenty trillion tones of ice move across the north arctic every day. These huge moving glaciers eventually form melt streams that pour into the sea, causing sea-water levels to rise. If current trends continue, experts predict that by the end of this century global sea-water levels may rise by fifty-seven centimetres, and consequently many islands and low-lying coastal regions may be submerged.

8.1.13. Discuss Future Developments

Example

What will follow in the future as a consequence of the current state of affairs or policies? For example, what will be the likely outcomes of the prescriptions imposed by the World Bank and the IMF on developing countries to open their economies to free-market forces? Increasing rates of widespread poverty, conflicts, social and political upheavals leading to local displacement, and mass cross-border world migration will be inevitable developments of such policies.

8.1.14. Point out limitations and implications for further study

Academic research must be conducted with a high standard of integrity and faith. Sometimes the results of research, especially in scientific empirical research, do not concord with the assumptions or premises posed in the thesis or may yield only partial validity. In such situations, the researcher must tell his audience why this is so—what has gone wrong. The researcher has to tell about the limitations of the research, and "Addressing the Limitations" is the best strategy to use. (Writing Tutorial Services, Indiana University–Bloomington 2010).

Example

> The questionnaire designed for this research is based on an estimated sample of about three hundred respondents. That is the minimum number that we considered to be sufficiently representative to give the right information we needed to validate the assumptions made. Unfortunately, we received only eighty-five completed questionnaire papers. This is the main limitation of this research. The results, therefore, should be taken with care, and further research will be needed to validate the results obtained from this study.

8.2. What not to include in conclusions

Avoid these common mistakes when writing your conclusion:

- ○ Avoid writing a vague conclusion that is not related to the topic.
- ○ Don't introduce new information. New information should be included in the body.
- ○ Avoid using trite expressions such as "In conclusion", "To conclude", "Finally", and "Therefore". Instead, state your meaning directly.
- ○ Avoid making your conclusion too crammed with details. Make it short and simple enough to convey your final message.
- ○ Avoid writing a conclusion paragraph that lacks coherence and unity. Write your conclusion in an exemplary coherent

and unified paragraph with a clear topic sentence, body, and end.

- Avoid ending the paragraph with a different topic.
- Don't forget to write a conclusion. Sometimes students forget to write a conclusion.
- Avoid stating your thesis for the very first time in the conclusion.
- Don't add any pictures or other illustrations. Conclusions are written with words only.
- Avoid being apologetic or unconfident about the work you have done. Stand fast to what you have found or not found. You have made your voice heard.

Chapter References

Addressing the Limitations)pamphlet, 2010). Writing Tutorial Services, Indiana University–Bloomington., Centre for Innovative Teaching and Learning, Wells Library Learning Commons. Last updated 12 October 2010.

Freedman, Leora, and Jerry Plotnick (n.d.). "Introductions and Conclusions". University College Writing Centre, University of Toronto. Accessed 15 March 2017. http://advice.writing.utoronto.ca/wp-content/uploads/sites/2/intros-and-conclusions.pdf.

Nesbitt-Johnston Writing Centre (2014). "Conclusions". The Trustees of Hamilton College, Hamilton College, Clinton, New York. Accessed 14 November 2016. *https://www.hamilton.edu/documents/Conclusions.pdf*

Palmer, Richard (2002). *Write in Style: A Guide to Good English.* 2nd ed. Routledge.

Sweeney, Teresa, and Fran Hooker (2005). "Strategies for Writing Effective Conclusions", in *Home Academic Resource Center Writing Tips.* Webster University Writing Center. *http://www.webster.edu/academic-resource-center/*

The Writing Studio, Colorado State University (2014). "Tips for Writing a Good Conclusion". http://writing.colostate.edu/files/classes/7998/file_b4a54838- fc40-1691-86bb6f50fa6b3141.pdf.

The Writing Centre at the University of North Carolina (2009). "Introductions". https://writingcenter.unc.edu/tips-and-tools/introductions/. Accessed 2nd Sep. 2016.

———, "Conclusions". Accessed 14 November 2016. https://writingcenter.unc.edu/tips-and-tools/conclusions/.

CHAPTER 9

Writing in-Text Citations and Lists of References in APA Style

Abstract: This chapter focuses on the important issue of proper documentation of sources; an essential requirement in academic research. Documentation of sources is a two-pronged process: it requires (1) accurate in-text citations throughout the body of research, and (2) a corresponding reference list at the end, listing all the sources the writer has used in the body. The two interrelated processes are ridden with complexity and a daunting amount of small details. This has been particularly accentuated by the differing methods of using them in the various "Referencing Styles". This chapter delineates the methods and details on how to write in-text citations and a reference list in the APA (American Psychological Association) style, and extensive examples are included for illustration.

Keywords: in-text citations, list of references, bibliography, referencing styles, APA style

Referncing styles: a general overview

The various referencing styles deal with two basic documentation processes; namely in-text citations and the list of references at the end of the paper. In-text citations appear in the body of the research to acknowledge the authority of the information the writer has used. Such citations should give accurate details of sources in brief; containing the author's family name, year of publication, and, in cases of quotations, a page number (e.g., "(Adams 2008: 89)"). However, these brief notes should also appear in full bibliographical detail in the list of references at the end of the paper. The example of in-text citation above appears in the list of references as follows:

Adams, George (2008). *Plagiarism in Higher Education Institutions: a study on students' ethical behavior at college and future ethical behavior in the workplace.* Oxford, Oxford University Press.

Students often think it is enough to include in-text citations as a way to avoid plagiarism. In-text citations alone are not enough; they must also appear in full details in the list of references.

The list of references is a listing at the end of the paper of all the sources the researcher has used and referred to in the body of the work. This includes sources from which the researcher has obtained information, and also those from which she or he has gained only ideas. A bibliography, on the other hand, lists all the sources the writer has used, including both those she or he has cited and those she or he has only consulted. The list gives an indication of the scope of the sources of information, gives a measure of the depth and rigour of the academic work, and tells about the researcher's credibility, integrity, and adherence to academic ethics and conventions. Those engaged in academic research are required to exercise utmost care to both acknowledge the sources and include a corresponding list of references at the end. Students often think that fulfilling one or the other of the two documentation requirements is enough to safeguard against plagiarism. The two documentation processes are necessary, and students and researchers need to be sure how to write citations and references properly.

9.1. Documentation and in-text citations

Documentation refers to the required academic practice of crediting authors of the original sources from which the writer has gained either information or ideas. Documentation is an essential feature of academic writing that is required for the work to gain credibility and for the writer to avoid the offence of plagiarism.

Documentation is carried out through two main methods of recording source details:

1. Through in-text citations in the body of the document
2. In the list of references at the end of the document

9.1.1. In-text citations

Include the following brief information about a source within the text of your document:

- the name of the author or authors
- the date of publication
- the page number (see below for further information)

In-text citations are placed within round brackets at the beginning or the end of a sentence (before the concluding punctuation). For example: Pegrum, (2009) examines the future of electronic technologies in education.

9.1.2. List of references at the end

At the end of your paper, include a unified list of all the sources you have cited in the body. Various names are used to denote references: "reference list", "works cited", "bibliography", or simply "references". A bibliography is most inclusive; it lists all the sources the writer has used, whether cited or only consulted. Begin your list of references on a new page, and title it using any of the titles given above or according to your supervisor's preference. Each reference stands alone as a single entry in the list, and entries should be indented and separated by a space from one another (hanging indent and double space in APA). Each entry should include the essential bibliographic details required according to the referencing style used in the document.

There are several systems of referencing, most common of which are APA (American Psychological Association) style, Harvard style, MLA (Modern Language Association) style, the Vancouver system, the New Oxford Style, the footnote/endnote system, the MHRA (Modern Humanities Research Association) system, Chicago style, and Turabian style. Each of the various referencing styles is used in particular academic disciplines. APA style, for example, is most often used in disciplines within the natural, social, and behavioural sciences; Harvard style is most commonly used in the sciences and social sciences; and MLA style is mostly used in the humanities, English studies, and the liberal arts. There are a few major and many minor differences between them. The basic rule here is that consistency matters. Be consistent with the use of small details, such as font size, punctuation, and brackets all through the work. However, the essential bibliographic details required across the various styles include the following:

- – authors' names
- – dates of publication
- – titles of sources (books, journal articles, chapters in books, etc.)
- – volume numbers, issue numbers, and page numbers for journal articles
- – names of publishers
- – places of publication
- – website addresses for internet sources
- – database names and websites
- – access dates to website internet sources

The way these bibliographic details are recorded varies according to the type of source.

For a book source with one author:
Fowler, H. W. (1965). *Modern English Usage,* 2nd edition, revised by Ernest Dowers. Oxford University Press.

For an article in a journal:
Smith, Pete & Chris Rust (2011), "The potential of research-based learning for the creation of truly inclusive academic communities of practice", in *Innovations in Education and Teaching International, Vol. 48, No. 2, May 2011, pp. 115–125.*

9.2. Parenthetical referencing: an overview

A concise summary is given of the three most commonly used referencing and citation styles: the APA (American Psychological Association), Harvard, and MLA (Modern Language Association) referencing and citation styles. The three referencing styles share a common core in citations, namely that all three include the three elements essential for in-text citations—(1) author, (2) date and (3) page number—but differ in the way they organize and order the elements in the use of parentheses, quotation marks, and full stops. Moreover, referencing and citation styles have many differences in the way they organize required bibliographical information when writing the list of references at the end. For the benefit of students and researchers, the APA style is presented below, with a summary on the two documentation processes of how to write (a) in-text citations and (b) lists of references.

9.3. The APA (American Psychological Association) referencing and citation style

APA style is widely used in the natural, social, biological and earth sciences; specifically, it is used in psychology, anthropology, economics, business, education, and linguistics. It requires that all in-text citations appear in full bibliographical detail in the list of references at the end. This is to help readers and those interested to locate your sources of information if they want to read further on the topic, or to verify information for accuracy and validity. In-text citations are inserted in the body of research, contained within round brackets. The list of references is included at the end of the paper.

9.3.1. In-text citations in APA style

Generally, APA style uses the following rules when citing only ideas in summaries and paraphrases.

The following items are required:

1. the author's name (or authors' names in cases of multiple authorship)
2. date of publication (1 & 2 when summarizing or paraphrasing ideas)
3. page number (this is especially important when quoting information)

(University of North South West Sydney 2016)

Citing sources with one author

For ideas summarized or paraphrased in the writer's own words, the citing may come at the beginning or end of the summary or paraphrase, giving in brief form only (1) the author's family name and (2) the year of publication; for example: "in their research, the authors (Nonis & Swift 2001) have established that there is a strong connection between academic dishonesty at college and dishonesty in the workplace."

Or the citation may come at the end:

> Encouraging students to adhere to the rules of honest academic practice is the responsibility of both the teacher and the educational institution (Nonis & Swift 2001).

Note that when a citation initializes a paraphrase, the author's family name comes first, followed by the publication year within parenthesis, and the rest of the paraphrase follows naturally and ends with a full stop. If the citation comes at the end, both the author's name and the year are contained within parentheses, and the final full stop falls outside the parenthesis.

For direct quotations, in addition to the author's name and the publication year, the page number must be included.

Example

> Michael Wilson (2014, p. 1) explains the philosophical foundations of authentic leadership and their implications for leadership practice and continuing professional development, and emphasizes "the contribution of virtue ethics by identifying key moral and intellectual virtues associated with authenticity and how they can provide an ethical framework for action guidance in the school leadership context."

Or the citation may come at the end:

> Explaining the philosophical foundations of authentic leadership and their implications for leadership practice and continuing professional development, he emphasizes "the contribution of virtue ethics by identifying key moral and intellectual virtues associated with authenticity and how they can provide an ethical framework for action guidance in the school leadership context" (Wilson 2014, p. 1).

Citing sources with more than one author

If two or more authors author a source, they should be cited in the order in which they appear in the source, separated by "and" in running sentences, and by "&" when in parenthesis

Example

- Rujoiu, O. and Rujoiu, V. (2014) state that ...
- (Rujoiu, O. & Rujoiu, V. 2014)

Citing sources with more than three authors

If more than three authors author a source, they should *all* be cited the first time they are mentioned in the order in which they appear in the source, separated by commas. Subsequently they may be listed only by the first author plus "et al" (meaning "and others").

Example

- (First entry) Russell, Tony, Allen Brizee; Elizabeth Angeli; Russell Keck; Joshua M. Piaz (2016)
- (Subsequent entries) Russell, Tony, et al. (2016)

Citing sources with no author

If the source has no author name, the title of the work should stand in the place of the author. However, titles can sometimes be too long to conveniently fit; therefore, a shortened version of the title would suffice.

Example

The Oxford English Corpus (2016)

Citing sources with no date

For sources which have no dates, especially e-sources and journals, the abbreviation n.d. (no date) is included with the author's name.

Example

- Aaqib (n.d.) argues that ...

Citing two authors on the same subject or topic

If multiple authors have written different sources on the same subject or topic, they should be cited alphabetically, separated by semicolons, and they should be given different entries in the list of references at the end.

Example

- (Abdulateef, 2005; Ahmed, 2008)

Citing multiple authors on the same subject matter or topic

If multiple authors have written different sources on the same subject matter or topic and included in one parenthesis, they should be cited in the order in which they appear in the list of references at the end of the paper.

Example

- (Musaab & Mohammad, 2009; Fatima & Mizna, 2008)

ACADEMIC RESEARCH WRITING

Citing a secondary source referred to by another author

If a secondary source is referred to by another author, both sources should be cited, with the primary source cited first, followed by the secondary source preceded by the phrase "cited in ..."

Example

Bill George, for example, states that "Authentic leaders genuinely desire to serve others through their leadership. They are more interested in empowering the people they lead to make a difference than they are in power, money, or prestige for themselves" (George 2003, p. 12, cited in Wilson 2013, p. 484).

Citing a reference cited by someone else

Sometimes you need to cite a source you have not read but found cited by someone you have read. In this case, you need to include both authors in the citation, but the cited author's name appears only in the citation, but not in the list of references. The list of references should include only the author you have read.

Example:

Bill George (as cited in Wilson 2013) argues that ... (University of Western Australia Library Guides 2016)

9.3.2. Writing the list of references in APA style

The List of References comes at the end of the paper, listing all the sources the writer has cited in the body. Here, full bibliographical details of each source are entered, including the authors' names, dates of publication, place of publication and publisher details, paper title and subtitle, journal volume and issue number, website details and access dates, databases, encyclopedia entries, and wikis. The reference list is arranged alphabetically according to authors' family names.

Book: Single author

> Senge, P. M. (1990). *The Fifth Discipline: The Art and Practice of the Learning Organization.* New York: Currency Doubleday.

Book reference with two authors

> Murray, R. & Sarah M. (2006). *The Handbook of Academic Writing: A Fresh Approach.* New York: Open University Press.

Book reference with three authors or more

> Butler, Eugenia, Mary Ann Hickman, Patricia J. McAlexander, & Overby Lalla (1995). *Correct Writing* (6th ed.), Heath and Co., Lexington, MA.

Book reference with no author

> *Roget's College Dictionary* (4th ed.). (1985). New York: New American Library.

Book by a corporate author

The Arbinger Institute. (2000). *Leadership and self-deception: Getting out of the box.* San Francisco: Berrett-Koehler.

Referencing a translated book

Schuon, Frithjof (1953). *The Transcendent Unity of Religions,* P. Townsend (trans.). London: Faber and Faber.

Referencing a chapter in a book

Abdoun, A. H. (1991). "Agricultural Machinery and Equipment Supply"; in Craig, G. M. (ed.) 1991: *The Agriculture of the Sudan;* Oxford University Press.

Edited book

Duncan, Wu, (Ed. 1012) (4th edn.) *Romanticism: An Anthology.* Chickester, West Sussex: John Wiley & Sons.

Referencing a chapter in an edited book with two editors

Abdel Raziq, E. M. 1986. "The Supply and Demand of Agricultural Labour", in Zahlan, A. B. and Magar, W. Y. (eds.). *The Agricultural Sector of Sudan: Policy and Systems Studies,* London, Ithaca Press.

Book reference with no date

Plato's Republic (n. d.) Translated by Benjamin Jowett, Provided by the Internet Classics Archive.

Available online at URL: *http://classics.mit.edu//Plato/republic.html*

Journal article in print: single author

Sternberg, Robert J. (2009). "Ethics and Giftedness"; *High Ability Studies, Vol. 20, No. 2,* December 2009, 121–130.

Journal article in print: multiple authors

Trevor S. Harding, Donald D. Carpenter, Cynthia J. Finelli, and Honor J. Passow (2004). Does Academic Dishonesty Relate to Unethical Behavior in Professional Practice? An Explanatory Study*"; SciEng Ethics, April 2004, Vol. 10, No. 2, pp: 311 – 24.*

Journal article online: Digital Object Identifier supplied

Wilson, Michael (2014). "Critical Reflection on Authentic Leadership and School Leader Development from a Virtue Ethical Perspective"; in *Educational Review, 2014, Vol. 66, No. 4, pp: 482–496,* School of Education, University of Leeds, Leeds, UK. *http:// dx.doi.org/10.1080/00131911.2013.812062*

Journal article online: No DOI supplied

Toor, Rachel (2012). "Becoming a 'Stylish' Writer", *Chronicle of Higher Education, 00095982, 7/6/2012, Vol. 58, No. 40:* Database: Academic Search Complete, *http://search.ebscohost.com/?authtype=cookie,ip,uid,* revised: 07/2015

Journal article online: from a database

Zinsser, William (2009). "Visions and Revisions: Writing "On Writing Well" and Keeping It Up-to-date for 35 Years", *American Scholar, 00030937, Spr. 2009,*

Vol. 78, No. 2, Database: *EBSCOhost Academic Search Complete, retrieved 23rd Jan. 2017.*

Article online: electronic database freely available on the Web

BetterEvaluation, "Combine Qualitative and Quantitative Data", web page: *http:// www.betterevaluation.org/en/plan/describe/ combining_qualitative_and_quantitative_data;*

Paper in conference proceedings in print

Al-Bashir, A. B. R. (1991). "People on the Move: Immigrants, refugees and displaced masses, and their impact on the society", Paper presented to the Second International Sudan Studies Conference; Sudan: Environment and People, held at the University of Durham 8-11 April 1991.

Paper in conference proceedings online: electronic database

Hjelsvold, R., & S. Vdaygiri. Web-based personalization and management of Interactive video. *Proceedings of the Tenth International World Wide Web Conference,* 1–5 May 2001, Hong Kong. WWW10. Retrieved July 19, 2001, from http://www20.org/cdrom/ papers/405/index.html

Unpublished dissertation

Abdel Aziz, O. F. The Production and Marketing of Dura and Sesame in the Eastern Central Rain-lands of the Sudan: The contrast between the public and private sectors. Unpublished PhD. thesis, University of Leeds, 1979.

Article in an Online Magazine

Schneider, C. (2001, July 21). "The Goodwill Games: How to tackle FASB's new Merger rules." *CFO.com* [Online]. Retrieved October 17, 2001, from *http://www.cfo.com/FASBguide*

Newspaper article in print

Heather, S. Daniel B. & Jennifer R. (2018, Oct. 18). Theresa May signals willingness to extend transition period: PM open to staying in customs union for longer but offered EU nothing new on Irish border. *The Guardian.*

Newspaper article online

Banerjee, N., & A. C. Revkin. (2001, July 21). OPEC leaders indicate they are set to cut output again. *The New York Times on the Web* [Online]. Retrieved August 14, 2001, from http://www.nytimes.com/archives

Web page

Data Collection, Processing, and Analysis. Local Area Planning: Geography Notes. Web page. *http://www.nios.ac.in/media/documents/316courseE/E-JHA-31-10A.pdf.*

Wikis

Macron Campaign Emails. (n.d.). In *WikiLeaks. Retrieved Dec.20, 2018, from https://wikileaks.org/macron-emails/.*

Blogs

Council of Writing Program Administrators (CWP) (2014). Best Book Award, [web blog post], retrieved from: *http://wpacouncil.org/node/7019*, site maintained by Charlie Lowe.

Chapter References

American Psychological Association (APA) (2010). *The Publication Manual of the American Psychological Association*, 6th ed. Washington, DC: American Psychological Association. ISBN-10: 1-4338-0559—6.

Larson, Kelly A. (2004). "APA Documentation: Name and Year". The Purdue OWL, Purdue University Writing Lab. Updated 16 March 2004.

Snooks & Co. (2002). "Methods of Citation", chapter 12 of *Style Manual for Authors, Editors and Printers*, 6th ed. University of Tasmania Library Guides, http://utas.libguides.com/ld.php?content_id=21757697.

University of North South West Sydney (2016). "The American Psychological Association (APA) Referencing System (a Guide)". Last updated 28 June 2016. Accessed 17 September 2016. doi: H:\Guide to Academic Writing Files\UNSW Current Students.html.

University of Western Australia Library Guides (2016). "APA Citation Style: Introduction." Last updated 14 March 2016. http://guides.is.uwa.edu.au/ap.

Wikipedia (n.d.). "Parenthetical Referencing". Text available under the Creative Commons Attribution-ShareAlike Licence. Accessed 14 September 2016.

CHAPTER 10

Writing In-text Citations and the List of References in Harvard Style

Abstract: This chapter focuses on the important aspect of proper documentation of sources; an essential requirement in serious research. Documentation of sources is a two-pronged process: it requires (1) accurate in-text citations throughout the body of research, and (2) a corresponding reference list at the end, listing all the sources the writer has cited in the body. The two interrelated processes are ridden with complexity and a daunting amount of minute details. This has been particularly accentuated by the differing methods of using them in various "Referencing Styles". This chapter delineates the methods and details on how to properly write in-text citations and a reference list in the Harvard system, and extensive examples are included for illustration.

Keywords: in-text citations, list of references, bibliography, referencing styles, Harvard system

10.1. Introduction to the Harvard style of referencing and citations

Harvard style of referencing and citations (sometimes also called "parenthetical referencing") is an umbrella term to refer to referencing systems that use author-date-page parenthetical notations for crediting sources of information inserted in the body of an academic paper. The Harvard style has an interesting history of evolution. Its origin can be traced back to a singular incident of citation in a paper by the renowned zoologist Edward Laurens Mark (1847–1946), Hersey professor of anatomy and director of the zoological laboratory at Harvard University. In 1881 Mark wrote a paper on the embryogenesis of the garden slug, in which he included an author-date citation within parentheses on page 194; this is the first known instance of such a reference. Until then, and for some time afterwards, according to an article in the *British Medical Journal*, "references appeared in inconsistent styles in footnotes, referred to in the text using a variety of asterisks, daggers and other printers' symbols" (Chernin 1988, p. 1). Later, the story goes, a visiting English academic visited Harvard Library and was impressed by the referencing system used there, which, upon his return to England, he dubbed the "Harvard system" rather than "Mark's system" to attribute it to the originator.

There are two versions of the Harvard System.

1. A version that uses author-date references is preferred in the sciences and social sciences and is recommended by the American Psychological Association (APA).
2. A version that uses author-title references is used in the arts and humanities and is recommended by the Modern Language Association.

In-text citations in the Harvard system require three pieces of information: author, date, and page number (the latter in case quotations are included). These elements are inserted within parentheses at the beginning or end of a sentence, starting with the author's last name followed by the year of publication to acknowledge the source in brief (Smith 1954). In case the information includes a quotation, a page number or range is added (Smith 1954, 89). However, this brief form of citation in the body must appear in full bibliographical details in the list of references at the end, including in addition to the author's last name and the year of publication, other details about the publisher, place of publication, edition, journal volume and issue number, and page range; also website details for internet sources.

10.2. In-text citations in Harvard style

Harvard in-text citations when summarizing, paraphrasing and quoting

Generally, Harvard style uses the following rules when citing only ideas in summaries and paraphrases. Required are

1. the author's family name (or names, in case there are more than one),
2. date of publication, and
3. page number (though a page number is not required if you refer to the general idea of a source).

Example

(Smith, 2011, 38).

Or, in a sentence context,

Smith (2011, 38) concludes that ...

Harvard style requires that all in-text citations must appear in full bibliographical details in the list of references at the end. This is to help readers and those interested locate sources of information if they want to read further on the topic or to verify information for validity and accuracy.

Citing sources with one author

For ideas summarized or paraphrased in the writer's own words, the citation may come at the beginning or end of the summary or paraphrase, giving in brief form only (1) the author's family name and (2) the year of publication.

Example

Walbridge (2009) stated that …

Or the citation may come at the end:

Ancient Greek philosophy has had great influence of contemporary educational and political thought (Walbridge 2009).

For one author and a short quotation of less than thirty words

The quoted material runs as an integral part of the paragraph, contained within quotation marks. In addition, the author's family name, the date, and the page number or range must be included within round brackets.

Example

> In a study on the political inclinations of liberals and conservatives, it is found that "In both the United States and the United Kingdom, more intelligent children are more likely to grow up to be liberals than less intelligent children" (Kanazawa 2010, p. 2).

In long quotations (thirty words or more), the quote stands as a separate block and follows the guidelines below:

o   The quotation must be an exact copy of the original text, word for word.
o   It is separated from the rest of body paragraphs and hangs in the middle.
o   It is written single spaced and in a font smaller than the text in the body paragraphs.
o   It is indented on both the right and left margins.

- ○ No quotation marks are used.
- ○ This marks the quote as independently highlighted text that stands out clearly as a block.

Example

In a study on the political inclinations of liberals and conservatives, it is found that

> in both the United States and the United Kingdom, more intelligent children are more likely to grow up to be liberals than less intelligent children. For example, among the American sample, those who identify themselves as "very liberal" in early adulthood have a mean childhood IQ of 106.4, whereas those who identify themselves as "very conservative" in early adulthood have a mean childhood IQ of 94.8. (Kanazawa, 2010, p. 2)

Citing sources with two or three authors

If two or three authors coauthor a source, they should be cited in the order in which they come in the source, separated by "and" if provided in running sentences, or by an ampersand if provided parenthetically.

Example

> Writers should consider carefully the differing needs and expectations of diverse types of audiences to help them decide on what style to use, what structure a text should take, and what to include or not to include (Anson & Schwegler 2011, p. 2).

Citing sources with more than three authors

If more than three authors coauthor a source, use only the first author's family name plus "et al" (meaning "and others").

Example

Original reference

Johns, Beverley H., Mary Z. McGrath and Sarup R. Mathur, 2008 Lanham, MD, Rowman & Littlefield (2010), *Ethical Dilemmas in Education: Standing up for Honesty and Integrity*, ISBN13: 978-157-88-6783-7. © 2010, Kristján Kristjánsson.

In text:

A number of studies have highlighted the important and urgent need to reinstate the ethics of honesty and integrity in schools and colleges (Johns et al. 2010).

Citing sources with no author and no editor

For sources with no author and no editor, the title is used in the position of the author or editor. The title may be shortened to the main tile if it is long.

Example

Greenhouse Effect: Measuring CO2 Emissions (*Greenhouse Gas Emissions IPCC* 2008).

Citing sources with no date

For sources which have no dates, especially e-sources and journals, the abbreviation "n.d." (meaning "no date") is included with the author's name.

Example

Mamdani (n.d.) argues that …

Citing two authors on the same subject matter or topic

If multiple authors have written different sources on the same subject or topic, they should be cited alphabetically, separated by semicolons, and given different entries in the list of references at the end.

Example

(Amin 1989; Bush 1996)

Citing multiple authors on the same subject referred to collectively

If multiple authors have written different sources on the same subject and are included in one parenthesis, they should be cited in the order in which they appear in the list of references at the end of the paper.

Example

A score of studies on the pragmatic function of virtue ethics in businesses (Wilson 1013; Ciulla 2005; Mendonca and Kanungo 2007; and Milton Friedman 1970), revealed that ethical leadership makes good business sense, because leadership virtues, such as commitment, technical expertise and industriousness, can be soon rendered ineffective by such leadership vices as arrogance, insensitivity and untrustworthiness.

Citing a secondary source referred to by another author

When a secondary source referred to by another author needs to be cited, both sources should be cited, with the primary source cited first, followed by the secondary source preceded by the phrase "cited in ..."

Example

Hussien (as cited in Quafoor 2008, p. 32) stated that ...

However, in the list of references, you should cite only the source you have used (Quafoor, in this case, and not Hussien). It is always better to find the original source and cite it.

Citing different sources by the same author written in the same year

If an author has more than one source of the same year, the different sources are distinguished by lower case letters in the reference list. For example, Dana Driscoll has two publications in 2012 which appear in the list of references as Driscoll, Dana 2012a and 2012b. Such sources should be cited accordingly in the body.

Example

On writing (Driscoll 2012a) and on style (Driscoll 2012b) ...

Citing a chapter in an edited book

The author of a chapter is cited followed by the date of publication of the edited book; the full bibliographical details of the edited book appear in the reference list, including the title of the chapter as well as the title of the edited book, the name of the editor, and the year of publication and the edition number, if other than the first.

Example

> *Handbook of Qualitative Research*, 2nd ed., an edited book, includes a discussion on data collection, processing, and analysis (Norman 1994) …

Corporate author—when the author is also the publisher

The name of a corporate author is to be entered in full with an abbreviation in the first instance; then, in all subsequent citations, only the abbreviation is used.

Example

> An analysis of mean global temperatures by the Inter-Governmental Panel on Climate Change (IPCC 2005) has shown a steady rise in surface temperatures over the last 100 years and recommends that carbon emissions must be reduced to levels below …

Then, in all subsequent in-text citations, only the abbreviation is entered:

> The IPCC (2005) obliged governments to set limits to their carbon emissions at levels below …

Approximate date of publication

Example

> More recent information on the topic (Qayyum c. 2011) suggests that ...

Print Dictionaries and Encyclopedias

Example

> According to one definition of "Euthanasia" (*Webster's Collegiate Dictionary* 1985, p. 429) ...

> Dictionaries and encyclopedias appear in the reference list as follows:

> *Webster's Collegiate Dictionary*, 6th ed. (1985), "Euthanasia", Merriam Webster Publishers, Massachusetts, p. 429.

Articles in Print Journals

Example

In-text citation:

> Holowchak, M. (2013) argues that there is a paradox in civil service ...

> In reference lists, details about editions, volume numbers, and page numbers should be included in parenthesis after the title of the paper.

> Holowchak, M. (2013), "The Paradox of Public Service: Jefferson, Education, and the Problem of

Plato's Cave", in *Studies in Philosophy and Education*, January 2013, vol. 32, no. 1: pp. 73–86.

Electronic Dictionaries and Encyclopedias

Example

The encyclopedia has an English-Arabic translation facility (Encyclopaedia Britannica 2017) that gives readers …

In reference list:

Encyclopaedia Britannica (2017), English–Arabic Translation, Encyclopaedia Britannica, Inc. file:///I:/Encyclopedia%20Britannica%20_%20 Britannica.com.html.

Figures, Tables, Graphs, Maps, or Charts

Cite each of these as you would a book. Include the type of entry immediately after the title.

Example

Graphs

The internal processes were well described (Kaplan & Norton 2004), which led to …

In reference list:

Kaplan, R. S. & Norton, D. P., 2004, "Internal processes deliver value over different time horizons", graph, in *Strategy maps: converting intangible assets into tangible outcomes*, Harvard Business School, Boston, Massachusetts, p. 48.

Maps

To locate a property just outside the Australian Capital Territory, use the 1:100,000 map produced by Geoscience Australia (2004), which covers …

In reference list:

Geoscience Australia [NATMAP] 2004, *ACT region, New South Wales and Australian Capital Territory*, map, Geoscience Australia, Canberra.

Website—entire website

Example

The new website of the Department of Education, Employment and Workplace Relations (DEEWR 2009) includes useful information on current government education policy.

In reference list:

Department of Education, Employment and Workplace Relations 2009, DEEWR, Canberra, viewed 21 November 2009, http://www.deewr.gov.au/

Wikis

Include the date retrieved, since the information in these sources is likely to change at any time.

Example

Grammar for accuracy in prose writing ('Grammar/ Usage' n.d.) …

In reference list:

"Grammar/ Usage" (n.d.), *Wikipedia: the Free Encyclopedia*; available under the Creative Commons Attribution-ShareAlike License, accessed Oct. 1, 2016, https://en.wikipedia.org/wiki/Grammar// https://en.wikipedia.org/wiki/Usage.

10.3. Writing the List of References in Harvard Style

Titled "List of References" or simply "References", the list comes at the end of the paper on a new page, listing all sources the author has cited in the body. The list is arranged alphabetically according to authors' family names, followed by the first names initialized or in full. If the author has more than one entry in the list, the works of that author are arranged chronologically starting with the earliest published work. The author's name is then followed by the date of publication. In case an author has more than one publication in the same year, the works are distinguished by lower case letters (for example, "Saleem 2008a" and "Saleem 2008b") and are arranged alphabetically in the list according to the work title, disregarding articles (a, an, the). Sources that have no date are indicated by "n.d".

Books (print and online)

One author

Example

Adams, G. 2008 *Plagiarism in Higher Education Institutions: a Study on Students' Ethical Behavior at College and Future Ethical Behavior in the Workplace.* Oxford, Oxford University Press.

Two or more authors

List all authors in the list of references.

Example

Cargill, M. & Patrick O'Connor 2009, *Writing Scientific Research Articles*, Wiley-Blackwell, ISBN 978-1-4051-8619-3.

Works and editions (for editions other than the first) should be included.

Example

American Psychological Association (APA) 2010, *The Publication Manual, 6th ed.* American Psychological Association, Washington, DC, ISBN-10: 1-4338-0559—6.

Edited books: Acknowledging editors, compilers, revisers or translators:

If the role of an editor (or compiler, reviser or translator) is of primary importance, list the work under those names. Use abbreviations such as "ed.", "eds.", "trans.", "rev.", "comp.", and "comps.".

Example

> Ahmad, S. E., Dreze, J. P., Hills, J. & Sen, A. K. (eds.) 1991, *Social Security in Developing Countries*. Oxford University Press.

Chapter in an edited book

Page numbers are not usually needed in the reference list (Style Manual for Authors, Editors and Printers 2002, p. 194).

Example

> Adler, P. A. & Adler, P. 1994, "Observation Techniques". In Norman K. Denzin & Yvonna S. Lincoln (eds.). *Handbook of Qualitative Research*, Thousand Oaks, CA: Sage.

> Gurdon, C. G.1991, "Agriculture in the National Economy" in Craig, G. M. (ed.) 1991. *The Agriculture of the Sudan*; Oxford University Press.

If page numbers are essential to accurately locate the source or are required for inclusion, they can be presented as the final item of the citation (e.g., "p. 10", "pp. 19–25", "pp. 21–6", "pp. 21, 31–5").

Editions

The edition (if other than the first edition) is included after the main title.

Example

> Anson, C. M. & Robert A. S. 2011, *The Longman Handbook for Writers and Readers, 6th edn*, Longman, Boston, ISBN 978-0-2005-74199-1.

Anonymous works (no author or editor given)

Use the title in place of the author name.

Example

> Conclusions 2014, Nesbitt-Johnston Writing Center, Hamilton College Clinton, NY, The Trustees of Hamilton College.

Conference proceedings

For papers collected and published as proceedings, include page numbers at the end of the citation.

Example

> Hay, R. and Rukuini Mandivamba, 1988, "SADCC (South African Development Coordination Conference) Proceedings on Food Security Strategies: Evolution and Role", *World Development*, vol. 16, no. 9, Sept. 1988.

Corporate authors:

The jurisdiction is not usually given for government agencies but is indicated by the place of publication.

Example

> AFESD (Arab Fund for Economic and Social Development) 1976: *Basic Programme for Agricultural Development in the Sudan*. (Summary and Conclusions). Kuwait.

Same author(s) for multiple works

For single author, entries start with the earliest date:

Example

> Brizee, Allen 2003, "Introductions, Body Paragraphs, and Conclusions for an Argument Paper", The Purdue OWL. Purdue University Writing Lab, last update: 14 Oct. 2003: https://owl.english.purdue.edu/owl/owlprint/724/.
>
> —— 2013, "Body Paragraphs: Moving from General to Specific Information", The Purdue OWL, Purdue University Writing Lab, last update: 25th Feb. 2013, https://owl.english.purdue.edu/owl/resource/724/02/.

For multiple-author entries beginning with the same name, list the one with the earliest date first. A long dash (2-em, approximately equivalent to 4–6 hyphens in length) can be used to replace that part of the author entry which is repeated. There is no space immediately after the dash.

Example

> Driscoll, D. L. 2013, "Parallel Structure", the Writing Lab and the OWL at Purdue and Purdue University, last Edited: 2013-03-22 09:01:32, https://owl.english.purdue.edu/owl/resource/623/01/.
>
> —— & Allen Brizee 2010, April, "What is Primary Research and How Do I Get Started?" The Writing Lab & the OWL at Purdue and Purdue University; last updated on 17th April, 2010.

Online book

Example

> Carlson, John W. 1012, *Words of Wisdom: A Philosophical Dictionary for the Perennial Tradition*; Amazon Paperback Books, March 15, 2016, https://www.amazon.com/Words-Wisdom-Philosophical-Dictionary-Perennial/dp/0268023700.

Journal articles

To reference journals, it is essential to include the volume number, issue number, or other identifier, and page numbers separated by commas where all these elements are available. If the journal issue has both a number and an identifier such as a month or quarter, choose one and use it consistently. If there is no volume number, the issue number or identifier should follow the journal title. The same rules used for book author referencing apply to journals.

One author

Both volume and issue numbers are available.

Example

> Dafermos, M. 2016, "Critical Reflection on the Reception of Vygotsky's Theory on the International Academic Communities", in *Cultural-Historical Psychology* 2016, vol. 12, no. 3, pp: 27–46.

Two or more authors

List all authors in the list of references.

Example

Cavaliere, Frank, J., Toni P. Mulvaney, & Marleen R. Swerdlow 2010, "Teaching Business Ethics after the Financial Meltdown: Is It Time for Ethics with a Sermon?" *Education, vol. 131, no.* 1, pp. 3–17.

No author given

Put the journal title in the position the author's name would otherwise take.

Example

Education and Plato's Parable of the Cave 1996. Originally appeared in Journal of Education, vol. 178, no. 3.

Internet journal article

Example

Bello, Iria 2016, Cognitive Implications of Nominalizations in the Advancement of Scientific Discourse, International Journal of English Studies (IJES). vol. 16, no. 2, pp: 1–23. Servicio de Publicaciones, Universidad de Murcia, *IJES* <http://revistas.um.es/ijes, accepted: 08/10/2016>.

Full-text journal article from an electronic database

Example

Charlton, Claire 2006, "Just a Click Away: Online Writing Labs at Universities Offer Free Help with Grammar, Style, Editing and Other Issues",

Kalmbach Publishing, 00439517, Sep. 2006, 9, Database: Academic Search Complete. <http://search.ebscohost.com/?authtype=cookie,ip,uid>.

Newspaper articles

Example

Heather, S, Daniel B, & Jenifer R. 2018, "Theresa May signals willingness to extend transition period: PM open to staying in customs union for longer but offered EU nothing new on Irish border". *The Guardian*, Oct. 18.

Web documents and sites

Web documents

Web documents use the following format: author/editor or compiler, year of the most recent version, title, version number (if applicable), description of document (if applicable), name and place of the sponsor of the source, viewed day, month, year, <URL either full location details or just the main site details>.

Example

BetterEvaluation, "Analyze Data", web page, BetterEvaluation, accessed 7th Dec, 2017, <http://betterevaluation.org/plan/describe/look_for_patterns>.

Websites

Websites use the following format: author (the person or organization responsible for the site) year (that the site was created or last revised), name and place of the sponsor of the source, viewed day month year, <URL>.

Example

> Council of Writing Program Administrators (CWP) 2014, Best Book Award, [web blog post], retrieved, site maintained by Charlie Lowe, from: <http://wpacouncil.org/node/7019>.

Helpful hints for Web documents:

- You must specify the date on which you accessed the item, since Web documents can change or disappear at any time.
- If a Web document includes both a date of creation and a date it was last updated, use only the date it was last updated.
- If you find a document on the Web which is a series of linked pages, use the information from the main, or "home", page.
- If you have trouble identifying the title, look at the top of the Web page above "File" on your browser.
- The date a Web document was created is usually listed at the bottom of the document.

Advantages and disadvantages of the Harvard system

- One of the biggest advantages of the Harvard system is its flexibility to be adapted to various renderings in citations and in the list of references to suit different demands, while at the same retaining the principal features. Variations in the use of punctuation marks, capital letters, italics, boldface, and brackets are generally tolerated as long as they follow a consistent pattern throughout the document.

- Readers who are familiar with important publications in their field are more likely to recognize works in the body text citations without the need to check dates in the reference list.
- In the author-date system, readers can easily identify works that are outdated as well as those that are current.
- The author-date system is much more convenient than those systems that use numbers in in-text citations to refer to the reference number as it appears in the list of references. The latter can cause great frustration when and if a change in the numbering in the list of references occurs, as then a corresponding change in citations will have to follow. The author-date system is free of this "scourge".
- The main disadvantage of the parenthetical system is that it takes up space, and the presence of many citations in the same place can distract readers and obstruct understanding.
- The date of publication may not be that important, since in the arts and humanities many works are known by their authors and can go through various revisions and editions such as renders inclusion of date unnecessary and sometimes redundant. For example, in "(Plato 1912)", the date would be of little significance, since Plato's works have gone through many translations and editions. A more suitable way is to cite information that is more useful to the reader (e.g., "Plato, the Republic, Book III, p. 129") (Wikipedia [n.d.], "Editing Parenthetical Referencing").

Chapter References

Chernin, Eli (1988). '"The Harvard System": a Mystery Dispelled'. *British Medical Journal* vol. 297, 22 October 1988.

Snooks & Co. (2002). "Methods of Citation", chapter 12 of *Style Manual for Authors, Editors and Printers*, 6th ed. University of Tasmania Library Guides. *http://utas.libguides.com/ld.php?content_id=21757697*.

University of Southern Queensland (2016), *Harvard AGPS Referencing Guide*. Wiley, Australia. Retrieved 6 October 2016.

University of Sydney University Library (2012). *Your Guide to Harvard Style Referencing*, Accessed 18 September 2016. https://library.sydney.edu.au/subjects/downloads/citation/Harvard_Complete.pdf.

University of Tasmania Library (2009). *Referencing and Assignment Writing: Harvard, Online Guide*. University of Tasmania. 25 February 2009. http://utas.libguides.com/referencing.

Wikipedia (n.d.). "MLA Handbook". Accessed 9 January 2017.

Wikipedia (n.d.). "Parenthetical Referencing". Text available under the Creative Commons Attribution-ShareAlike License. Accessed 14 September 2016.

CHAPTER 11

Writing In-text Citations and a Works Cited List in MLA Style

Abstract: This chapter deals with the important issue of proper documentation of sources—an essential requirement in serious research. Documentation of sources is a two-pronged process; it requires (1) accurate in-text citations throughout the body of research, and (2) a corresponding reference list at the end, listing all the sources the writer has cited in the body. The two interrelated processes are ridden with complexity and a daunting amount of minute details. This has been particularly accentuated by the differing methods of using them in the various referencing styles. This chapter delineates the methods and details how to properly write in-text citations and a list of works cited in Modern Language Association (MLA) style, and extensive examples are included for illustration.

Keywords: in-text citations, works cited, referencing styles, MLA style, MLA concept of containers, MLA core elements

11.1. The history and evolution of MLA style

The inception of MLA style was a thirty-one-page document titled *MLA Style Sheet*, which came out in 1951. The *MLA Style Sheet* then developed into the *MLA Handbook for Writers of Research Papers, Theses, and Dissertations*, which was published in five editions spanning the years between 1977and 1999. In the sixth edition, which appeared in 2003, the title was changed to *MLA Handbook for Writers of Research Papers*. (Wikipedia [n.d.], "Parenthetical Referencing"). In 2009, the seventh edition came out. This edition had a number of changes; most notably that it no longer recognized a default medium and instead called for listing the medium of publication, whether print, web, or CD, in every entry in the list of works cited. It recommended against listing URLs and stated a preference for italics over underlining. Additionally, the seventh edition included a website containing the full text of the book. Eventually the seventh edition was superseded by the eighth edition, which was published in April 2016 with major changes in the way of writing the list of works cited.

According to the MLA, *MLA Handbook for Writers of Research Papers* (1977–2009) is a publication of the Modern Language Association mainly intended for classroom instruction. It is used "worldwide by scholars, journal publishers, by academic and commercial presses". The purpose is to provide "guidelines for writing and documentation of research in the humanities, such as English studies, the study of other modern languages and literatures, including comparative literature; literary criticism; media studies; cultural studies; and related disciplines" (Wikipedia [n.d.], "MLA Handbook").

11.2. The eighth edition of the MLA handbook

As of April 2016, the eighth edition of the *MLA Handbook* came into effect as the authoritative system of scholarly documentation to replace the guidelines contained in its seventh-edition predecessor and the *MLA Style Manual*. Following the advent of the eighth edition of the *MLA Handbook* in spring 2016, the MLA stated that the *MLA Style Manual* would be declared out of print effective 1 September 2016. (Wikipedia [n.d.], "MLA Handbook"). Also, the MLA Style Center states that "the eighth edition's system of documentation supersedes the guidelines set out in the seventh edition and in the *MLA Style Manual*" (Modern Language Association, MLA Style Center, 2016). The eighth edition includes a number of important changes, especially in the area of lists of references. The principles that govern in-text citations in MLA style, however, remain largely unchanged; only a few details have been added, mainly for the purposes of clarification, but retaining the essential features of the former style used in the seventh edition.

The professed purposes behind the changes include a more heightened sensitivity to addressing the professional needs of scholars in the era of digital information, and a quest for a more flexible approach to documentation that moves away from a restrictive set of rules towards a few universal general guidelines that will help writers create their own documentations more easily. In the new edition, the MLA recommends "a universal set of guidelines" for writers to apply, which gives them "the tools to intuitively document sources" (MLA Style Center, 2016). The MLA identifies what it calls "core elements"—a set of nine elements to serve as guides for creating a list of works cited. Here are the nine core elements:

1. Author
2. Title of source
3. Title of container
4. Other contributors
5. Version
6. Number
7. Publisher
8. Publication date
9. Location

In essence, the eighth *MLA Handbook* edition gives two fixed major elements for documentation (author and title of source) and seven variable minor ones subsumed under the generic term "containers" in set order.

11.3. MLA's list of core elements

The mainstay in the new changes in MLA style is that the list of core elements constitutes a core common to all documentation styles and therefore are listed in a particular order, with the punctuation marks following each element. The punctuation marks are limited to only commas and full stops to separate the different parts of the entry. The MLA core elements are shown in the nine entries below.

MLA core elements for documentation: meaning and method of entry

Core Elements

1. Author

   Each entry starts with the first (or only) author's last name, followed by a comma and any other names, and ending with a full stop (e.g., Doerksen, D.).

2. Title of source

   The title of the source follows the author's name, ends in a full stop, and is written in italics or within quotation marks, depending on the type of source; book titles and websites are italicized (e.g., Eliot, T. S. *Dante, Selected Essays*. New York: Faber and Faber.). Journal articles and media sources are contained within quotation marks (e.g., "Let There Be Peace': Eve as Redemptive Peacemaker in Paradise Lost, Book X").

3. Title of container

   "Container" is a generic term used to refer to a larger category which contains a primary individual source. Containers can be series, websites, or other larger bodies which contain other smaller containers. Containers are italicized and are followed by commas.

   Example

   Milton Quarterly

4. Other contributors

These are others who contributed to the source and should be given due credit. They include editors, illustrators, translators, etc. Their names should be included in the documentation whenever necessary. In the new MLA style, the words "editor", "illustrator", and "translator" are written in full and not abbreviated.

5. Version

The source may appear as an edition or version of an original or earlier work, and this should be reflected in the citation.

6. Number

In many instances, especially with journal and magazine articles, the source appears as part of a numbered sequence, such as a multivolume book or a journal with both volume and issue numbers. These details and numbers should also be reflected in the citation (e.g., vol. 32, no. 4).

7. Publication

There may be one or more publishers disseminating the work to the public. If there is more than one publisher, both should be included in the citation, separated by a forward slash (/)

Example

> Lucas, F. L. (1968). "On the Fascination of Style". Essay. (*Holiday*, March 1960). Reprinted in *The Odyssey Reader: Ideas and Style*, 1968 / and in *Readings for Writers*, ed. Jo Ray McCuen and Anthony C. Winkler, New York, 2009.

8. Publication date

Some sources may have different publication dates, especially when a source has both a print version and an electronic one. In such cases, the date that is most relevant to the paper, or else the original date of the work, should be included.

9. Location

Location refers to the specific page number(s) on which the source is located within a book, a journal, an encyclopedia, or other types of collections, and it should be recorded as accurately as possible (e.g., 124–130. DOI:10.1111/j.1094-348X.1997.tb00499.x) For online sources, the location should include a URL.

Example

> Paulesu, E, et al. "Dyslexia: Cultural Diversity and Biological Unity." *Science*, 291, 5511 (2001), 2165–2167. <http://www.sciencemag.org/content/291/5511/2165.full.pdf?sid=e7fcb20f-73c5-49a5-bbc4-f8efd0123b40>.

11.4. The new concept of containers

An important new concept in the eighth edition is what is called "Containers". "Containers" is an elastic generic term used to refer to all and every broader category under which is subsumed the individual primary source to be documented. The concept of containers is a crucial new concept around which a list of works cited is now to be written in MLA style. Essentially, it traces the primary source to its various origins and locates it in what is termed a "container"—that is, the larger unit within which the primary source and its secondary source are located. A poem by John Coleridge or a novel by Joseph Conrad, for example, may be contained in an anthology of romantic poetry or a collection of stories, with the poem and novel being the primary sources and the anthology and the collection being the containers. There might be larger containers to contain other containers, such as databases and electronic libraries.

For example, "Ode to a Nightingale" is the title of a primary source—a poem by John Keats—that comes under the container *An Anthology of Romantic Poems*. Keats's "Ode to a Nightingale", in the list of works cited, would appear as the main source, while *Romanticism: An Anthology* would be the container. The container is written in italics and is followed by a comma; then follow other contributors, publisher details, the publication date, and, finally, the page number or range.

Example

> Keats, John. "Ode to a Nightingale". *Romanticism: An Anthology*, edited by Duncan Wu, 4th ed. Chickester, West Sussex: John Wiley & Sons. 2012, pp. 1464–66.

The container can be any larger category, such a series, collection, or website, within which is contained the individual primary source. Sometimes a container may be within a larger container. Articles may be published in specialized journals, such as the *Journal of Education* or the *Journal of Mental Health*, which in turn are contained within a larger database, such as EBESCOHost. It is necessary to cite both containers to help readers locate relevant sources.

Example

> Stankiewicz, Mary Ann. "Perennial Promises and Pitfalls in Arts Education Reform." *Arts Education Policy Review*, Nov/Dec 1997, vol. 99, no. 2, pp. 8–14. H:\EBESCOComplete

Files*Perennial promises and pitfalls in arts education reform EBSCOhost.htm.*

Other Contributors:

In addition to the author, there may be other contributors to the source who should also be credited, such as editors, illustrators, translators, etc. If their contributions are relevant to your research, or if they are necessary to identify the source, include their names in your documentation. Note that in the eighth edition, terms like "editor", "illustrator", "translator", etc., are not abbreviated.

11.5. In-text citations in MLA style

The MLA uses parenthetical citations, not footnotes. When you quote or paraphrase someone else's work, you provide the author's name followed by the page number or range in parentheses, generally at the end of the sentence. There is no punctuation mark between the name and the page number. If you mention the author in the sentence itself, you need only give the page number. You do not need to cite page numbers if you are referring to an entire work, or if the work is only one page long. The table below shows how in-text citations are recorded in various situations.

Table (2) How to Insert in-Text Citations in MLA Style and Examples

In-text citation case	How to cite	Example
Book with one author	Both (author last name + page #) inside parentheses	On neo-Platonic Tradition, (Algis 139) points out …
	Only (page #) inside parentheses	Algis points out (139) …

Book with two or three authors	(Author's last name & last author's last name + page #) inside parentheses	On business students' academic practices (Bagraim and Pulker 331) found that ...
	Only (page #) inside parentheses	Bagraim and Pulker (331) found that ...
Book with more than three authors	(First author's last name + et al. + page #) inside parentheses	Calling for ethics in education (Cavaliere et al. 3) suggest that ...
	Only (page no) inside parentheses	Cavaliere et al. (3) suggest that ...
Book with a corporate author	Both (organization name + page #) inside parentheses	High-income segments (Department of Statistics 136) show ...
	Only (page #) inside parentheses	Department of Statistics (136) shows ...
Book with an editor	Both (editor's last name + page #) inside parentheses	The conference of "Learned Journals addresses" (Cornett 184) stated that ...
	Only (page #) inside parentheses	Cornett (184) stated that ...
Chapter in an edited book	Both (author's last name + page no.) inside parentheses	In the African Sahel (Amin 221) reports ...
	Only (page #) inside parentheses	Amin (221) reports ...
Print journal article	Both (author's last name + page #) inside parentheses	In inclusive academic communities (Smith 115) suggests that students ...
	Only (page #) inside parentheses	Smith (115) suggests that students should be initiated ...

E-journal article	Both (author's last name + page #) inside parentheses	Investigating correlation between academic dishonesty and workplace dishonesty, (Nonis and Swift 69) established that …
	Only (page #) inside parentheses	Nonis and Swift (69) established that …
Print newspaper article	Both (author's last name + page #) inside parentheses	Reporting on the explosion, (Chris 18) revealed that …
	Only (page #) inside parentheses	Chris (18) reported that the explosion was …
Online newspaper article	Only (Author's last name) inside parentheses	Another reporter (Schwan) found that …
Page on a website	(Use first few words of the page title) inside parentheses	Accordingly, most common misspellings (The Oxford English Corpus) occur because …
Website	(Author's last name / website name) inside parentheses	For example, (Toor/http://search.ebscohost.com) corroborates that …
Blog	Only (author's last name) inside parentheses	Computer checkers sometimes strain the relationship between editors and their clients (Gina) complained …
Government agency publication	Both (organization name + page #) inside parentheses	Evaluating the national assessment program (Senate Standing Committee on Education 223) recommended that …
	Only (page #) inside parentheses	The Senate Standing Committee on Education (223) recommended …

Parliamentary and legal material	Only (abbreviated form of title) inside parentheses	The bill on Public Law 480 (PL 480) was passed ...
Theses	Both (author last name + page #) inside parentheses	The research (Fadlalla 8) supports earlier studies ...
	Only (page #) inside parentheses	Fadlalla (8) contributed ...

11.6. Writing a list of Works Cited in MLA style

The new guidelines in the eighth edition introduce a number of important changes that depart from previous features of the seventh edition. The MLA states that "previously, a writer created an entry by following the MLA's instructions for the source's publication format ... That approach has become impractical today" and explains that this is because "publication formats are often combined ... or are undefinable" and concludes with the most important change that "[i]n the new model, the work's publication format is not considered. Instead of asking, 'How do I cite a book [or ... Web page]?' the writer creates an entry by consulting the MLA's list of core elements." The list of core elements, in fact, effects a fundamental change in the way the list of works cited is written. The important thing to consider is the core elements and how to order them, paying no attention to the original format of the source. Because of this fundamental change, the list of works cited in the new approach is markedly different from that produced by previous versions (Modern Language Association of America 2016d). The following examples illustrate the new style.

A source in a single container: An essay in a journal

Elements of entry	Example
1. Author	Holowchak, M.
2. Title of source	"The Paradox of Public Service: Jefferson, Education, and the Problem of Plato's Cave."
3. Title of container	*Studies in Philosophy and Education,*
4. Other contributors	_
5. Version	_
6. Number	vol. 32, no. 1,
7. Publisher	_
8. Date of publication	Jan. 2013
9. Location	pp. 73–86.

(MLA Style Center 2016b)

This entry would appear in the list of works cited as follows:

Holowchak, M. "The Paradox of Public Service: Jefferson, Education, and the Problem of Plato's Cave." *Studies in Philosophy and Education, vol. 32, no. 1,* Jan. 2013, pp. 73–86.

A Source in two containers: A Journal Article

- ○ Author: Stankiewicz, Mary Ann
- ○ Title of source: "Perennial Promises and Pitfalls in Arts Education Reform."

227

Container 1

- o Title of Container: *Arts Education Policy Review*
- o Other Contributors
- o Version
- o Number: vol. 99, no. 2
- o Publisher
- o Publication date: Nov/Dec 1997
- o Location: pp. 8–14.

Container 2

- o Title of Container: EBESCO Complete Files\Perennial promises and pitfalls in arts education reform EBSCOhost.htm
- o Other Contributors
- o Version
- o Number
- o Publisher
- o Publication date
- o Location

In the list of Works Cited, this entry would appear as follows:

Stankiewicz, Mary Ann. "Perennial Promises and Pitfalls in Arts Education Reform." *Arts Education Policy Review*, Nov/Dec 1997, vol. 99, no. 2, pp. 8–14. H:\EBESCO Complete Files\Perennial promises and pitfalls in arts education reform EBSCOhost.htm.

ACADEMIC RESEARCH WRITING

Chapter References

Citation Producer Blog. (2012, July). "Understanding and Writing in the MLA Format Style." Accessed 22 February 2017. http://citationproducer. com/article/understanding-and-writing-in-the-mla-format-style/

Modern Language Association. *MLA Handbook. https://www.mla. org/MLA-Style.*

Modern Language Association of America (2016a). "Formatting a Research Paper". MLA Style Center. Retrieved 22 January 2017. https://MLA%20Style%20Center.htm.

——— (2016b). "What's New in the Eighth Edition". MLA Style Center. Accessed 21 January 2017. https://style.mla.org/.

——— (2016c). "In-Text Citations". MLA Style Center. Accessed 20 January 2017. https://style.mla.org/.

——— (2016d). "Works Cited: A Quick Guide". MLA Style Center. Accessed 20 January 2017. https://style.mla.org/.

Russell, Tony, Allen Brizee, Elizabeth Angeli, Russell Keck, Joshua M. Piaz, Michelle Campbell, Rodrigo Rodriguez-Funtes, Daniel P. Kenzie, Ausan Wegener, and Maryam Ghafoor (2016). "MLA Formatting and Style Guide". The Purdue OWL, Purdue University Writing Lab. Last edited 12 September 2016.

Snooks & Co. (2002). "Methods of Citation". Chapter 12 of the *Style Manual for Authors, Editors and Printers*. 6th ed. University of Tasmania Library Guides. http://utas.libguides.com/ ld.php?content_id=21757697.

Tonkin, Humphrey (2010). "Navigating and Expanding the MLA International Bibliography". *Journal of Scholarly Publishing*. April

229

2010. DOI: 10.3138/jsp.41.3.340. file:///H:/EBSCO%20New%20 Files/Navigating%20and%20Expanding%20the.pdf.

University College Dublin Library (2011). "MLA Referencing Style". 25 July 2011. Accessed 17 September 2016.

University of Colorado: The Writing Center (2017). "How-to Guides." http: //www.ucdenver.edu/academics/colleges/CLAS/ Centers/writing/resources/Pages/guides.aspx.

Wikipedia (n.d.). "MLA Handbook". Accessed 9 Jan. 2017.

Wikipedia (n.d.). "Parenthetical Referencing". Text available under the Creative Commons Attribution-ShareAlike License. Accessed 14 September 2016.

CHAPTER 12

The Language of Academic Writing

Abstract: This chapter deals with one of the essential features of academic research writing—namely, accuracy of language. Accuracy of language demands that good research is written in correct language in terms of grammar, sentence structures, verb and tense forms, and types of phrases and clauses. Therefore, a good knowledge of basic grammar is necessary to writing good research papers. The chapter gives a concise English grammar required to write in correct English. It gives a summary of the basic types of English tenses, subject-verb agreement, the use of active and passive forms, and the various types of phrases and their uses, such as prepositional phrases, noun phrases, gerund phrases, and infinitive phrases. Accuracy of language is essential in writing good academic research papers because it ensures clarity of meaning and transparency of the intended message.

Keywords: types of English tenses, subject-verb agreement, the compound sentence, English tense forms, active and passive voice, types of phrases, articles

Good research should be written in correct language and in the proper academic style. Linguistic accuracy and stylistic appropriateness remain essential for good research writing, alongside integrity of the author, reliability of information, credibility of evidence, depth of content, and honesty in acknowledgements, citations, and referencing. However, language accuracy understandably cannot be dealt with in any exhaustive manner in a work such as this one, whose main focus is on academic research, of which language forms only one part, important as it is. For this reason, this chapter deals with those salient features of language with direct relevance to broader issues of common concern in research writing. In particular, the chapter will be selective in dealing with common linguistic features which pose difficulties to writers and are commonly known to be problematic, causing common errors across a wide spectrum of written material. Following are some of the problematic grammar and language issues of direct relevance to correct writing; writers in the English language are cautioned when writing them.

Language elements

- correct sentence structure and length
- subjects, verbs, and complements
- subject-verb agreement
- tense, voice, and mood
- active and passive voice
- phrases, clauses, and sentences
- adjectives and adverbs
- articles

12.1. Types of sentences in English

The sentence is the basic unit of writing; a group of sentences about an idea or thought form a paragraph, and a number of paragraphs make an essay. There are three types of sentences in English:

1. The simple sentence
2. The compound sentence
3. The complex sentence

A sentence requires three basic elements: at least one subject, one verb, and the expression of a complete thought. A sentence begins with a capital letter and ends with a full stop (.), a question mark (?), or an exclamation mark (!).

12.1.1. The simple sentence:

The simple sentence has three basic elements:

1. It has at least one subject (the subject is who or what performs the action).
2. It has at least one verb (the verb is the action or state that relates to the subject).
3. It has a complete meaning (the subject and verb express a complete idea or thought).

Example

The man who is standing there.

This is not a sentence even though it has a subject ("the man"), and a verb ("is standing"). It is not meaningful.

Tameem apologized.

This is a complete sentence with a subject ("Tameem") and a verb ("apologized"), and it is meaningful.

The man who is standing there is my uncle.

This is a complete sentence; it has a subject ("the man") and a main verb ("is standing") and gives a complete meaning.

Although the simple sentence must have at least one subject and one verb, the different combinations of these two elements can cause confusion. The simple sentence may have more than one noun or pronoun as a subject, or more than one verb.

Examples

Amjad and Khalid are close friends. ("Amjad" and "Khalid", two nouns, form the subject).

Or

They study and socialize together. ("Study" and "socialize" are two verbs relating to the subject "they".)

Or

Amjad and Khalid study and socialize together. (Here there are two nouns forming the subject and two verbs.)

In many situations, writers forget to include a subject or a verb in a sentence, resulting in a sentence fragment. Sometimes they may include a subject and verb and think that the sentence is complete, but on closer reading the sentence does not have a complete meaning.

Other more complex forms of the English sentence are

A. the compound sentence and
B. the complex sentence

12.1.2. The compound sentence

The compound sentence is formed of two main clauses joined together by a coordinating conjunction (e.g., "and", "but", "or", "for", "so", "nor", "yet"). The two clauses are separated by a comma. Each of the two clauses can stand alone as an independent sentence complete in its own right.

Examples

It was cold and rainy, yet the travellers continued their trek uphill.

This can be rewritten in two separate sentences:

It was cold and rainy. Yet, the travellers continued their trek uphill.

Sometimes the two main clauses are combined in one sentence without a conjunction and a semicolon is used instead:

Badr works very hard; he works eight overtime hours a day to earn some extra money.

12.1.3. The complex sentence

The complex sentence is formed of one main clause and one or more dependent clauses; the two clauses joined together by (1) subordinating conjunctions (e.g., "before", "after", "since", "if"), by (2) relative pronouns ("who", "which", "that", "what", "when", "where"), or by (3) punctuation.

Examples

The aeroplane had already taken off before we arrived at the airport.

(The two clauses are joined by the subordinating conjunction "before".)

The man who was presented on TV yesterday **is our neighbour.**

(The two clauses are joined by the relative pronoun "who".)

If oil prices rise, **the prices of other products will also rise.**

(The two clauses are joined by a comma.)

Note that the main clauses (**marked in bold**) can stand alone as complete sentences in their own right, while the dependent clausescannot; hence they "depend" on the main clauses to give meaning.

Examples:

> *Before* we arrived at the airport. (Does not provide a complete meaning.)

> *Who* was presented on TV yesterday. (Does not provide a complete meaning.)

> *If* oil prices rise. (Does not provide a complete meaning.)

These clauses do not make complete sentences even though each contains a subject and verb. This is because they do not make a complete meaning or thought. Writers often mistake such clauses to be complete sentences, resulting in the common error called "sentence fragments".

Good writing should have sentence variety. Good writers vary the structure and length of their sentences. They include a variety of simple, compound, and complex sentences, as well as long and short sentences with varying levels of complexity depending on the subject of the writing. There is no standard length of a sentence; however, care should be taken not to cram the writing with short, repetitive sentences. Too many short sentences can be monotonous. It is also advisable to avoid using too many long, complex sentences to safeguard against making mistakes.

12.2. Basic English tenses and forms

There are three basic tenses in English—present, past, and future—and each has three forms, indicating time frames: (1) a continuous form indicating actions progressing in time, (2) a perfect form indicating completed actions, and (3) a perfect continuous form indicating actions that will be in progress at some point in time. Below are examples of the four basic verb tenses in English and their forms.

Examples of the Three Basic English Verb Tenses, Their Three Forms and Usage

Simple Tenses	Perfect Form	Continuous Form	Perfect Continuous
	Used for completed actions	Used for ongoing actions	For ongoing actions to be completed at a definite time
Present Tense			
Write/s	Have/has written	Am/is/are writing	Have/has been writing
Past Tense			
Wrote	Had written	Was/were writing	Had been writing
Future Tense			
Will write	Will have written	Will be writing	Will have been writing

12.3. Basic English tense forms

Example Sentences of the Four Basic English Verb Tenses and Forms

Basic Forms	Tenses	Examples
Simple Forms	Present Tense	Khalid writes the exam every semester.
	Past Tense	Khalid wrote the exam yesterday.
	Future Tense	Khalid will write the exam next week.
Continuous Forms	Present Continuous Tense	Khalid is writing the exam now.
	Past Continuous Tense	Khalid was writing the exam for three hours yesterday afternoon.
	Future Continuous Tense	Khalid will be writing the exam soon.

Perfect Forms	Present Perfect Tense	Khalid has written the exam.
	Past Perfect Tense	Khalid had written the exam already.
	Future Perfect Tense	Khalid will have written the exam.
Perfect Continuous Forms	Present Perfect Continuous	Khalid has been writing the exam.
	Past Perfect Continuous	Khalid had been writing the exam.
	Future Perfect Continuous	Khalid will have been writing the exam.

12.4. Subjects and Verbs in Sentences

A sentence must have at least a subject and a verb, and it must also have a complete meaning. The subject and verb must agree in the sentence; otherwise, the sentence is not correct. This is called "subject-verb agreement".

Subject-Verb Agreement

The subject and verb in a sentence must agree on five counts: three counts in person, and two counts in number.

Three persons:

1. First person (I, we)
2. Second person (you, you)
3. Third person (he, she, it, the boy, they, the girls)

Two numbers:

1. Singular
2. Plural

ACADEMIC RESEARCH WRITING

Subject-verb Agreement Relationships in Number and Person

Person	Example	Number	Subject	Verb Agreement			
				Present	*Past*	*Perfect*	*P. Part.*
First Person	I	Singular	I	Am	Was	Have	Done
Second Person	We	Plural	We	Are	Were	Have	Done
	You	Singular	You	Are	Were	Have	Done
	You	Plural	You	Are	Were	Have	Done
Third Person	He		He	Writes	Wrote		Written
	The boy	Singular	The boy			Has	
	Sara/She		Sara/She	Sleeps	Slept		Slept
	It		It				
	They	Plural	The boys	Play	Played	Have	Played
	The boys		They	Sleep	Slept		Slept

12.5. Tense and voice

Tense

"Tense" refers to the use of the verb in the sentence as it expresses the time at which the action occurs—in the present, past, or past-unto-the present (the latter case using the participle). Accordingly, there are three main types of tenses in English:

Type	Common meaning	Example
Present	sometimes referred to as verb 1	Joe *speaks* Vietnamese.
Past	sometimes referred to as verb 2	The president *spoke* eloquently.
Past participle	sometimes referred to as verb 3	Sara has *spoken* softly to me.

Knowledge of the three forms of a verb tense—present form, past form, and past participle—and when to use them is essential basic

239

knowledge that will allow you to avoid many unnecessary writing errors which might otherwise result from using the wrong tense. The importance of tense is that it helps the writer express different thoughts, ideas, and events as they occur in time sequence, and the various verb forms of present, past, and past participle help us do just that. Students are frequently exposed to a variety of activities and exercises to drill them in the use of the different verb conjugations and to memorize those conjugations. In almost every book on grammar, it is possible to find lists of English verbs of common usage and their conjugations according to the three tense forms.

Voice

There are two types of voice for a verb: active and passive.

Voice refers to the use of the verb in the sentence in relation to the role of the subject; it indicates whether the subject is the doer of the action or the receiver. When the doer of the action is referred to as the subject of the sentence, the verb is said to be in the active voice; and when the subject is the receiver, the verb is in the passive voice. As such, the active form emphasizes the doer, while the passive emphasizes the receiver of the action.

Examples

Naji invited his friends to dinner.

The verb "invited" is in the active voice because the subject, "Naji", did the action of inviting. The emphasis is on the doer, "Naji".

His friends were invited to dinner (by Naji).

The verb "were invited" is in the passive voice because the subject "His friends" received the action of inviting and the emphasis is on the receiver.

Note that the passive form of the verb consists of two parts: the verb "be" and the past participle form of the main verb ("were invited"), together making a verb phrase. Confusion sometimes occurs with the passive voice.

12.6. Active and passive verbs

It is advisable to use active verbs because they are more direct, emphatic, and more concise. Passive verbs are also necessary in writing, especially in situations where the "doer" of the action is unknown or is unimportant.

12.6.1. Active verbs

Active verbs are used in sentences in which the subject is the doer of the action.

Examples

Mohammad took Majid to hospital immediately after the accident.

In addition to books and stationery, the bookstore sells computers and electronics.

In the two examples above, the subject Mohammad did the action of taking, and the bookstore does the action of selling.

12.6.2. Passive verbs

The passive voice is used when the subject of the sentence is not doing the action of the verb but is receiving it. The passive voice is widely used in scientific writing, in which the identity of the subject is often unimportant. Passive verbs are formed from the verb "be" preceding the past participle form of the main verb (e.g. "is done", "was done", "were done", "has been done").

Examples

> A large-scale investigation was carried out to determine the cause of the plane crash.

> Good news has been circulating recently that a new drug for diabetes has been developed.

> A South African tribal chief was pickpocketed at a busy underground station in London.

In the first and second examples above, the recipients of the action (the investigation and the new drug) are more important than those doing the action; therefore, they become the central focus (the subject) of the sentences. In the third, however, the doer of the pickpocketing action is unknown in so crowded a place as an underground metro station—possibly a place teeming with stalking pickpockets.

12.6.2.1. *Common errors of usage with the passive form*

- Forgetting the "be" part of the verb phrase, such as in "The criminal caught by the police" (forgetting verb "was")
- Writing the wrong tense of the main verb, often using the past instead of the past participle

Example

> Good words <u>are spoke</u>. (incorrect: past participle "are spoke")

> Good words <u>are spoken</u>. (correct: past participle "are spoken")

- In some situations, intransitive verbs are used with the passive voice. Intransitive verbs (e.g., "happen", "look", "occur", "seem") do not take an object and therefore do not have a passive form.

Example

The accident was happened by fast driving.

"Happen" is intransitive, does not take an object, and has no passive form.

Example

Our friend was received the prize of the contest.

"Our friend" doing the receiving is placed in the receiving end, and vice versa for the prize. To correct the sentence, the verb should either be in the active or the passive:

Our friend received the prize. (This is active, since our friend does the receiving.)

Or

The prize was received by our friend. (This is passive, since the receiving falls on the prize.)

12.6.2.2. *The passive voice is used in certain contexts*

The passive voice is used in some of the following contexts:

- When the actual doer is not known:

The dinosaurs were wiped out millions of years ago. (What caused it is unknown.)

- When it is unnecessary or unimportant to mention the actual doer:

It has been found that exposure to the sun in the early morning is good for health. (It is unnecessary or unimportant to say, for example, "doctors or scientists found that ...").

- When the writer does not want to mention the actual doer:

The meeting was cancelled. (This could be used instead of "The manager cancelled the meeting.")

- To convey facts:

It has been proved that sugar, and not fats, is the main cause of heart problems.

- To make wording more neutral and impartial:

Better solutions for environmental problems could be found. (This is more neutral than to say "governments can find better solutions".)

- Used for hedging or mystification:

Parts of the new building are not yet fully completed as required by the contract.

Here this is indended to hedge and mystify against the contractor's implied failure to meet the standards stipulated by the contract.

- To make the wording noncommittal (to avoid responsibility):

It is reported that the recent increase in the number of traffic accidents is mainly due to bad road construction.

This is done to avoid responsibility and accountability. If the sentence is written in the active voice, revealing the identity of the reporter, the government or municipal authorities might take legal action against the reporter for tarnishing their good name.

12.7. Phrases: types and uses

Unlike a sentence or a clause, a phrase is a group of words without a main verb that therefore does not have a complete meaning. Understanding how phrases function in the writing process helps writers use them properly and correctly in their writing. Phrases in English are of different types, the most common of which are

- prepositional phrases,
- noun phrases,
- gerunds,
- infinitives,
- verb phrases, and
- phrasal verbs.

12.7.1. Prepositional phrases

A prepositional phrase is a group of words that begins with a preposition to indicate place, time, direction, or manner. Examples of prepositions include "on", "in", "at", "over", "to", and "under". Combined with other words, these prepositions form prepositional phrases (e.g., "on the table", "in the room", "at the beach", "over the counter", "to school", "under the tree").

Use	Example
Showing place	The students go *to school* every morning.
Showing time	They go early *in the morning.*
Showing direction	Their school is *across the road from the hospital.*
Showing manner	They enter classes quietly and *in order.*

Besides the preposition, which is the main part, a prepositional phrase may contain an article

("a", "an", "the"), a noun, a pronoun, or an adjective, but it can never contain a subject, verb, or object.

Being able to correctly write and identify prepositional phrases is particularly important to allow writers to easily check their sentences in terms of tense and subject-verb agreement. Sometimes writers confuse the object of a prepositional phrase with the object of the main sentence verb. Take a sentence like this, for example: "Abdallah discusses with the manager the low overtime rate." Here "the low overtime rate" is the object of the main sentence verb "discusses", and "the manager" is the object of the preposition "with". Confusion may occur when the writer considers "with the manager" to be the object of the main verb "discusses". Knowing that the prepositional phrase does not make an object of the main sentence verb, the writer can leave it out and read the sentence without it, to check and correct if there is disagreement between the subject and the main verb. Knowledge of prepositional phrases is especially relevant to the tasks of editing and proofreading.

12.7.2. Noun phrases

A noun phrase consists of a noun plus a modifier or modifiers, and it functions as a subject, object, or complement in a sentence.

Examples

> *One aspect of the concept of globalization* involves free movement of labour and capital.

Here "One aspect of the concept of globalization" is the noun phrase, which functions as the subject of the verb "involves".

Speculations have propelled *the prices of property* to unprecedented levels.

Here "the prices of property" is the noun phrase, which functions as the object of the verb "have propelled".

"Symbiosis" is *a medical term* that refers to organisms mutually feeding on one another for survival.

Here "*a medical term*" is the noun phrase, which functions as a complement of the verb "is".

12.7.3. Gerund phrases

A gerund is formed of the "-ing" form of a verb and always functions as a noun. A gerund phrase consists of a gerund plus its modifiers, and it functions as subject, object, or complement in the sentence.

Examples

Being physically and mentally fit is an essential requirement for successful athletes.

Here "Being physically and mentally fit" is the gerund phrase, which functions as the subject of the verb "is".

Good health requires exercising on a regular basis.

Here "exercising on a regular basis" is the gerund phrase, which functions as the object of the verb "requires".

One of the biggest challenges that face new college students is *deciding on the right accommodation.*

Here "deciding on the right accommodation" is the gerund phrase, which functions as the complement of the verb "is".

12.7.4. Infinitive phrases

An infinitive is formed of "to" plus a verb (e.g., "to respond"). An infinitive phrase consists of an infinitive plus its modifiers, and it functions as a noun, adjective, or adverb.

Examples

To arrive safely home demands careful and defensive driving.

Here "To arrive safely home" is the infinitive phrase, which is a noun and functions as the subject of the verb "demands".

Good citizenship is a value that presupposes citizens *to have honesty and integrity.*

Here "to have honesty and integrity" is the infinitive phrase, which functions as the adjective for the noun "citizens".

To carry out his duties professionally, a doctor has routinely to do night shifts and be on standby for emergency cases.

Here "To carry out his duties professionally" is the infinitive phrase, which functions as the adverb of the verb "carry out".

12.7.5. Verb phrases

A verb phrase consists of a main verb and its auxiliary or helping verb (e.g., "can be", "would entail", "are risking"). A verb phrase can function only as the predicate of a sentence.

Examples

> Digging gold out from deep underground mines *can be* a very high risk job.

> It *would entail* high probability of mine collapse or serious injuries from rigging and loading machines.

> Indeed, mine workers *are risking* their own dear lives for a little cash.

12.7.6. Phrasal verbs

Phrasal verbs are different from verb phrases in that phrasal verbs consist of a verb plus a particle, unlike verb phrases, which consist of two verbs—one main verb and one helping, or auxiliary, verb. An example of a verb phrase is "could break", but "break down" is a phrasal verb. Phrasal verbs are used to create special meanings. For example, the verb "break" can be attached to different prepositions to form phrasal verbs (e.g., "break up", "break down", "break into"), each time giving a completely different meaning. Because of this quality of creating special meanings, phrasal verbs are very useful in writing; they enable the writer to express complex ideas and relationships concisely and vividly. Below is a list of common phrasal verbs and examples:

Phrasal Verb	Meaning	Example Sentence
Come across	Meet by accident	I *came across* an old friend in downtown Riyadh whom I haven't seen since high school.
Come down	Fall, drop	The prices of property *came down* by 10 per cent in the last two years.
Go over	Review, revise	The students *go over* the last chapters of the book in preparation for the final exam.
Go through	Have an experience	Tameem has *gone through* a very difficult experience after having lost his job.
Drop by	Visit for a short time	I'll *drop by* your place on my way home after work tomorrow.
Think about	To consider	Would you like to come to the party? *Think about* it and let me know.
Think over	Consider carefully	The father said to his son: "I want you to *think over* your decision to study engineering. I know you are not good at maths".
Put on	Wear (clothes)	Every year, we *put on* new clothes on Eid days at the end of the holy month of Ramadan.
Put up	Tolerate, bear with	My next-door neighbours are too loud and noisy. I can't *put up* with it any longer.
Try out		"*Try out* that blouse before paying," the mother said. "It looks smaller than your size."
Set in motion		The new tax policy has *set in motion* a whole range of negative changes in the economy.

12.8. Articles

The articles "a", "an", and "the" create a lot of confusion. Many writers are often not sure when to use one—especially regarding the use of the definite article "the". Below are some guidelines on when to use these articles.

12.8.1. The definite article "the"

The article "the" is used with both singular and plural nouns; it is much more problematic than the articles "a" and "an". There are contexts where "the" makes a big difference in the meaning of a sentence. In others, its presence or otherwise doesn't affect the meaning. Generally, "the" is used and is not used in the following contexts:

Used to refer to a specific noun	"What are you looking for, Saeed?" "I'm looking for *the* car keys."
Used after the first mentioning of a noun	A strong storm is coming this direction. *The* storm is forecast to last for three hours.
Is used with superlative forms of comparison	*The* highest price, *the* longest day
Is not used with common words that refer to materials	The house is built of *stone, brick, and wood.*
Is not used with plural count nouns when referred to generally	*Businesses* all around the world compete for new markets.
Is not used with abstract nouns but is used when referring to a particular one	*The* justice of law, *the* beauty of sunset

12.8.2. The indefinite articles "a" and "an"

The article "a" generally denotes a singular noun; that is, a noun that refers to one thing (for example, "a book" means "one book"). Sometimes the noun is separated from the article by an adjective (e.g., "a thick book"). Sometimes, however, the adjective modifying the noun begins with a vowel letter, in which case "an" is used instead of "a" (e.g., "an amazing book"). Therefore, "an" is used with singular nouns that begin with vowel letters (e.g., "an apple", "an orange") or with singular nouns preceded by an adjective that begins with a vowel letter.

Examples

a story; an appearance

but

an unbelievable story; an unusual appearance

Chapter References

Butler, Eugenia, Mary Ann Hickman, Patricia J. McAlexander, and Overby Lalla (1995). *Correct Writing.* 6th ed. Lexington, Massachusetts: Heath and Co.

D'Youville College Learning Center (2012). "Prepositions and Prepositional Phrases". The Purdue OWL, Purdue University Writing Lab.

Escalas, Maggie (2000). "Summary of Verb Tenses". The Write Place. St. Cloud State University. Last updated 22 September 2000.

Westphal, Donella (2000). "Active and Passive Verbs". The Write Place. St. Cloud State University. Last updated 8 February 2000,

Wikipedia (n.d). "Grammar". Available under the Creative Commons Attribution-ShareAlike License. *https://en.wikipedia.org/*

——— (n.d.). "Usage". Available under the Creative Commons Attribution-ShareAlike License. Accessed 1 October 2016. https://en.wikipedia.org/wiki/Usage.

CHAPTER 13

Clauses, Adjectives, Adverbs, and Punctuation

Abstract: This chapter is a continuation of Chapter 12 on the "Language of Academic Writing", highlighting the other elements of accurate language use such as clauses, adjectives, and adverbs. Related to these is the proper use of punctuation. Knowledge of the types and uses of clauses is indeed elusive to many writers; and therefore, it is important to know how to write them correctly. The two basic types of clauses are discussed: the dependent and independent (main) clauses; and how to combine them by coordinating and/ or subordinating conjunctions, and by relative pronouns. There are some common errors which writers need to avoid when writing clauses. The use of adjectives is also problematic to some writers. A good list of adjective endings is given to aid writers recognize them. Sometimes, confusion arises in the use of adjectives and adverbs, and writers are alerted to distinguish between the two when writing sentences. An important element of accurate writing is the proper use of punctuation. Punctuation breaks the continuity of the written material into chunks of meanings, and is therefore essential to the clarity of argument. Writers need to know how to properly use punctuation, such the full stop (full stop), the comma, semi-colon, the quotation marks, brackets (parenthesis), etc.

Keywords: dependent and independent (main) clauses, coordinating and subordinating conjunctions, relative pronouns, adjective endings, adverbs, punctuation, the comma, the full stop (period), semicolon, brackets

13.1. Dependent Clauses and Types

A clause is a group of words that may contain a subject and a verb, and may or may not have a complete meaning. Clauses in English are of two main types: *dependent* and *independent*. An independent clause has a subject and verb and can stand alone as a sentence complete in its own right, but it can also be added to another minor clause—a dependent clause. The dependent clause has a subject and a verb but does not give a meaning unless it is attached to another main clause. Below are examples of dependent clauses and their reasons of dependency.

Clause	Type	Reason of dependency
Unless it is attached to a main clause	Dependent clause	Has subject and verb, but no meaning
a dependent clause has no meaning	Independent clause	Has subject and verb, and has meaning

The two clauses above may be combined in one sentence by the subordinating conjunction "unless": "Unless it is attached to a main clause, a dependent clause has no meaning."

Types of Dependent Clauses

13.1.1. Noun clause

A noun clause is a dependent clause used as the subject of the sentence.

Example

> *What the manager plans to do* can put the entire construction project at risk.

13.1.2. Adjective clause

An adjective clause is a dependent clause that modifies a noun or pronoun.

Example

The TV show, *which was presented on Friday nights,* is very interesting.

13.1.3. Adverbial clause

An adverbial clause is a type of dependent clause which functions exactly as an adverb modifying a verb, an adjective, or another adverb. Adverbial clauses can be used to express time, place, condition, cause, or manner.

Example

I visit my grandparents in the countryside whenever I feel bored of the restless city life.

13.2. Combining dependent and independent clauses

Dependent and independent clauses can be combined in a number of ways to form vigorous sentences. The special value of these clauses is that they allow the writer to express the relative value and weight of the ideas carried in the two clauses. Weightier ideas are reserved for main or independent clauses, whereas minor ideas are appended in the dependent clauses. The ways by which dependent and independent clauses can be combined include

Academic Research Writing

1. coordinating conjunctions ("and", "but", "so", "or", "nor", "yet");
2. subordinating conjunctions ("although", "however", "unless", "if", "whereas", "since", "because"); and
3. relative pronouns ("who", "whom", "which", "that", "whose", "what").

13.2.1. Combine by coordinating conjunctions

Coordinating conjunctions combine clauses of equal weight—that is, independent clauses that each can stand alone as an independent sentence. The combined sentence may begin with either clause, with no difference in meaning; the connecting word serves as a "coordinator" between the two clauses and is preceded by a comma.

Examples

> Space exploration is very ambitious. Space exploration is too expensive to sustain.

> Space exploration is very ambitious, but it is too expensive to sustain.

> Space exploration is too expensive to sustain, but it is very ambitious.

The first example above consists of two independent clauses (sentences) of equal weight. They can be combined beginning with either of the two, and the meaning remains the same. The second and third examples both begin with one of the two clauses and are combined by the coordinator "but." The two parts carry equal weight, still giving the same meaning.

13.2.2. Combine by Subordinating Conjunctions

Subordinating conjunctions combine two clauses; one dependent and one independent, to make one sentence. The two clauses are not of equal weight; the independent clause carries the major idea, while the dependent clause carries the minor idea and *depends* on the other to be meaningful (thus it is *dependent*). The connecting word "subordinates" the minor to the major, thus the term "subordinating". Subordinating conjunctions include "although", "unless", "however", "if", "moreover", "since", "nevertheless", "because", "when', "on the other hand", "therefore", "then", and "thus").

Examples

It was cold and rainy; nevertheless, the travellers continued their trek uphill.

The example above has one independent clause (sentence) and one dependent clause. The independent clause carries the main idea and can stand alone as a sentence; while the dependent clause carries the minor idea and cannot stand alone as a sentence.

The two clauses can be combined beginning with either of them.

The retired professor bought an antique house in a remote suburb. He likes the serenity of the countryside away from the restless city.

1. The retired professor bought an antique house in a remote suburb because he likes the serenity of the countryside away from the restless city.

2. Because he likes the serenity of the countryside away from the restless city, the retired professor bought an antique house in a remote suburb.

Example (1) above begins with the independent clause, and the subordinating connector "because" links it to the dependent clause. In this case, no comma is used. Example (2) begins with the dependent clause connected to the main clause by the subordinating conjunction "because", indicating the minor weight of the dependent clause and its subordination—that it is meaningless without the main clause to which it is attached. A comma is used when the sentence begins with the dependent clause.

13.2.3. Combining by Relative Pronouns:

Relative clauses, as an example of dependent clauses, are introduced by relative pronouns and are used to modify a word or phrase in the independent clause. The modified word is called the "antecedent". Relative pronouns include "who", "whom", "which", "that", "whose", and "what".

Example:

The woman *who presents the TV family show* is our neighbour.

The main clause, "The woman is our neighbour", is a complete sentence in its own right. The relative clause, "who presents the TV family show", begins with the relative pronoun "who" and modifies "the woman", which is the subject of the main clause (sentence).

There are two types of relative clauses: *restrictive* clauses and *nonrestrictive* clauses.

Restrictive relative clauses

In restrictive relative clauses, the relative pronoun and the rest of the clause form an integral part of the sentence because they add essential information to the antecedent in the sentence; therefore, they are not separated by a comma. That is, without the restrictive relative clause, the rest of the sentence does not have a complete meaning.

Example

> The bank manager was the man during whose era the bank was fined eight million dollars for violating sanctions against countries supporting terrorism.

The restrictive relative clause "during whose era the bank was fined eight million dollars for violating sanctions against countries supporting terrorism" adds essential information to the sentence. If it is removed, the rest of the sentence—"The bank manager was the man"—will have an incomplete meaning.

Nonrestrictive relative clauses

Nonrestrictive relative clauses, on the other hand, add unimportant information which can be omitted without affecting the meaning of the sentences. Because they add information only for more clarity, nonrestrictive relative clauses are set apart from the rest of the sentence by commas.

Example

> The man, *whom we met yesterday,* was the bank manager I told you about.

The nonrestrictive relative clause "whom we met yesterday" adds unimportant information. If it is removed, the rest of the sentence—"The man was the bank manager I told you about"—is still a complete, meaningful sentence.

13.3 Common errors to avoid when writing clauses

Clauses are important and useful in writing. They enable the writer to express ideas clearly and logically to show the relative weight of ideas and their relationships. However, care should be exercised to avoid some very common mistakes in writing clauses. Some of these errors (which will be discussed in more detail in the chapter "Common Language and Style Errors") include sentence fragments, comma splices and run-on (fused) sentences.

12.3.1 Sentence fragments

Sentence fragments occur when a writer treats a dependent clause as a complete sentence (e.g., "When the time comes.") This is not a meaningful sentence. To correct, a main clause is needed to complete the meaning (e.g., "When the time comes, the project will be fully operational").

13.3.2. Comma splices

A comma splice occurs when a writer joins two independent clauses by only a comma.

Example

> Tariq works very hard, he works overtime in another company to earn extra income.

To correct a comma splice, the two independent clauses may either (a) be separated by a full stop, making them two separate sentences, or (b) be joined by a semicolon into one sentence.

Example

Tariq works very hard. He works overtime in another company to earn extra income.

or

Tariq works very hard; he works overtime in another company to earn extra income.

13.3.3. Run-on (fused) sentences

Run-on (fused) sentences occur when there is no punctuation used to separate two independent clauses; both are fused together as one sentence.

Example

People in farming communities remain emotionally healthy they support each other when in need.

Run-on or fused sentences can be corrected by using the correct punctuation to separate the two fused clauses.

People in farming communities remain emotionally healthy. They support each other when in need.

or

People in farming communities remain emotionally healthy; they support each other when in need.

13.4. Adjectives

Adjectives are words that modify or describe nouns (words used to identify people, places, objects, and ideas) and pronouns (e.g., "he", "she", "they"). Adjectives appear in various positions in a sentence. As a general rule, adjectives describe nouns or pronouns.

- Adjectives may come after articles (e.g., "the", "a", "an") (e.g., "Thamir bought *a red* car.").
- Adjectives may come before a noun (e.g., "The sun is like a *golden ball.*").
- They can come after certain stative verbs (e.g., "feel", "look", "seem", "appear") (e.g., "He looks tired.").
- Adjectives are formed mostly from nouns (e.g., "national" [from "nation"], wooden [from "wood"] and "thirsty" [from "thirst"]).
- Adjectives are also formed from verbs (e.g., "excited" and "exciting" [from "excite"], and "break" [from "broken"]).
- Sometimes a noun can function as an adjective when it modifies another noun (e.g., "A tennis ball is quite small", in which the noun "tennis" functions as an adjective modifying the second noun, "ball".

13.4.1. Adjectives formed from verbs

There are some troubling issues in writing adjectives. One vexing problem is the confusion in writing adjectives derived from the participles of verbs, namely; the "-ed" and "-ing" forms (e.g., "excited", "exciting"). Students often confuse the use of the two verb-adjective forms.

Example

The film was *exciting.*

not

The film was *excited.*

To dispel the confusion, adjectives formed from past participle ("-ed") verb forms, such as "frightened", "thrilled", and "confused", usually describe human feelings toward the thing described.

Examples

The child was *frightened* of the horror film.

Dona was *thrilled* by the news of her dazzling success.

Students were *confused* about which question to answer.

Adjectives formed from the present participle (-ing) verb forms, such as "frightening", "thrilling", and "confusing", describe the objects that cause the feeling.

Examples

The horror film was *frightening* [to the child].

Dona found the news of her dazzling success *thrilling.*

The question was written in a *confusing* way [for students to answer].

13.4.2. Order of adjectives

Another equally troubling issue is the order of adjectives when more than one adjective is used in a sentence. Sentences can include more than one adjective; each adjective adds specific function in the sentence. Adjectives appear in a particular order according to their function. Adjectives add meanings to denote size, age, colour, quality, shape, or origin, and are written in the following order:

Opinion	Size	Age	Shape	Colour	Origin	Material	Purpose
O	S	A	SH	C	O	M	P
A beautiful	spacious	old	square	white	Thai	wooden	guest house

Although in theory this is the right order, it is not customary to use more than three adjectives in a sentence at a time. Moreover, it is not always easy to memorize the order of adjectives when writing, which often leads to murky sentences. The order can be shortened to the acronym: OSASH COMP for easy memorization.

13.4.3. Adjective endings

It is helpful for students and writers to know how to recognize adjectives and use them properly in their writing. One useful way of recognizing adjectives is by knowing their endings. Below is a list of the most common adjective endings and examples.

adjective endings	examples
-ful	beautiful; useful
-ous	famous; serious
-tive	positive; active
-less	fearless; spotless
-able	durable; portable
-ible	terrible; legible

-ic	Arabic; Atlantic
-ese	Burmese; Congolese
-ent	prominent; imminent
-y	noisy; spicy
-al	formal; nominal
-ing	exciting; refreshing
-ed	excited; terrified
-ive	coercive; explosive
-ish	feverish; Turkish
-an / ian	Republican; Brazilian
-ant	fragrant; reluctant

13.5. Adverbs

Adverbs describe verbs, adjectives, or other adverbs and explain how something happens or in what manner or degree it happens.

Examples

The workshop was organized for company employees to teach them how to drive defensively. ["Defensively" is an adverb describing the verb "to drive". It answers the question "how?"]

The new Mercedes Benz is prohibitively expensive. ["Prohibitively" is an adverb describing the adjective "expensive"; it answers the question "How expensive?"]

The short-story writer writes extremely well. ["Well" is an adverb describing the verb "writes", and "extremely" is another adverb describing the adverb "well". It answers the question "To what degree?" The most common adverb form is the "-ly" form added to adjectives. It is easy to identify.]

Another important aspect closely related to both language and style is correct punctuation. Punctuation, again, remains a subject which writers and researchers need to know exactly how to use properly for the sake of correctness and clarity of meaning. Sometimes, however, good research and brilliant ideas can be blurred just because of improper punctuation. The section below is devoted to the salient features of punctuation marks, and their proper usage.

13.6. Punctuation

Punctuation is important in writing for its function in breaking sentences into meaningful units, marking the beginning, end, and other breaks that are necessary to clarify meaning and make it easy for the reader to follow. Just as a speaker pauses while speaking to vary tone and signal direction of meaning, so does a writer's use of punctuation. In the absence of proper punctuation, sentences may be confusing, and meaning difficult to follow, sometimes resulting in a complete breakdown in communication. Proper use of punctuation is especially important in academic research writing, since clarity of meaning is an essential criterion of formal scientific writing. For these reasons, research writers will be best advised to have a grasp of the main types of punctuation and the basic rules on how to use them properly in their writing. This section gives guidelines on the following punctuation marks and uses:

1. Comma
2. Full stop
3. Colon
4. Semicolon
5. Quotation marks (inverted commas)
6. Parentheses and brackets
7. Hyphens
8. Apostrophes

13.6.1. Comma

The comma is used to mark breaks in a sentence, separating words, phrases, and clauses. This clarifies the connections and relationships between the different components in the sentence, making it easy to understand. Commas are used to separate elements of sentences in the following situations:

- to mark off introductory words and phrases
- to separate items in lists
- to separate clauses
- to mark off direct speech
- to mark off certain parts of a sentence
- to mark off appositives
- with "however" as a contrastive conjunction

A comma marks a slight break between different parts of a sentence. Used properly, commas make the meanings of sentences clear by grouping and separating words, phrases, and clauses. Many people are uncertain about the use of commas, though, and often sprinkle them throughout their writing without being clear about the basic rules governing the use of commas.

Following are the main cases when you need to use a comma.

Using commas to mark off introductory words and phrases

Words and phrases that introduce sentences are separated from the rest of the sentence by a comma.

Examples:

There are a number of reasons why Thailand is one of the preferred tourist destinations for thousands of tourists every year. First, there is the Grand Palace of the Thai royal family built in 1789.

At the same time, Thailand exemplifies ancient Buddhist traditions in the way people lead their lives and in the style of architecture.

Using commas to separate items in lists

Put a comma between the different items in a list; the list may consist of nouns, verbs, or phrases, as in the following sentences:

Grandmother bought me a blouse, leather belt, a scarf, and cream-coloured baggy pants.

The wandering group shouted, yelled, and cried loudly for help.

Sometimes the comma is not used before the last item of the list. But this can be confusing. Look at the example below:

Majid loves pizza so much, especially pizza with mushrooms, chicken, garlic and cheese and onions.

In this sentence, it is not clear whether the last three items (garlic, cheese, and onions) are three different types of pizza or two. The use of a final comma in such sentences in necessary to clarify the meaning:

Majid loves pizza so much, especially pizza with mushrooms, chicken, garlic and cheese, and onions.

The above sentence indicates that "garlic and cheese" is one type of pizza made up of two components. Without the use of the comma, the meaning is not clear.

Using commas in quotations

A comma is used to separate a phrase introducing a direct quotation.

Example

Abdulla said, "I'm completely broke."

"I wonder," he went on, "if I can get a loan from the bank."

Using commas to separate clauses

Commas are used to separate clauses in sentences containing dependent and independent clauses that begin with a dependent clause.

Example

Because of the terrible weather, conditions, we postponed the trip to next week.

But no comma is needed if the sentence begins with the main clause.

Example

We postponed the trip to next week because of the terrible weather conditions.

Commas in restrictive and nonrestrictive relative clauses

Restrictive relative clauses contain information that is essential to the overall meaning of the sentence. If such information is removed, the meaning will not be clear.

Example

Only patients who were operated on by surgeon
Kamal will be discharged today.

No commas are used with restrictive relative clauses because
they are essential to the sentence. If you remove the relative clause
("who were operated on by surgeon Kamal") from the sentence, the
meaning will not be clear. It contains information essential to the
meaning of the sentence.

Nonrestrictive relative clauses, on the other hand, contain
information that is not essential to the overall meaning of a sentence,
and therefore they can be omitted without affecting the meaning.

Example

The main sections of the exam, which was
conducted yesterday morning, consisted of a
definitions section, MCQs section, and a short essay
writing section.

Commas are used before and after a nonrestrictive relative clause
to set it apart as unessential information. If you remove the clause
"which was conducted yesterday morning", the rest of the sentence
still makes perfect sense; the clause only adds extra information that
is not necessary.

Example

The main sections of the exam consisted of a
definitions section, MCQs section, and a short essay
writing one.

Using commas to mark off parts of a sentence

Sentences in natural language settings usually contain parts that only add extra unessential information which does not affect the meaning of the sentence if removed. Commas are used in such sentences to mark off those parts that contain extra unnecessary information.

Example

Amin's book, *Indigenous Farming Communities*, is now available on Amazon.

The phrase *"Indigenous Farming Communities"*, set apart by commas, contains unnecessary information, indicating that Amin has only this book. The same sentence without the commas has a different meaning:

Amin's book *Indigenous Farming Communities* is now available on Amazon.

Here the added part is essential, as it distinguishes which of Amin's books is now available on Amazon.

Using a comma with "however" as a contrasting conjunction

"However" is used in sentences to denote two different meanings: one "in contrast", and another "in whatever manner". Consider these two examples:

Sara wants to buy that stylish leather bag; however, it is too expensive for her to afford.

Sara wants to buy that stylish leather bag however expensive it may be.

Using commas to mark off appositives

Appositives are words or phrases that follow a noun and define or explain it. Appositives are set off from the rest of the sentences by commas.

Example

A stethoscope, a device used to listen to heartbeats, is an indispensable companion of every doctor.

13.6.2. Full Stop (British English) / Period (American English)

The full stop is usually used to mark the end of declarative sentences (statements), but it has other uses. It is used in the following situations:

To mark the end of a declarative sentence that is a complete statement

The twins Jim and Jack lived apart for forty years from the day they were born. Surprisingly, they bought the same type of car, and married ladies having the same name, Linda.

Sometimes, however, full stops are used for the purpose of emphasis at the end of clauses and phrases that are not complete sentences.

They kept pushing on their trek. Day in and day out for several days.

For abbreviations in various contexts

- Abbreviated forms of the months: "Jan." "Feb." "Sept." "Dec."
- Entities: "org.", "co."
- Morning and evening times of day: "a.m."; "p.m."

For abbreviations that end in a full stop, no second one is needed

Example

> The audience comprises a wide spectrum of society: artists, writers, comedians, singers, brands designers, etc. All come with an eye both for pleasure and benefit.

13.6.3. The colon

The colon is used in three situations:

1. To introduce a list of items

   Example

   > The inventory list includes the following items: fifty-two chairs, twenty-eight desks, twelve computer units, and one printer.

2. Between two independent clauses that are organically connected

   Example

   > Those were trying times for my grandmother as an immigrant: she had to battle with the odds of discrimination, no job, and a series of illnesses.

3. Before a direct quotation

   Example

   > Tariq remembers: "My grandfather has always been in love with the desert. He has never lived away

from the old brick-and-wood house built by his great-grandfather near a beautiful oasis deep in the Great Sahara Desert of the African Sahel."

13.6.4. The semicolon

Semicolons are used widely to combine two independent clauses in one sentence; the two clauses otherwise can be separated into two separate sentences.

Example

> The driver changes gears; the gearbox transmits power from the engine to increase the car's speed.

The above example can be rewritten as two sentences separated by a full stop.

Example

> The driver changes gears. The gearbox transmits power from the engine to increase the car's speed.

Another use of the semicolon is to separate a group of elements contained within another group in the sentence, where the elements in the primary group are separated by commas, while the major groups are separated by semicolons.

Example

> The panel consists of experts in the fields of construction, materials, and safety; lawyers in business law, company law, and civil law; and experts in public and environment health.

Above, a major group "of experts" (separated by commas between its members) is separated by a semicolon from the other major group, "lawyers", (also separated by commas within its members), which is separated again by a semicolon from a third major group: "health and environmental experts".

13.6.5. Quotation marks (American English) / inverted commas (British English

British and American English use quotation marks (inverted commas) differently. In British English, single quotation marks ('…') are the norm, whereas in American English the norm is double quotation marks ("…").

Quotation marks are used in the following situations:

a. In direct quotations

Example

The jury agreed on the verdict, and the judge uttered the sentence "The evidence presented to this court proves beyond doubt that you have committed the hideous crimes of assault and robbery. Therefore, you are sentenced to three years' imprisonment under hard labour."

b. For quotations within quotations

Sometimes a quotation is embedded within a quotation. In this situation, American and British English use different quotation marks to identify the two quotes. In American English, single quotation marks are used for the internal quote.

Example

> Jowett, in his translation of *The Republic*, notes that "*The Republic*, together with Roseau's *Emilee* are the two most influential works ever written on the philosophy of education. Plato persuasively argued that 'the best guardians must be given the best education' to prepare them rule the polis in the best interest of all citizens."

The same quotes in British English would be written within single quotation marks for the direct quote, and double marks for the embedded quote.

Example

> Jowett, in his translation of *The Republic*, notes that 'The Republic, together with Roseau's Emilee are the two most influential works ever written on the philosophy of education. Plato persuasively argued that "the best guardians must be given the best education" to prepare them rule the polis in the best interest of all citizens.'

c. to mark off a word or phrase quoted or referred to within a text

Example

> Martin, father of the positive psychology theory, has written extensively on the concept of "flow".

13.6.6. Parentheses and brackets

There are three types of brackets used: round (...), square [...], and angled < ... >. The different types of brackets are used to convey different messages to the reader about the text being enclosed within them.

Uses of round brackets ("parentheses" in American English)

In in-text citations

Perhaps the most important use of round brackets (parentheses) is in the documentation of sources in the body of a piece of writing, especially in academic writings, referred to as "in-text citations". In-text citations refer to the insertion of bibliographic details, such as authors' names and dates of sources, in the body of a document. Such details are usually enclosed within round brackets or parentheses, giving them the name "parenthetical citations". Parentheses are also used to mark off information that isn't essential to the overall meaning (i.e., material contained within them that, when removed, leaves the sentence complete and meaningful).

Example

Having moved with my family to Khartoum (the capital of Sudan) in 1992, I spent the major part of my childhood there.

The history of the Continent (Europe) is rife with wars and bloodshed, as the two world wars testify.

Round Brackets are also used to add a comment by the writer for clarification:

Debate still goes on about the moral issues involved in euthanasia (also called *mercy killing*): the act of putting to death painlessly or allowing a person or animal to die to end suffering from an incurable painful disease or condition.

Uses of square brackets

Square brackets (*called brackets in American English*) are mainly used to add words by a writer who is not the original writer and insert them in the original text for the purpose of clarification:

"This view of science refers to the positivistic or natural science model or quantitative [sometimes called empirical] research approach".

In this example, the primary text is a quotation from original source, the qualifying clause enclosed within the square brackets *[sometimes called empirical]* is added by the secondary writer giving a definition to clarify the concept *"quantitative"*.

Use of angled brackets

Angled brackets are mainly used to enclose URLs and websites addresses.

Example

Education Policy and Management, vol. 32, no. 1, February 2010, 111–13. ISSN 1360-080X print/ISSN 1469-9508. online DOI: 10.1080/13600800903440600. URL: *<http://www. informaworld.com>*.

13.6.7. The Hyphen

Hyphens are used to join together elements of words. Hyphens are used in three main situations:

1. the formation of compound words
2. the joining of prefixes to main word stems

3. the indication of word breaks

("Punctuation" 2017)

Hyphens in compound words

Hyphens are used in compound words to indicate a strong connection between the combined words, showing that the words form a unified meaning between them.

Examples

> a good-willed fellow
> a soft-spoken character
> a cleft-chinned youth
> a law-abiding person

Hyphenated compound words

Hyphenated compound words include different combinations formed of (1) adjectives added to present participles ("-ing" verb forms), (2) adjectives added to past participles ("-ed" verb forms), (3) nouns added to adjectives, (4), and nouns added to verbs. The list below illustrates the different combinations of hyphenated compound words.

Adjective + present participle	Noun + past participle	Noun + adjective	Noun + verb
smart-looking	stone-built	power-hungry	to roller-skate
sharp-thinking	bed-ridden	frost-free	to court-martial
far-reaching	wind-generated	pizza-crazy	to snare-trap
fast-selling	mule-tempered	user-friendly	to gas-heat

Hyphens joining prefixes to main word stems

Hyphens are also used to link prefixes to main word stems. These hyphenated words used to be in common usage in the past, especially where the prefix ends in a vowel and the main word begins with a similar vowel (e.g., "co-operate", "pre-exist"). Current usage, though, favours one-word forms (e.g., "cooperate", "preexist").

Hyphens are also used to separate prefixes from names and dates.

Examples

Neo-Platonism

post-war era

Hyphens used to split words

Hyphens are also used to split normal words when such words are to be divided at the marginal ends of written lines. Splitting words at margin lines arbitrarily can be confusing to the reader. For example, "co- ntemporary" and "man- agement" are confusing when split at random. Words should be split according to syllables, or in a place where the split does not cause confusion to the reader. The examples above should be divided as "con- temporary" and "manage- ment".

Other hyphenated words

Hyphens are also frequently used to describe age and time.

Examples

His grandfather is a seventy-five-year-old man.
Droughts reoccur in one-hundred-year-cycles.

Hyphens are also used to stand for an omitted common element of a word appearing in a succession of similar elements. The hyphen is used in all but the last element of the group.

Example

> Fuel prices have increased two-, three-, and four-fold over the last three years.

13.6.8. Apostrophe

The apostrophe is one of the most commonly used punctuation marks; however, students and many others have difficulty using it correctly. It would be helpful to know that an apostrophe is written in one or the other of two cases, and you need to distinguish which of the two you intend to use. It is used

1. to indicate possession, and
2. to indicate omission

Using the apostrophe to indicate possession

To indicate possession, an apostrophe is inserted followed by the possessive *s.*

Example:

> Our house is only one block away from my uncle's supermarket.

However, an apostrophe is used for possession in various ways, and you need to be familiar with the rules of how to use it correctly. It is used with the following:

1. Singular nouns and most personal names
2. Personal names that end in -*s*
3. Personal names that end in -*s* but are not pronounced with an extra s; just add an apostrophe after the -*s*
4. Plural nouns that end in -*s*
5. Plural nouns that do not end in -*s*
6. Pronouns

Below are shown the various rules of usage of the apostrophe indicating possession.

Use	Rule	Example
Singular nouns	Insert apostrophe + *s*	the company's headquarters
Most personal names	Insert apostrophe + *s*	Ahmed's car
Personal names that end in -*s*	Insert apostrophe + *s*	Charles's dear wife Diana
Personal names ending in a silent *s*	Insert apostrophe without adding an *s*.	Camus's best work
Plural nouns ending in -*s*	Insert apostrophe after the *s*.	the female students' common room
Plural nouns not ending in -*s*	Insert apostrophe + *s*	the children's playroom
With pronouns	Insert *s* without apostrophe	his book; its tail

Using apostrophe to indicate omission

An apostrophe is also used to indicate the places of missing letters. Below are some examples:

I'll = I will
He won't = he will not
You shouldn't = you should not
I'm = I am

283

You're = you are
It isn't = It is not.
She didn't. = She did not
Shop 'n' save = Shop and save

Confusing "it's" and "its"

"It's" and "its" cause a lot of confusion in writing. The confusion stems from writers' uncertainty whether or not to insert an apostrophe. Remember these two rules to dispel the confusion:

1. In "it's", the apostrophe is used for *omission*, either for "it is" or "it has".

Examples

> It's 12:00 midnight [it is 12:00].
> It's been so lovely [it has been].

To differentiate between the two, look at the word following the *s*. If the *s* is followed by the past participle of a verb, the omission indicates "it has"; otherwise it indicates "it is".

2. *Its* (without an apostrophe) indicates possession by the pronoun "it".

Examples

> Its windows overlook a beautiful park.
> Its trees are trimmed every few months.

Chapter References

"Punctuation" (2017). The Oxford English Corpus and Oxford Dictionaries. The Oxford English

Corpus (web page). Accessed 20 February 2017, https:// en.oxforddictionaries.com/the-oxford-english-corpus// https:// en.oxforddictionaries.com/punctuation.

Butler, Eugenia, Mary Ann Hickman, Patricia J. McAlexander, and Overby Lalla (1995). *Correct Writing*, 6th ed. Lexington, Massachusetts: Heath and Co.

Perelman, Leslie C., James Paradis, and Edward Barret (1998). *The Mayfield Handbook of Technical Scientific Writing*. Mountain View, California: Mayfield Publishing Co. ISBN 1-55934-647-7.

CHAPTER 14

The Style of Academic Writing

Abstract: Appropriateness of style is the second essential feature besides accuracy of language required in correct academic writing. Style involves the writer's careful choice of words or diction, level of formality, and use of syntax to convey specific meanings not typically mediated through the normative usage of words. The style of academic writing has to meet certain criteria of formality, objectivity, neutrality, and impartiality. Additionally, it should also meet requisite academic conventions of precision, brevity, clarity of focus, complexity of concepts, and organized structure. An important feature of academic style is the necessity of documenting sources of information. The chapter explains the various elements of good style and gives suggestions with extensive examples on how to achieve them. The chapter also explains the types of bad style to avoid, such as bad diction, clichés, vagueness, redundancy, and slang words.

Keywords: style, academic style, diction, word choice, conciseness, connotation, redundancy, wordiness, clichés, vagueness, slang, sentence openings

Style refers to the writer's special choice of words, usage, level of complexity and formality, turn of phrase, syntax, and tone to convey specific meanings. There is no one correct or standard style; however, each writer has his or her own distinctive way of expression—his or her unique signature. Style is the way we use features of the language selectively to convey meanings within the constraints of generally accepted norms of usage, diction, grammar, and structures.

In his book *Style,* Lucas (1955) accords proper style the place it deserves. He devoted three successive chapters to the same heading: "Courtesy to Readers". The subheadings are on clarity, brevity and variety, urbanity, and simplicity. There are what he calls "blustering signatures that swish across the page like cornstalks bowed before a tempest". There are other "cryptic signatures, like a scrabble of lightning across a cloud, other ... florid signatures ... [and] humble, humdrum signatures". There are also other signatures that are "courteously clear, yet mindful of a certain simple grace and artistic economy – in short, of style." (Lucas 1968, p. 1)

14.1. Academic style

While Lucas (1968) talks about writing style in general, academic writing has its unique features which distinguish it from other writing styles. The style of academic writing is a distinct form of professional writing used mainly by academic experts to express complex thoughts in their disciplines of expertise. It is characterized by a neutral, objective tone; by a formal, precise, and unbiased language; and by a clear focus on the subject of investigation.

14.2. Features of academic writing style

Academic writing has to meet certain requirements in language, style, and conventions. Following are some of the important features of academic writing styles.

14.2.1. The overall picture

Academic writing is formal, concise, objective, and documented, and it has a logical flow. The various sections are connected consistently and meaningfully through well-developed and organized paragraphs for better readability and clarity of meaning. Information should be properly documented inside the body text and referenced at the end of the document.

14.2.2. The tone of academic writing

Throughout your research paper, you should maintain a neutral, objective stance with regard to the positions of other authors. You should be faithful to the information you borrow from others to support your argument, without loading their opinions or skewing them towards the direction or purpose of your own argument. You are expected, as an academic investigating a subject, to be objective and authoritative, distancing yourself from personal biases and feelings.

14.2.3. The diction of academic writing

"Diction" refers to the choice of words a writer uses. It is important that writers in academic fields are aware of a number of issues related to the choice of correct words to use. First, you should be aware of the formality or otherwise of the words. You should also possess a good repertoire of the vocabulary used in the specific discipline you are writing in, sometimes called "jargon". For example, writing in law requires that the writer have a good knowledge of legal language; another writing in the aerospace field needs a quite different diction. Moreover, writers need to be sensitive to the slight shades of meaning that words may impart. Words have what are called "literal" meanings—the direct, immediate meanings of words. Words also have what are called "figurative", or imbedded, meanings, sometimes called "connotations", which are extra meanings the writer wants to load onto the same word. In academic writing, use a clear, direct language that is free, as much as possible, from jargon and loaded meanings.

14.2.4. Language clarity and organizational structure

It is important in academic writing that you use a language that is both clear and well-structured for readability and clarity to aid the reader in following the flow of the argument. This requires that the sentences carry the meanings in clear, transparent, precise, and concise language. At the same time, the paragraphs are structured in a way that presents the argument in a coherent, systematic manner. The reader can follow the chain of argument easily through the ideas contained in topic sentences in each of the paragraphs, and can see the supporting evidence that the writer is able to enlist in support. Clarity demands that you avoid language that is vague and imprecise. For example, expressions like "people, "the organization", and "they" are not precise. Also avoid contractions (e.g., "aren't", "I'll") and shortened expressions, such as "com" and "org". Write the full word instead: "company", "organization".

14.2.5. Adherence to academic conventions

An essential characteristic of academic writing is strict adherence to the academic conventions and traditions. A basic requirement in this regard is accurate citations of sources of information in the body text, with a corresponding detailed listing of all cited sources at the end of the document. In-text citations require that the writer credit all sources of information she or he has used, whether these be ideas, general information, or direct quotations. These again should be reflected in full bibliographic details in the list of references at the end. This two-pronged documentation procedure makes for both credibility of information and trustworthiness of the author, since it makes it possible to verify writers' sources of information to guard against plagiarism.

11.2.6. Verifiability of evidence and strength of argument

One of the fundamental principles of academic research is that it should lend itself to verification to ascertain its validity or otherwise. Researchers should base their work on an understanding of an existing body of knowledge, with the aim of contributing to it and expanding it with new insights of their own individual efforts. For this reason, in academic research, ideas and opinions should be backed up by solid facts and sound evidence that can stand up to testing and verification. The more solid the evidence and the more rigorous the work, the more the argument gains validity and trust. Strive, therefore, to enlist sound evidence, sufficient support, and persuasive reasoning to lend strength to your argument.

14.2.7. Thesis formula

Good academic research starts from a thesis properly formulated as an idea or question for inquiry. The motivation behind such an academic quest is the spirit for love of knowledge and curiosity to arrive to a better understanding of the subject under investigation. The aim may be to prove or disprove some idea, to establish a new line of thinking or support one, or to find new ways of doing things or answers to riddling questions.

14.2.8. Complexity and higher-order thinking (HOT)

A distinguishing characteristic of academic research writing is what is termed "higher-order thinking skills". These are a set of qualities that employ idiosyncratic cognitive abilities and organizational skills to describe complex thoughts and processes and render them accessible to others for better understanding of the phenomenon investigated. These individual traits include cognitive aptitudes to comprehend, solve, organize, and deal with ideas and abstract concepts. Moreover, academic writing style has some generally accepted features; it has to be formal, accurate, impartial, objective, and precise.

14.2.9. Formality of style

Formal writing is composed of paragraphs that are clearly structured, each with a topic sentence, followed by supporting sentences to elaborate on the topic. It should also be free of the use of contractions (e.g., "didn't", "they'll"); the full forms of contracted words should be used instead (e.g., "did not", "they will"). Formal vocabulary is used instead of informal vocabulary. For example, "children" is more formal than "kids", "apologize" is more formal than "sorry", and "fabricate" is more formal than "make up". Formal style uses more cautious, more moderate, and less emotionally-charged language. For example, words such as "hate", "love", and "awful" are charged with strong emotions, which raises issues of impartiality and objectivity. Instead, more moderate words (e.g., "dislike", "like", and "unacceptable") are better.

Another aspect of formal style is that it should be appropriate to the area of expertise of writing. Vocabulary should clearly carry the meanings embedded in the technical terms that are generally used in that discipline of study (e.g., medicine, law, accounting, psychology), as well as in the specific field or topic of study within that discipline (e.g., neurology within medicine, criminal law within law, and positive psychology within psychology). It is therefore important that when choosing words, writers be careful about the meanings of the technical terms they use. Often a word has a different meaning in another discipline. For example, the word "passive" can be used as a technical term in physics, as well as in disciplines such as electrical engineering. However, it has different meanings in linguistics (as in the terms "passive verb" and "passive voice").

14.2.10. Objectivity, neutrality, and impartiality

The style of academic writing is objective and impersonal, which means that it avoids expressing personal feelings. In order to express your point of view and still write in an objective style, you can use some of the following language strategies:

1. Move information around in the sentence to emphasize things and ideas instead of people and feelings. For example, instead of writing "I believe the model is valid, based on these findings", write "These findings indicate that the model is valid" or "The following section will show how the model is validated by the findings."
2. Avoid evaluative words which are based on non-technical judgments and feelings, such as "badly", "disappointment", and "amazing". Instead use technical evaluations related to academic or discipline-specific criteria and values, such as "valid", "inaccurate", "reliable", "clearly demonstrates", "rigour", and "outdated".
3. Avoid intense or emotional evaluative language. Instead use more moderate and graded evaluative language. For example, instead of writing "Parents who smoke are obviously abusing their children", write "Second-hand smoke has some harmful effects on children's health."
4. Use modality to show caution about your views or to allow room for others to disagree. For example, instead of writing "I think second-hand smoke causes cancer", write "Second-hand smoke _may_ cause cancer", or "There is evidence to support the possibility that second-hand smoke increases the risk of cancer."
5. Find authoritative sources (e.g., authors or researchers in books or articles) who support your point of view, and refer to them in your writing. For example, instead of writing "Language is, in my view, clearly something social", write "As Halliday (1973) shows, language is intrinsically social."

Different disciplines often have quite different expectations about how objective or subjective a piece of writing can be. In the discipline of education, for example, it is often acceptable to refer to your experiences directly through pronouns (e.g., "I", "me", "my"). On the other hand, in many science disciplines, this would usually *not* be acceptable. It is wise to find out about the writing style expected in your discipline or disciplines by browsing recent articles in some authoritative journals in the field.

14.3. Conciseness and how to achieve it

"Conciseness" simply means economy of expression—the expression of ideas in the fewest possible words. Conciseness also makes for clarity, brevity, and ease of understanding, allowing the reader to follow your argument easily without having to read unnecessary words. It is the unique signature of good writers to engage audiences and get the message across in exactly the right words, briefly and succinctly. In his famous work *The Elements of Style,* Strunk stresses that "vigorous writing" should be concise—that a sentence should contain exactly the words needed to carry the meaning and no unnecessary words, and the same with a paragraph. The writer should strive to "make every word tell" (Strunk 1918, p. 12).

Again, Lucas (1955) emphasizes the importance of concise and clear language. In particular, he emphasizes clarity and brevity. Clarity demands that the writer remain truthful and honest to himself and to others, and brevity that he or she should be respectful to readers and sensitive enough not to waste their time unnecessarily. Clarity, brevity, and honesty remain cornerstones in Lucas's concept of good style. He learned the importance of clear and concise language from experience, having spent six years in a war department. He learned that if the message to be sent out was "too wordy, the communication channels might choke." But if the message was not clear, the results might be disastrous (Lucas 1968, p. 1). So, after six years of this experience, Lucas came out convinced of the importance of clarity and brevity as features of good style.

How to achieve conciseness

A good number of linguistic techniques can be used effectively to achieve conciseness. These include the use of the active instead of the passive form, the use of positive instead of negative statements, the omission of padding words and phrases, and the varying of the use of both short and long sentences. The following paragraphs discuss these linguistic features that may be used to achieve conciseness.

14.3.1. Use the active voice

The active voice is usually more direct, more vigorous, and more concise than the passive voice. for example, "The retired officer remembers the days of the war with silent grief for lost comrades" (active), is better than "The days of the war are remembered with silent grief for lost comrades [by the retired officer]" (passive). And "My mother made us a delicious cheesy pizza" (active), is better than "A delicious cheesy pizza was made for us by my mother" (passive).

The use of the active voice makes strong, direct, and vigorous sentences. This, however, does not mean that the passive voice should never be used. In many contexts, the passive is frequently convenient and sometimes necessary. The example below shows that the passive voice expresses the idea better than the active:

The city council tore down the old building blocking the river view. (active)

The old building blocking the river view was torn down. (passive)

The passive voice in the sentence is clearly superior to the active, since it emphasizes the action itself (tearing down the building) which is more important than who did it (the city council). The passive voice is better used in contexts where the agent doing the action is unknown or unimportant (as in the example above).

14. 3.2. Put statements in positive form

Writing in an assertive, positive form makes for good, strong sentences. Writers are advised to "avoid tame, colorless, hesitating, non-committal language" (Strunk and White 2000, p. 12). Writers should strive to use words in their affirmative meanings, and not as a way of denying or dodging the subject.

Negative form	Positive, assertive form
He doesn't usually come on time.	He is often late.
He puts on a lot of stuff to hide his true character.	He is hypocritical.
She was not at all interested.	She was indifferent.
He bears a heavy heart for his brother's good fortune.	He is envious of his brother's success.
It is not much use trying to persuade him.	It is useless trying to persuade him.

Negative statements are inherently weak because they give only half the truth (what is not) and fall short of giving the other half (what is). The result is that the reader is left dissatisfied at having been told only half the truth. As a general rule, "it is better to express a negative in positive form" (Strunk and White 2000). Thus, one should make the following substitutions:

- "dishonest" instead of "not honest"
- "trifling" instead of "not important"
- "forgot" instead "did not remember"
- "ignored" instead of "did not pay any attention"

14.3.3. Omit needless words

Although a good writing style should be concise, many expressions in common English usage violate this principle. Below is a list of commonly misused wordy expressions and their concise equivalents.

Wordy	Concise
➤ there is no doubt / no doubt	√ doubtless
➤ in a hasty manner	√ hastily
➤ he is a man who …	√ he
➤ this is a subject which	√ this subject
➤ owing to the fact that	√ since/because
➤ in spite of the fact that	√ though/although
(Strunk and White 2000)	

As a general rule, positive statements are more concise than negative ones, and sentences written in the active voice are more concise than those written in the passive voice. It is also more concise to combine a succession of thoughts in one sentence by using connectors and cohesive devices than to present them in a series of separate sentences.

14.3.4. Avoid a succession of loose sentences

Parading long successions of short sentences connected by coordinating conjunctions (e.g., "and", "but", "so") and sometimes by coordination (using "when", "while", "who", "that", "which", etc.) is one of the most common types of inappropriate style errors

Example

> Before the invention of printing, books were very expensive. Books were also difficult to get. Many

workers worked hard to produce books. Workers used pens and pencils, and they used ink to write. They wrote on animal skins. Books took a long time to produce and also took great effort. That is why books were expensive before the invention of printing.

The paragraph above is an example of bad style because of the short sentences that render it monotonous. Such paragraphs can be greatly improved by restructuring the sentences into longer ones combined by conjunctions, by proper punctuation, and by cohesive devices.

Example

Before the invention of printing, books were very expensive and difficult to get. Book production involved many workers who worked hard, using pens, pencils, and ink to write on animal skins. Books took a long time and great effort to produce; therefore, they were expensive before the invention of printing.

14.3.5. Combine sentences for conciseness, variety, and clarity

A succession of short sentences is monotonous and tedious. Moreover, a series of short sentences may not show fully the many relationships between the ideas carried in them. Combining such sentences will make for conciseness, variety, and clarity. Following are some ways to combine sentences.

- Combine sentences of repeated subjects or verbs. If adjacent sentences contain the same subject or the same verb, combine two or more of them in a single, concise sentence. This can be done by omitting repeated items.

- Omit a repeated subject.

Examples

> The coach adopted a completely new reshuffling strategy for the team. The coach decided to bring Majid in on defence and Abdallah on deep offence.

> The coach adopted a completely new reshuffling strategy for the team and decided to bring Majid in on defence and Abdallah on deep offence.

- Omit repeated subjects and verbs.

Examples

> The college council is meeting to discuss arrangements for the upcoming semester. The council is also meeting to consider an extension to the existing student parking.

> The college council is meeting to discuss arrangements for the upcoming semester and to consider an extension to the existing student parking.

- Omit repeated subjects and verbs, and use adjectives.

Examples

> The manager called for a meeting to discuss the overtime rate. The meeting was unscheduled. The meeting was ad hoc and unattended. It was adjourned.

Few people attended the unscheduled meeting called for to discuss the overtime rate, so it was adjourned.

- Omit repeated subjects and verbs and use adverbs.

Examples

The travellers trekked uphill the final five hundred metres. The travellers were very tired and weary from the long trek. But finally they succeeded in making it to the summit in the end.

The travellers trekked uphill the final five hundred metres, very tired and weary, but they successfully made it to the summit in the end.

14.3.6. Combine sentences of equal weight

Coordinating conjunctions are used to combine adjacent sentences that contain ideas of equal importance. Coordinating conjunctions (e.g., "and", "but", "so", "or", "nor", "yet") join sentences of equal weight and create different relationships between two ideas; each is used to convey a certain meaning: "and" is used to convey addition; "but", contrast; "so", result or consequence; "or", choice or preference; "nor", negative addition; and "yet", contrast. The combined sentence may begin with either of the two adjacent sentences, with the coordinating conjunction preceded by a comma.

Examples

The strike divided the town, and it strained labour–management relations.

Negotiators resolved the strike, but the town remained divided.

Coping with environmental issues is a necessary part of industrial studies, for industries affect the environment.

Industries affect the environment, so coping with environmental issues is a necessary part of industrial studies.

The environment cannot sustain constant resource depletion; nor can it recover quickly from wide-scale resource extraction.

Businesses can design their own programs for recording statistical data, or they can use purchased, predesigned programs.

The urban economic sector has been hard hit by the recession, *yet* rural economies remained largely intact.

Sentences can be joined with a semicolon. A semicolon needs complete sentences on either side of it that have complete meaning and can stand by themselves. Use a semicolon when you want to keep two closely related ideas in one sentence.

Sentences can be joined by using a semicolon with a transitional word and a comma. Some common transitional words are as follows:

- "However" (has the same meaning as "but")

Example

The actress's performance electrified the audience; however, lighting and sound problems diminished the play's overall impact.

ACADEMIC RESEARCH WRITING

- "furthermore" (has the same meaning as "in addition")

Example

> The project required extensive research; furthermore, budget cuts reduced the available funds.

- "Instead" (has the same meaning as "rather")

Example

> Neither bold colours nor heavy lines made the painting striking; instead, the sheer size of the canvas drew attention.

- "consequently" (has the same meaning as "as a result")

Example

> The speech required preparation and an in-depth analysis of the situation; consequently, the student surveyed the population on the issue.

- "nevertheless" (has the same meaning as "however")

Example

> The recently established bio-social theory helps us see the evolution of human behaviour with a new perspective; nevertheless, few scientists endorse it.

14. 3.7. Combine sentences of unequal weight

Subordinating conjunctions are used to combine adjacent sentences that contain ideas of unequal importance. Subordinating conjunctions ("because", "since", "though", "although", "until", "if", "when", "while", etc.) join sentences of unequal weight, such that a minor clause is subordinated to a main one by a subordinator, creating a relationship of "dependency". The minor clause is said to be dependent on the independent main clause. If the sentence begins with the dependent clause, a comma is used to combine the two clauses, but no comma is used when the sentence begins with the main clause.

Examples

There has been great damage in the outer skirts of the town because of the heavy rains.
[main clause   dependent clause]

Because of the heavy rains, there has been great damage in the outer skirts of the town.
[dependent clause   main clause]

Subordinating conjunctions can be used to signal one of the following relationships between two ideas showing meaning and usage:

- "because", "since": show causal relationship
- "so that": shows result
- "before", "after", "when", "while", "as soon as", "until", "since": show time relationship
- "unless", "provided that", "if", "as though": show conditionality
- "although", "even though", "though", "while": show contrastive relationship

14.3.8. Reduce redundancy and wordiness

Wordiness (padding and redundant empty words) occurs when writers want to pad their writing with empty phrases, sometimes because of a lack of clarity of ideas. Conciseness, therefore, can be achieved by incorporating several strategies during the writing if writers are aware of the common wordiness patterns and of the individual patterns of wordiness typical of their own writing. (See "Patterns of wordiness and examples of how to correct them" in chapter 15, "Common Language and Style Errors and How to Correct Them.")

14. 3.8.1. *Vary sentence length*

Using long, complex sentences in academic writing helps express different ideas and relationships concisely. However, long, complex sentences are more likely to lead to mistakes in grammar, subordination, and subject-verb agreement. Short sentences, on the other hand, are clear and are less likely to cause errors; but a succession of short sentences can be dull and monotonous. The best way to achieve harmony is to use both long and short sentences to give your style a varied rhythm and twist. To achieve variety, follow the strategies below.

14. 3.8.2. *Vary rhythm by alternating short and long sentences*

Alternating between short and long sentences allows the writer to shift emphasis in order to focus more on ideas that need to be brought to the fore. It also creates an engaging mood for the reader in place of a monotonous mood if otherwise a monotone of dull short sentences is used.

Example

Nature poetry was associated with love of life. It was also about the abandonment of study in youth, and romantic love. This is recorded in the famous anthology of medieval lyrics. These lyrics spanned the age from 1159–1250. These lyrics owe much to Celtic, to Arabic, and to Pagan sources. One of these lyrics "Benedictbeuern" is an impressive example.

revision:

Nature poetry was associated with love of life, abandonment of study in youth, and romantic love. The famous anthology of medieval lyrics, spanning the age from 1159–1250, includes "Benedictbeuern", an impressive example of these lyrics, which owe much to Celtic, Arabic, and Pagan sources.

14.3.8.3. *Vary sentence openings*

Most often, sentences start with common words, such as articles (e.g., "the", "a", "an") or pronouns (e.g. "you", "he", "it"). A rhythmical use of such patterns can make sentences dull and may cause a reader to feel bored, so varying opening words and phrases can revitalize your writing. The example below gives a good list of alternative openings for a fairly standard sentence, illustrating the possibilities of ways to vary your sentence openings.

Example

It was a great surprise that I met Khalid at exactly the same spot where we met two years ago.

Possible varied openings:

Surprisingly enough, I met Khalid at exactly the same spot where we met two years ago.

Khalid and I had the greatest surprise when we came across each other at exactly the same spot where we met two years ago.

To our great surprise, and at exactly the same spot, Khalid and I came face-to-face exactly where we met two years ago.

Our greatest surprise was when Khalid and I saw each other again at exactly the same spot where we met two years ago.

Meeting each other again at exactly the same spot where we met two years ago, Khalid and I had the greatest surprise of our lives.

14.4. General guidelines on style

Below are some general guidelines which should help writers avoid many of the most common style errors in academic writing.

1. Use formal instead of informal or colloquial vocabulary.
2. Hedge your identity and feelings by avoiding evaluative adjectives and adverbs, such as "lovely", "awful", "interesting", "wonderful", etc.
3. Choose words carefully and precisely to convey exactly the intended meaning.
4. Use language cautiously and in a tentative tone. Avoid absolute, declarative language.
5. Use the full forms of words instead of contractions (e.g., "do not" instead of "don't" and "we are" instead of "we're").
6. Writers should strive to avoid asking questions. In research writing, you are expected to give affirmative statements to explain your subject, not to raise questions.

7. Formal writing is continuous—that is, it is composed of sentences forming paragraphs in a continuously connected argument. Therefore, loose, fragmented writing, such as numbered or bulleted points, are not appropriate in academic writing.

14.5. Diction

Diction is word choice. Good choice demands that words are accurate, appropriate to the purpose of writing, and understood by the reader. Good diction also carries meanings both explicit and implicit (i.e., both overt denotations and meaning implied by connotations). Diction carries different levels of formality (formal, informal, colloquial, and slang), and connotations may carry positive or negative meanings.

"Diction" comes from the Latin word "*dictionem*" (nom. *dictio*), meaning "an expression or word", and "in its original, primary meaning, [it] refers to the writer's or the speaker's distinctive vocabulary choices and style of expression in a poem or story ..." (Wikipedia [n.d], "Diction"). Diction has a number of concerns, of which register is foremost. Words are either formal or informal in social contexts, and there are positive or negative meanings imbedded in the choices of words and syntax.

Examples

Formal Diction	Informal	Colloquial	Slang (very informal)
are not angry	aren't angry	not angry	ain't ticked

In addition to the level of formality, diction may also connote positive or negative meanings:

Positive	Negative
He is sturdy.	He is fat/heavy.
She is slim.	She is skinny/thin.

14.5.1. Connotations

Connotations are the implied added emotional meanings imbedded in words beyond and between their literal meanings. Connotations play a big role in the search for the "right word" because sometimes they may convey meanings not intended by the writer if not chosen carefully.

Example

> The manager handles the company affairs with utmost care and meticulousness. He pays attention to time, detail, and fairness in treating employees. He is firm, strict, and fair. He is a very bossy manager.

Above, the adjective "bossy" is out of context with the rest of the language used to describe the manager ("careful", "meticulous", "punctual", "fair", "firm", "strict") all of which conveys positive meanings. "Bossy" is an outlier in this context, implying a negative connotation. A more appropriate description would be "He is the perfect example of a good leader."

Words denoting similar literal meanings may carry quite different implied meanings, or connotations. The list below includes words with similar literal meanings that carry shades of different feelings or connotations.

Positive	Neutral	Negative
relaxed	inactive	lazy
prudent	timid	cowardly
modest	shy	mousy
time-tested	old	out-of-date
dignified	reserved	stiff-necked
persevering	persistent	stubborn
up-to-date	new	newfangled
thrifty	conservative	miserly
self-confident	proud	conceited
inquisitive	curious	nosy

14.5.2. Types of bad diction to avoid

Diction distinguishes good writing from bad writing. Therefore, it is important for writers to avoid the following common types of bad diction:

- clichés or triteness (worn-out phrases and expressions)
- vagueness (language that has more than one possible meaning)
- wordiness (unnecessary words that add nothing to the meaning)
- slang (casual colloquial language)

14.5.2.1. *Clichés or triteness*

Clichés and triteness comprise worn-out phrases and expressions that have lost their "original freshness" from too frequent usage in newspaper headlines, captions, public speeches, and pretentious writings. Below is a list of common clichés in English.

scared out of my wits	last but not least	frightened to death
at the speed of light	get to the bottom of it	take the tiger by the tail
nerves of steel	if only walls could talk	think outside the box
fit as a fiddle	few and far between	thick as thieves
lasted an eternity	like a kid in a sweet shop	read between the lines
kicked the bucket	dead as a doornail	haste makes waste
spill the beans	nipped in the bud	

14.5.2.2. *Vagueness*

Vagueness refers to words that have more than one possible meaning. Usage of vague words indicates unclear thoughts. The common use of collectives, abstractions, general terms, and undefined terms are instances of vague diction. Vagueness can be sensed in common words, such as *"asset, factor, phase, case, nature, character, line and field"* (Butler et al. 1995, p. 315). Such words have basic meaning, and if used in other contexts, they should be used with caution. Instead, usage of more precise diction is necessary to avoid vagueness.

14.5.2.3. *Wordiness*

Wordiness is the use of unnecessary words that add nothing to the meaning but are mere paddings in writing. Again, wordiness is another indicator that thoughts are not clear, such that the writer struggles to express the ideas clearly and concisely, ending up using too many unnecessary, sometimes empty, words to make up for the lack of clarity.

Wordiness, as a common type of bad diction, results from a number of instances: excessive predication, redundancy, and jargon. Excessive predication is the too-frequent use of coordinating conjunctions (e.g., "and", "but", "so") typical of college students' writing. Redundancy is unnecessary repetition (i.e., the repetition of the same ideas in different words, with the writer going in circles without adding substance to the meaning. Jargon, the specialized language of professionals, is spurious in that it is far from precise or brief.

14.6. Word choice: slang vs. formal language

People use slang in everyday conversations. While this is perfectly acceptable, using slang in academic discourse is not acceptable. Academic discourse requires formal language as an important feature. Slang and colloquial language are casual and informal, which make them unfit for a formal academic tone. Below is an example of inappropriate slang words:

Original paragraph

My neighbour Sara is a very nosy person. She always pokes her nose in other people's private affairs. I sometimes tell her to bugger off when she starts her nonsense talk.

Revised paragraph:

My neighbour Sara is an intrusive person. She often meddles with other people's private affairs. I sometimes tell her to heed when she starts her empty talk.

14.7. Tone and voice

Two more features of writing style (also of speech) are tone and voice. *Tone* refers to the writer's attitude in addressing his or her audience and conveying the message in a formal, informal, serious, humorous, objective, subjective, rational, or emotional mood. Essentially, the writer varies the tone to suit the situation in ways that appeal to the audience, at the same time reserving a degree of freedom to express himself or herself. *Voice*, on the other hand, is the writer's unique mark—his or her "signature". Tone varies to suit the occasion, but voice is the writer's inner drive that always marks his or her thoughts as uniquely his or hers. (Wheaton College Writing Center 2009)

Examples

"Don't play what's there; play what's not there."
—Miles Davis

"The notes I handle no better than many pianists. But the pauses between the notes—ah, that is where the art resides." —Arthur Schnabel (1882–1951), German-born US pianist

These two musicians expressed the same thought in their own unique voices.

ACADEMIC RESEARCH WRITING

Chapter References

Bailey, Stephen (2015). *Academic Writing: a Handbook for International Students*, 4th ed. Oxford: Routledge.

Bairstow, Jeffrey (2012). "Good Writing is Clear Thinking Made Visible", *Laser Focus World* 76, October 2012, PennWell Corporation.

Bălcescu, Nicolae (2013). "Writing Well – A Must in the Military Profession" Marioara PATEŞAN. Social-Behavioural Sciences, pp. 60–66. Revista Academemie Fortelor Terestre no. 1 (69), 2013; EBSCOFiles/WRITINGWELLAMUST.pdf.

Butler, Eugenia, Mary Ann Hickman, Patricia J. McAlexander, and Overby Lalla (1995). *Correct Writing*, 6th ed. Lexington, Massachusetts: Heath and Co.

Campbell, Anthony (2000). Review of *Style* by F. L. Lucas. EBSCOhost Login, accessed 2 January 2017. http://www.acampbell. org.uk/bookreviews/r/lucas.html.

Driscoll, Dana Lynn, and Allen Brizee (2012). "Appropriate Language: Overview". The Writing Lab & The OWL at Purdue and Purdue University. Last updated 4 June 2012. Accessed 27 October 2016. *https://owl.english.purdue.edu/writinglab/*

Literary Devices: Definition and Examples of Literary Terms (2016). Blog. Accessed 11 October 2016. https://literarydevices.net/.

Lucas, F. L. (1955). *Style,* 2nd ed. London: Cassell.

———— (1968). "On the Fascination of Style". Essay. *Holiday*, March 1960, reprinted in *The Odyssey Reader: Ideas and Style*, 1968, and in *Readings for Writers*, ed. Jo Ray McCuen and Anthony C. Winkler.

311

New York, 2009. Accessed 2 January 2017. http://www.mrbauld.com/stylelc.html.

"Organizing Academic Research Papers: Academic Writing Style" (n. d.). Sacred Heart University Library and Colorado Technical College Writing Center. Accessed 18 December 2017. https://library.sacredheart.edu/c.php?g=29803&p=185910.

Schroeder, Carrie Jean, and Donella Westphal (2000). "Connotations", created for St. Cloud State University, St. Cloud, Minnesota. Last updated 23 August 2000. Accessed 23 August 2000. URL: http://leo.stcloudstate.edu/grammar/connotations.html.

Silvia, Paul J. (2007). *How to Write a Lot: A Practical Guide to Productive Academic Writing*. Washington, DC: American Psychological Association.

Strunk, William (1918). *Elementary Principles of Composition, The Elements of Style*. Wikisource. Accessed 18 February 2017. Page last modified 15 November 2014; available under the Creative Commons Attribution-ShareAlike Licence, *https://en.wikisource.org/wiki/The_Elements_of_Style/Principles*

Wheaton College Writing Center (2009). "Style, Diction, Tone, and Voice". Accessed 11 October 2016. *H:\Guide to Academic Writing Files\Unit 2 Ch. 5 - Style\Style Only Files\Style, Diction, Tone, and Voice _ Wheaton.html*.

Wikipedia (n.d.). "Diction". Retrieved 11 October 11 2016. Accessed 11 February 2017, https://en.wikipedia.org/w/index.php?title=Diction&oldid=731051895.

——— (n.d.). *"The Elements of Style"*. Retrieved 23 January 2017. https://en.wikipedia.org/w/index.php?title=The_Elements_of_Style&action.

———— (n.d.). "Usage". Available under the Creative Commons Attribution-ShareAlike License. *Accessed 1 October 2016. https:// en.wikipedia.org/wiki/Usage.*

Zinsser, William (2009). "Visions and Revisions: Writing 'On Writing Well' and keeping it up-to-date for 35 years". *American Scholar* vol. 78, no. 2, spring 2009. EBSOhost Academic Search Complete. Retrieved 23 January 2017.

CHAPTER 15

Common Language and Style Errors

Abstract: This chapter discusses the common errors in language and style that writers are likely to make in their writings. The chapter divides these common errors into five groups. First there are sentence fragments, which writers generally mistake for complete sentences. Examples of sentence fragments are presented so writers can avoid them. Another group of common errors includes sentences with wrong punctuation: run-on and fused sentences, comma splices, dangling and misplaced modifiers, and parallel structures. The chapter explains the best ways to correct such wrong sentences by using proper punctuation, conjunctions, and subordination. A third group includes confusing words of quantity, such as "many", "much", "a lot", "few", "a few", and "a little". A fourth group includes words of difficult and confusing spelling that are commonly misspelt. A fifth group involves the most common style errors (i.e., wordiness, redundancy, repetition, and padding).

Keywords: sentence fragments, run-on and fused sentences, comma splices, dangling and misplaced modifiers, parallelism, subordination, wordiness, redundancy, repetition

This chapter deals with the most common language and style errors that students and writers are likely to make and so are cautioned to take special care to avoid. Writers are also advised to be aware of their own specific error patterns. Such knowledge helps them more easily identify their mistakes and correct them. Common errors are grouped into five broad categories:

1. Sentence fragments and causes
2. Sentences with wrong punctuation

2.1. Run-on sentences
2.2. Fused sentences
2.3. Comma splices
2.4. Dangling modifiers and misplaced modifiers
2.5. Parallelism
3. Some confusing words
4. Commonly misspelt words
5. Common style errors

15.1. Sentence fragments

A sentence fragment is an incomplete sentence; but it is a fragment of a sentence—that is, one or another of the three essential elements that make a sentence (subject, verb, and meaning) is missing. The best way to judge a sentence fragment is to check whether it has the three elements, or if one of them is missing. If any one of the three elements is missing, the result is a sentence fragment. The following three examples illustrate the point:

> The brown hare between the bushes [has a subject but no verb].

> While preparing for the trip, forgot to take a spare tyre [has a verb but no subject].

> While we were preparing for the trip [has subject and verb but no complete meaning].

The best way to correct sentence fragments is to check them against the three elements and correct accordingly. Does the sentence have a subject? Does it have a main verb? Does it express a complete meaning?

Corrections

The brown hare hides between the bushes [includes the verb "hides'].

While preparing for the trip, we forgot to take a spare tyre [includes the subject "we"].

While we were preparing for the trip, we heard the forecast of bad weather conditions for the following three days [includes a main clause to complete the meaning].

15.1.1. Common causes of sentence fragments

A sentence fragment is an incomplete sentence which writers often mistake for a complete one. Following are some common causes that lead to sentence fragments.

15.1.1.1. *The present participle of verbs ("-ing")*

The present participle of verbs, the "-ing" form, is often confused for being the main verb in a sentence. A present participle cannot be the main verb in a sentence unless accompanied by the verb "be" ("am", "is", "was", "were", "be", "been") to form a two-word verb phrase.

Example

The young boy riding the bicycle at two o'clock in the afternoon.

Above, the writer has mistaken the "-ing" in "riding" to be the main verb and has therefore considered the sentence to be complete. In fact, this is merely a sentence fragment, since it contains no main verb. To correct it and make a complete sentence, the verb "be" has to be added.

Correction

The young boy was riding the bicycle at two o'clock in the afternoon.

15.1.1.2. *Infinitives of verbs*

An infinitive is formed by adding the preposition "to" to a verb ("to go", "to study", "to meet"). An infinitive does not express a complete action and therefore cannot be the main verb in a sentence. Infinitives, like gerunds, act either as subjects or complements in sentences; therefore, they require that the sentence have a main verb.

Example

The driver to arrive safely home.

Above, the writer has mistakenly used the infinitive "to arrive" as the main verb of the sentence, which it is not. This is another example of a sentence fragment. To make a complete sentence, either add another main verb or change the infinitive into a main verb by removing the preposition "to".

Correction

The driver drove carefully to arrive safely home.

or

The driver arrived safely home.

15.1.1.3. *Confusing the dependent clause and the main clause*

The subordinate relationship between a dependent clause and a main clause in a sentence can often lead to sentence fragments. This is partly due to the difficulty inherent in identifying subjects and verbs in complex sentences. The mistake arises mostly from subordinate clauses considered as complete sentences.

Example

Whenever Badi visits his grandfather.

Even though it has a subject ("Badi") and a main verb ("visits"), this clause is dependent and needs another main clause to complete the meaning. Often, however, students write this type of dependent clause construction as a complete sentence, thus falling into the common error of sentence fragments. To correct and make a complete sentence, a full main clause has to be added.

Correction

Whenever Badi visits his grandfather, he goes to see his grandfather's farm.

15.1.1.4. *Explanatory phrases*

Another common type of sentence fragment results from the use of explanatory phrases and words (e.g., "like", "such as", "for example") followed by a list of nouns. The mistake here arises from the absence of a verb; thus the sentence lacks the most essential part, the verb, and ends up as a sentence fragment.

Example

There are many things you can do to be successful in an interview. For example, good appearance, politeness, punctuality, and attention to the interviewer.

The second part is a sentence fragment that lists a number of actions but includes no verb. To correct this and make a complete sentence, a main verb has to be added.

Correction

There are many things you can do to be successful in an interview. For example, good appearance, politeness, punctuality, and attention to the interviewer are just some of the most important items for success in an interview.

15.1.2. Types of sentence fragments

- Fragment: Jubail University College offers several majors in engineering. Such as electrical, chemical, and mechanical engineering.
- Revised: Jubail University College offers several majors in engineering, such as electrical, chemical, and mechanical engineering.
- Fragment: The Wright Brothers were the first to fly in the air. Using a simple plane.
- Revised: The Wright Brothers were the first to fly in the air using a simple plane.
- Fragment: We are going to have a welcome-back party. As soon as they arrive.
- Revised: We are going to have a welcome-back party as soon as they arrive.

Some fragments are not clearly pieces of sentences that have been left unattached to the main clause; they are written as main clauses but lack a subject or main verb.

15.1.2.1. *No main verb*

- Fragment: The remains of the huge temple of the ancient history of Nubia in Northern Sudan.
- Revised: The remains of the huge temple tell of the ancient history of Nubia in Northern Sudan.

or

The documentary explains the mystery about the huge temple remains of the ancient history of Nubia in Northern Sudan.

- Fragment: The new drug not tested yet.
- Revised: The new drug is not tested.

or

The company declared that the new drug has not been tested yet.

15.1.2.2. *No subject*

- Fragment: Starting a new business, began searching for prospective customers.
- Revised: Starting a new business, the company's marketing team began searching for prospective customers.
- Fragment: Because of high fossil fuel consumption, has concentrated harmful gases in the atmosphere.

- Revised: High fossil fuel consumption has concentrated harmful gases in the atmosphere.
- Confusing preposition: Doing freelance work for a competitor got Phil fired.
- Rearranged: Phil got fired for doing freelance work for a competitor.

15.2. Common types of sentence fragments

15.2.1. Run-on sentences

A run-on sentence is an ungrammatical sentence that contains two (or more) sentences or clauses joined together as one without proper punctuation. The examples below illustrate the point.

Incorrect:

Support groups have been organized in almost all major cities and research efforts to isolate the AIDS virus have been given substantial funding.

Correct:

Support groups have been organized in almost all major cities, and research efforts to isolate the AIDS virus have been given substantial funding.

15.2.2. Comma splices

A comma splice occurs when two sentences or two independent clauses are joined together by only a comma. The two sentences are *split* by only a comma, resulting in an ungrammatical sentence. To correct the issue, the two sentences should be split either by a full stop, making them two sentences, or by a semi-colon.

Incorrect:

Jubail Municipal Authority aspires to make the city the cleanest and healthiest in the Middle East, the authority legislates for a fine of 300 Riyals on anyone who throws trash on the streets.

Correct:

Jubail Municipal Authority aspires to make the city the cleanest in the Middle East. The authority legislates for a fine of 300 Riyals on anyone who throws trash on the streets.

or

Jubail Municipal Authority aspires to make the city the cleanest in the Middle East; the authority legislates for a fine of 300 Riyals on anyone who throws trash on the streets.

15.2.3. Fused sentences

A fused sentence occurs when two sentences or two independent clauses are joined together with no punctuation at all. The two sentences are fused together incorrectly as one.

Incorrect:

Today's football match is going to be one of the hottest in the city the famous player Missey will play in the centre forward as main striker.

Correct:

The football match is going to be one of the hottest in the city; the famous player Missey will play in the centre forward as main striker.

Five methods can be used to correct comma splices and fused sentences:

1. Separate the clauses with a full stop.
2. Join the clauses with a semicolon.
3. Connect the clauses with a semicolon and a conjunctive adverb followed by a comma.
4. Connect the clauses with a comma and a coordinating conjunction.
5. Use a subordinating conjunction to make one clause dependent upon another.

Examples to illustrate the above

Example fused sentence

It was one of the biggest gatherings the city hall had ever had families attended the graduation ceremony to celebrate the success of their beloved daughters and sons.

Five possible corrections

It was one of the biggest gatherings the city hall has ever had. Families attended the graduation ceremony to celebrate the success of their beloved daughters and sons.

It was one of the biggest gatherings the city hall has ever had; families attended the graduation ceremony to celebrate the success of their beloved daughters and sons.

It was one of the biggest gatherings the city hall has ever had when families attended the graduation ceremony to celebrate the success of their beloved daughters and sons.

It was one of the biggest gatherings the city hall has ever had, and families attended the graduation ceremony to celebrate the success of their beloved daughters and sons.

In one of the biggest gatherings the city hall has ever had, families attended the graduation ceremony to celebrate the success of their beloved daughters and sons.

15.2.4. Dangling modifiers

Modifiers are descriptive phrases added to words to provide additional information. Modifiers should clearly point to the words they describe and should precede those words immediately. For example, in the sentence "Utterly exhausted, the plumber first dozed and then went into a deep sleep", "utterly exhausted" is a modifier clearly describing the subject ("the plumber") that immediately follows.

Dangling modifiers

A dangling modifier is a phrase or clause that does not modify any specific subject in the sentence. This occurs when the modifying phrase does not refer to the subject that it ought to modify but rather refers to some subject not intended by the sentence. For example, the sentence above may be put this way: "Utterly exhausted, I saw the plumber first doze and then go into a deep sleep." Here the modifying phrase "utterly exhausted" grammatically refers to the subject that immediately follows (I), which is not the intended subject of description. The intended subject is "the plumber"; therefore the modifying phrase "utterly exhausted" is left hanging in the air, not attached to its direct subject—hence the grammatical label "dangling modifier".

Below are some interesting examples showing the confusion dangling modifiers can cause.

> Chasing the squirrel barefoot, my feet became covered with dust.

The phrase "Chasing the squirrel barefoot" modifies the subject of the sentence ("my feet"), suggesting that "my feet" were chasing the squirrel on their own accord, independently of my will, such that they became "covered with dust". To correct the sentence, a suitable subject should be inserted. for example:

> Chasing the squirrel barefoot, I soon saw my feet covered with dust.

15.2.5. Misplaced modifiers

Misplaced modifiers occur when the modifying phrase is placed too far away from the word it modifies, such that it does not seem to modify the intended subject and the relationship between the two becomes unclear. It is a relationship of "wrong placement" between the modifier and the subject it modifies, hence the label "misplaced". A modifier should be placed as close as possible to the subject it modifies.

Example

> The lemon tree has been trimmed in the garden
> recently watered by the gardener.

The modifying phrase "by the gardener" is so far removed from its subject ("the lemon tree") that it is not clear whether it modifies "the lemon tree" or "the garden". To clarify the relationship between the two, the modifying phrase should be brought closer to the modified word.

Example

> The lemon tree has been trimmed by the gardener
> in the recently watered garden.

(For detailed examples on dangling and misplaced modifiers and revision, see appendix 3.)

15.2.6. Parallel structures

"Parallel structure" refers to the use of the same pattern of words to show that two or more ideas have the same level of importance. This can happen at the word, phrase, or clause level. Parallel structures are usually joined by coordinating conjunctions, such as "and" or "or." Errors often occur when writing words and phrases that are not parallel in the form of words (verbs, nouns, adjectives, infinitives, etc.). Below is a list showing examples of parallel and unparalleled structures.

Type of structure	Parallel	Unparalleled
Infinitives	John likes to swim, run, and play tennis. *or*	John likes to swim, run, and *playing* tennis.
Gerunds	John likes to swim, to run, and to play tennis. John likes swimming, running, and playing tennis.	John likes swimming, running, and *to play* tennis.
Nouns	The company recycles paper, glass, and wood.	The company recycles paper, glass, and *wooden*.
Adjectives	They arrived home tired, exhausted, and hungry.	They arrived home tired, exhausted, and *they want to eat*.
Adverbs	The job has been completed thoroughly, quickly, and timely.	The job has been completed thoroughly, quickly, and *took a short time*.
Phrases	Graduating students, their families, and their friends all gathered for the graduation ceremony.	Graduating students, their families, *and their friends coming*, all gathered for the graduation ceremony.
Clauses	With the work done, the time finished, and the workshop closed, all the workers went home.	With the work done, the time finished and the workshop *has closed*, all the workers went home.

15.3. Confusing words of quantity expression

Quantity expressions (e.g., "many", "much", "few", "a few", "less", "several", "a great deal", "lot of" and "a lot of", "some", "any", and "plenty of") create confusion on two counts: (1) being attached to count or non-count nouns, and (2) the level of quantity denoted by the word. The best way to dispel the confusion is to know how to

327

use them according to the noun they describe. Quantity expressions generally fall into three classes according to the noun they describe:

1. Those used with count nouns ("many", "several", "few", "a few").
2. Those used with non-count nouns ("much", "a great deal of", "little", "a little").
3. Those used with both count and non-count nouns ("some", "a lot of", "plenty of", "any").

"Many" is used to describe quantities of count nouns (e.g., "books", "houses", "trees"), and is followed by plural verbs (e.g., "Many books *are* sold", "Many houses *have* been affected by the storm").

"Much" is used to describe quantities of non-count nouns (e.g., "money", "sugar", "oil"); is followed by singular verbs, and is not usually used in affirmative sentences.

Examples

> The money spent isn't much.
> How much oil is wasted off shore?

Note that "many" and "much" are used to describe large quantities, whereas "few" and "less" are used with small quantities.

"A few," like "many", is used with count nouns.

Example

> A few cars are in the park.
> A few of the cars are in the park.

Note that "a few" and "a few of" are used to convey a positive meaning.

"Few" and "few of" (implying a low number) are used with count nouns.

Few people attended the gathering [implying a small number of people].

Few of the trainees took the course [implying a small number of trainees].

Note that "few" and "few of" are used to convey a negative meaning.

"Less", like "much", is used with non-count nouns (e.g., "Less sleep is bad for health"). These words follow idiomatic patterns, but the connotation changes.

Confusion may occur in the use of the phrases "a lot" and "a lot of" in spelling and in connotation. In spelling, "a" may be attached to "lot" to form "alot", a completely different spelling which is neither a verb ("allot") nor a quantifier ("a lot"). Confusion may also occur in the connotative use and meaning of the phrase "a lot of", which is used to give a general meaning, while "a lot of the" is used when the meaning is specific.

Examples

A lot of work has gone into the project [general work].
A lot of the work on the stadium project has been done [specific work on the stadium project].

15.4. Confusing and commonly misspelt words

Some words in English, denoted by the terms "homophones and homonyms" are generally confusing because they either have similar pronunciations but different spellings and meanings (*homophones*), or similar spellings but different pronunciations and meanings (*homonyms*). Writers sometimes use a word which is correct in spelling but has a different meaning, and vice versa. Below is a list of such confusing words.

15.4.1. Confusing pairs of words

1. accept (v) and except (prep)
2. compliment (n/v) and complement (verb)
3. effect (n) and affect (v)
4. flare (n) and flair (n)
5. economic (adj.) and economical (adj.)
6. its (pron.) and it's (pron. + verb)
7. lose (verb) and loose (adj.)
8. affective (adj.) and effective (adj.)
9. read (p. v) and red (adj.)
10. rise (intr. verb) and raise (trans. v)
11. site (n), cite (v) and sight (n)
12. title (n) and entitle (v)
13. there (*indicative*) and their (*possessive*)
14. write (v), rite (n) and right (n/adj.)

For more on commonly misused words, see appendix 1.

15.4.2. Confusing and commonly misspelt words

Incorrect spelling is one of the most vexing issues that faces writers at all levels. English spelling is problematic not only because many words have the same pronunciation and different spellings, but also because many more words are pronounced one way and written another. In addition, consonants are doubled in the middle of words and at the ends of words—when forming participles, for example. The list below shows examples of the most commonly misspelt words in English.

Wrong spelling	Corrected	Wrong spelling	Corrected
apearance	appearance	immediatly	immediately
apparantly	apparently	irresistable	irresistible

begining	beginning	neccessary	necessary
dissapear	disappear	noticable	noticeable
embarras	embarrass	occured	occurred
foriegn	foreign	paralel	parallel
finaly	finally	seperate	separate
disapoint	disappoint	tommorrow	tomorrow
happend	happened	truely	truly
harrassment	harassment		

For more on misspellings, see appendix 2.

15.5. Common style errors

Many common style errors fall into the following categories:

- wordiness
- redundancy
- padding
- repetition

15.5.1. Wordiness

"Wordiness" refers to the writer's use of unnecessary words that add nothing to the meaning. Wordiness bears negatively on the quality of writing in that it not only adds empty words but also interferes with the clarity of the message the writer intends to communicate, making it difficult for the reader to understand. Wordiness results from some bad style patterns, some of which are listed below.

15.5.1.1. *Use of the passive voice*

The passive voice is generally wordier than the active voice. Use the active voice instead; it is clearer, more direct, more forceful, and less wordy.

Example:

Passive

The trip was planned by my family to take place in mid-October.

Active

My family planned the trip to take place in Mid-October.

15.5.1.2. *Nominalization*

Nominalization is the act of forming a noun from a verb. For example, a writer may form "action" from the verb "act", or "pacification" from the verb "pacify". Using nouns is generally wordier than using verbs in sentences.

Example

Nominal	**Verbal**
The local authority took *action* immediately.	The local authority *acted* immediately.
They took a unanimous *decision*.	They *decided* unanimously.
They made a *recommendation*.	They *recommended*.

15.5.1.3. *Padding: empty words and phrases*

Many words and phrases in common English usage add nothing to the meaning. These are paddings which are mostly stuffed into writing unnecessarily in the form of redundant phrases and clichés, and they should be substituted by shorter, simpler words that convey the same meaning. Examples of such phrases include "at this point in time", which can be substituted by a single "now"; "for the purpose of", which can be substituted by "to + infinitive"; "because",which can be used instead of "due to the fact that"; and "if", which is far better than "in the event that".

15.5.2. Patterns of wordiness and how to correct them

As you read the following list, consider which patterns of wordiness are typical of your writing.

1. Filler phrases (e.g., "it is", "there is", and "there are" at the beginnings of sentences) often delay the true subject and verb in a sentence.
2. The indicative "this" at the beginning of a sentence should be omitted, and the sentence should be joined to the preceding one with a comma.
3. Constructions with relative pronouns (e.g., "which" or "that") should be changed to use an "-ing" word, or the relative pronoun clause should be removed altogether.
4. Use active verbs instead of passive verbs.
5. Prepositional phrases express ideas in unnecessarily long sentences. Instead use one-word modifiers.
6. Sentences can be combined by a colon or semicolon (e.g., when giving explanations or showing examples) instead of writing two separate sentences.
7. Combine adjacent sentences that share some elements, such as a common subject or verb.

8. The verb "be" is a weak form of expression when it occurs alone in a sentence. Replace it with a stronger verb.
9. Choose stronger verbs to replace auxiliary verbs (e.g., "should," "would," and "could").
10. Substitute nominal (e.g., "-tion", "-sion") constructions with verbal ones.
)Strunk and White 2000(

Below are examples illustrating the patterns of wordiness given above and their concise equivalents, in respective order.

Wordy Examples	**Concise**
1. It is expensive to upgrade computer systems.	Upgrading computer systems *is* expensive.
2. Chlorofluorocarbons have been banned from aerosols. *This* has lessened the rate of ozone layer's depletion.	Chlorofluorocarbons have been banned from aerosols, *lessening* the ozone layer's depletion.
3. The committee, *which* meets monthly, oversees accounting procedures and audits.	The committee, *meeting* monthly, oversees accounting procedures and audits.
4. Because the fluid, *which* was brown and poisonous, was dumped into the river, the company *that* was negligent had to shut down.	Because the brown, poisonous fluid was dumped into the river, the negligent company had to shut down.
5. Rain forests *are being destroyed* by uncontrolled logging.	Uncontrolled logging *is destroying* rain forests.
6. The president of the student senate was *in charge of* lobbying against the merger at the Minnesota Congress.	The student senate president *oversaw* lobbying the Minnesota Congress against the merger.
7. The theatre has *three main technical areas.* These areas are costumes, scenery, and lighting.	The theatre has three *main technical areas:* costumes, scenery, and lighting.

8. The director is concerned about *problems.* Typical *problems* may occur with lighting, sound, and props.

   The director is concerned about typical *problems* with lighting, sound, and props.

9. A new fire curtain *is* necessary for the stage

   The stage *needs* a new fire curtain.

10. The environmental council *could* see several solutions.

    The environmental council *saw* several solutions.

11. I submitted an *application* for the job.

    I *applied* for the job.

15.5.3. Repetition

Repetition is sometimes useful as a means of emphasizing a point or achieving parallelism in structure. Sometimes, however, repetition is an example of bad style, when words and phrases are repeated unnecessarily, blurring the clarity of meaning and slowing the reader down. Repetition often results from (a) a lack of appropriate coherence and (b) tautology Lack of coherence occurs when parts of the sentence (e.g., nouns and names) are repeated without properly using pronouns to refer back to their antecedents. To correct and smooth out the sentence to achieve coherence, pronouns are used to avoid repetition.

Example:

> The meeting with the director was a stormy meeting between the director and the staff in which the staff blamed the director for interfering with the staff's work.

Adding pronoun referents enhances clarity in the sentence and achieves coherence:

The meeting with the director was a stormy one between him and staff in which they blamed him for interfering with their work.

Tautology, on the other hand, occurs when different words are used to say the same thing. Tautology is an example of "padding"—a bad style of adding empty words and phrases needlessly, possibly done when the writer intends to "inflate" his or her writing. This also often occurs when the author is unclear about the message he or she wants to communicate, causing him or her go in circles while trying to grasp the elusive idea.

Example

In my view, I think that the match has been one of the best I have ever watched.

At the end, they finally got married, and for the rest of their lives they lived happily ever after.

Chapter References

Bailey, Stephen (2015). *Academic Writing: a Handbook for International Students.* 4th ed. Oxford: Routledge.

"Common Misspellings" (n.d.). Oxford English Corpus. Oxford Dictionaries.com. https://en.oxforddictionaries.com/spelling/common-misspellings. Accessed 10 November 2016.

Driscoll, Dana Lynn (2013). "Parallel Structure", the Writing Lab and the OWL at Purdue and Purdue University. Last edited 22 March 2013. https://owl.english.purdue.edu/owl/resource/623/01/.

Escalas, Maggie (1999). "Words That Confuse". The Write Place. St. Cloud State University. Last updated 5 October 1999. Accessed 10 November 2016.

Marchant, Becky (2000a). "Parallelism". The Write Place. St. Cloud State University. Last updated 27 June 2000, accessed 10 November 2016. http://leo.stcloudstate.edu/grammar/parallelism.html.

——— (2000b). "Common Causes of Sentence Fragments". Revised by Jill Cadwell and Donella Westphal. St. Cloud State University. Last updated 18 August 2000. http://leo.stcloudstate.edu/punct/fragmentcauses.html.

Schroeder, Carrie Jean (2000). "Dangling and Misplaced Modifiers". The Write Place. St. Cloud State University. Last updated 18 August 2000. Accessed 10 November 2016. http://leo.stcloudstate.edu/grammar/modifiers.html.

Wikipedia. "List of commonly misused English words". Available under the Creative Commons Attribution-ShareAlike License. Last modified on 14 September 2016. Accessed 10 November 2016.

——— *"The Elements of Style"*. Retrieved 23 January 2017. https://en.wikipedia.org/w/index.php?title=The_Elements_of_Style&action=edit&section=4.

PART III
Editing, Proofreading, Formatting, and Submission

CHAPTER 16

Editing and Proofreading

Abstract: Editing and proofreading are two related yet distinct revision processes required in good research. In editing, the writer attends to major editorial changes in the content, structure, style, and accuracy in in-text citations and references. In proofreading, the writer looks for and corrects minor errors in sentence structure, spelling, grammar, and punctuation. For both, the writer needs to establish a good strategy to get an effective and comprehensive revision. The chapter suggests ways to draw an effective strategy, breaking down the documents into chunks for revision, each to be devoted to a specific editorial theme, such as content, unity and coherence of argument, style, and overall organizational structure. Each of the revision themes could be accomplished in one or more sessions. It is strongly advised that, upon completion of a first draft, researchers allow themselves a reasonable lapse of time before embarking on the editorial stage. The chapter suggests an elaborate proofreading strategy to check and correct errors in language, grammar, vocabulary, style, spelling, and punctuation. Useful hints are also given on the strategies used in editing and revising by computer.

Keywords: editing, proofreading strategy, editing for content, editing for structure, editing for style, editing for gender bias, checking errors in language, style and punctuation, editing by computer

Editing and proofreading are two different revision strategies, but the terms are often used interchangeably. "Editing" refers to the first revision process, which writers undertake as soon they finish with the first draft of their paper. In this process, the writer addresses major changes in the overall paper structure, content, clarity, coherence and logic of thesis presentation, and the general organizational structure. Proofreading, on the other hand, involves looking for and correcting minor errors in grammar, sentence structure, spelling, and punctuation. Both revisions demand careful and close attention to be carried out in several sessions; sometimes a second reader may be necessary. Writers are strongly advised to allow themselves a reasonable lapse of time after finishing the first draft (a week or a few days) before starting a revision. Leaving your completed paper to rest for a while and distancing yourself from it gives you the chance to see it under a new light when coming back for revision and editing.

16.1. Editing

In the paragraphs that follow, a variety of useful strategies are suggested on how to edit and proofread your paper thoroughly before final submission. Editing can be carried out on different levels, as shown below.

16.1.1. Editing for content

The content comprises your thesis and the main claims you have put forward to support your thesis, including the types of evidence, proofs, reasons, statistics, and other kinds of details to make your arguments persuasive and convincing. When editing for content, ask yourself whether you have addressed the issues raised in the thesis adequately, logically, and consistently, or whether your argument is lacking in some important dimensions. Whilst editing for content, you are more likely to discover some important aspects that may need to be added, removed, rearranged, or modified to smooth out the "flow" of the argument.

16.1.2. Editing for clarity

Clarity is an essential feature of good academic writing and is mainly concerned with the degree to which the writer's language choices are accurate enough to carry the intended meanings and express ideas clearly and precisely. Therefore, to edit for clarity, the writer needs to go slowly and carefully over the paper, checking the ideas he or she wants to express and making sure that the words carry those ideas clearly and precisely, without ambiguity or opaqueness. Another important aspect of clarity is that writers should make every effort to define unusual and unfamiliar terminology. Sometimes common words acquire special meanings when used in certain contexts, and writers have to define such common words when they are used to connote special meanings.

16.1.3. Editing for paragraph unity and coherence

Paragraphs carry the ideas of the argument to be elaborated, such that each paragraph discusses one idea related to the main thesis. Each paragraph starts with a topic sentence stating the main idea under discussion, followed by supporting evidence and details. To edit for unity is to ascertain that all sentences in the paragraph are unified around the main theme contained in the topic sentence and that any sentences that do not relate to the topic are removed. To edit for coherence is to make sure that proper cohesive devices (transitional words, sequence words, and connectors) are in place to link paragraphs together, as well as the sentences within paragraphs, in a coherent way that reflects the logical flow of the argument. These relationships are the domain of paragraph-level editing.

16.1.4. Editing for overall organizational structure

The overall organizational structure is the general format of your paper—the main parts required to be present in the paper and the way they are organized in appropriate academic style to meet requisite academic conventions. Writers need to check that they have included an introduction, body paragraphs, and a conclusion, as well as that the introduction states the topic of the paper and includes a thesis statement at the end, giving the specific focus of the research. The body paragraphs should follow logically from the thesis statement, each paragraph presenting a single idea, thoroughly discussed and supported by sufficient detail, and all subsequent paragraphs should relate logically to the main thesis and to each other. Moreover, in the body paragraphs, writers should check that they have provided enough support backed by appropriate citations and referencing. Illustrations and graphics that may appear in the body should be numbered, labelled and referenced. Additionally, writers should check that their paper includes the following parts in order:

- title page (in proper standard format)
- table of contents (in proper standard format)
- list of tables or charts
- acknowledgements
- introduction
- literature review
- main body
- conclusion
- list of references
- appendix

16.1.5. Editing for style

Academic style has to be formal, objective, impartial, neutral, and precise; and when editing, writers need to check that the general tone of the paper meets these style features. Precise language requires the writer to remove padding, redundant words and phrases, and words that add nothing to the meaning. (For more on how to avoid wordiness and achieve conciseness, refer to chapter 14.)

16.1.6. Editing for gender-sensitive language

It is important to check your writing to make sure your style is free of gender bias. Writers should demonstrate that they are sensitive to gender differences in their writings. This should be reflected in their writing in their use of masculine and feminine pronouns, such as "he" and "she", and words that contain "man" but denote both sexes, such as "chairman." Being gender-neutral demands that writers use these words sensitively to show courtesy to both sexes. This can be done by specifying the gender pronoun as "he" or "she", according to the referent. Where the referent may refer to both sexes, such as "writer", you can use "he or she" or "she or he". Or, to avoid confusion, it is generally accepted to use the plural pronoun "they"; which is an agreement error in formal English, but is widely accepted for convenience. For words that contain "man", spell out the gender if it is known; otherwise use "person" instead (e.g., "chairperson"). A gender-neutral style of writing is not only sensitive and courteous; it is also more precise. The list below gives some of the commonly biased gendered nouns, and suggested neutral alternatives.

Biased	Neutral
man	person, individual
mankind	people, human beings, humanity
freshman	first-year student
man-made	machine-made, synthetic, artificial
the common man	the average person
chairman	chair, chairperson, coordinator, head
mailman	mail carrier, letter carrier, postal worker
policeman	police officer

(Gender-Inclusive Language, 2014)

16.1.7. Editing for references and in-text citations

Make sure that you have provided proper citations for all material you have used in the body of your research. These include ideas you have gained, information you have used, and texts you have either summarized, paraphrased, or quoted. Give proper in-text citations for the sources from which you borrowed such information, crediting authors and giving dates of publication. If, however, you use quotations, you need to acknowledge the author and source, and give the page number on which the quote appears in the original source.

When editing, it will be of great help to keep an eye on the types or errors you are likely to make and record these errors. Try to look at your errors to discern patterns that mark your writing. Your idiosyncratic pattern of errors will help you detect them easily and avoid them in future. For example, if you notice that you generally tend to have errors in subject-verb agreement, you can avoid this by paying careful attention any time you write a sentence to make sure that the subject and verb agree, until, with more practice, you are eventually able to get rid of the problem.

16.2. Proofreading

Proofreading is the final revision stage, in which one spots and corrects small errors in grammar, spelling, and punctuation. It is an important final editing activity to ensure that the paper is free of minor errors that may obstruct the clarity of meaning or give an impression of carelessness if otherwise not corrected. While presenting a good solid argument and novel ideas is a cornerstone to good academic practice, it is also important to present your work in neat and spotless language. However, going over the entire work and spotting small mistakes in grammar, spelling, and punctuation may seem both daunting and tedious. For precisely this reason, it is advisable to adopt a clear proofreading strategy to help carry it out effectively and systematically in the most economical amount of time.

An effective proofreading strategy requires the writer (1) to know the types of errors that are common in a wide range of writings and how to correct such errors, and (2) to be aware of the types of errors typical of his or her own writing. Such knowledge greatly helps in setting out a systematic proofreading strategy in which the writer lists the types of errors to be detected and corrected, prioritizing them from the most to the least serious of those typical of his or her writing.

16.2.1. An effective proofreading strategy

Generally, a comprehensive effective proofreading strategy needs to be developed to spot various types of small errors, including errors regarding language and style, punctuation, spelling, diction, and vocabulary choice, as well as issues concerning factual information. Facts can be wrong, which can be easily corrected by an editor or a groomed proofreader. More often, however, factual errors include subject-specific facts, which can be corrected by a specialist in the field. Because of the diverse nature of errors (in language, style, diction, spelling, and facts), it is not possible to check for them all in one reading. It is therefore advisable to do the revision in a number of proofreading sessions, each devoted to a group of related issues (for example, one for language, punctuation, and spelling; another session for style, diction, and vocabulary; and another for facts, both general and subject-specific).

General hints for an effective proofreading strategy

Researchers need to give time and consideration to proofreading their final drafts. Indeed, writers often think that by finishing their research paper, including all important ideas, and writing it in clear language, that is enough to guarantee acceptance of their work. But they should not forget that any piece of writing is likely to contain small errors that can be detected only on careful second and third readings, and which, if unchecked, could undermine the whole work. To put in place an effective proofreading strategy, writers need to consider these general points:

- Proofreading is an integral part of research just like any other important act, such as writing the introduction or conclusion.
- Leave a reasonable lapse of time between finishing writing the paper, editing, and proofreading it. This will give you time to look afresh at what you have written.
- Editing and proofreading are not exactly the same. In editing, focus on big chunks of the text for rearrangement and on sentence-level inaccuracies for correction.
- In proofreading, focus on word-level errors and read word by word, checking spelling, grammar, word choice appropriateness, word form, and place in the sentence structure.
- Editing and proofreading tasks cannot be accomplished hastily in one or two sittings. Be prepared to devote a good number of sessions to perform them satisfactorily.
- Don't rely entirely on spell checkers. These can be useful, but they are far from perfect.
- Grammar checkers are even more unreliable; since they have a limited inbuilt capacity of grammatical rules, they can't identify all errors and often make new ones.
- Proofread for one type of error at a time. This will help you give more focus to that particular error and correct it effectively.
- Read every word slowly and carefully, and also read loudly to hear how words sound together.
- Stop at every punctuation mark and check carefully to ascertain that it is appropriate.
- It is useful to read the document backwards. This is especially useful with checking spelling.

- Proofreading takes a lot of effort, as it involves checking many small things, some of which you may not be sure about. At every step, if you are not quite sure about something, it is always advisable to look it up in a dictionary or a thesaurus.
- With more practice, your proofreading efficiency will improve. Eventually you will be able to understand your own pattern of errors so you may pay attention and avoid them.

For an effective proofreading strategy, check the following most common types of errors.

- language errors
- errors of style and diction
- vocabulary
- spelling
- subject-verb agreement errors
- missing words
- errors in word order
- punctuation errors

16.2.2. Checking for errors

16.2.2.1. *Language errors*

Language errors include errors in grammar, tense, sentence structure, subject-verb agreement, pronoun agreement, singular and plural forms, word endings, and word order. Punctuation is also closely related to correct writing—especially sentences and clauses. Therefore, it is best checked alongside language errors. Because these errors share a common linguistic base, they could be conveniently checked in one proofreading session, in which it would be possible to detect these different types of errors without much difficulty, leaving other types of stylistic and factual errors to other reading sessions.

Subject-verb agreement errors

Subject-verb agreement errors occur when the two are not placed close to one another but are separated by intervening words or phrases. To correct subject-verb agreement errors, bring the two closer to one another, or isolate the main verb in the sentence so it becomes clear what verb would correctly agree with the subject.

Example

The number of reporters covering the war in Bosnia were estimated to be more than five hundred.

In the sentence above, the main plural verb, "were", is far removed from the singular subject, "number", resulting in a subject-verb agreement error. Obviously, the intervening modifying phrase "covering the war in Bosnia" separates the two elements and causes the error. To correct this, isolate the two elements to clearly identify number and tense. The subject, "number" (singular), requires a singular verb, "was", for agreement.

The number of reporters covering the war in Bosnia was estimated to be more than five hundred.

Pronoun agreement errors

Pronoun agreement errors are one of the most widespread types of errors in writing. In any sentence that contains a pronoun, that pronoun should refer back to a noun mentioned earlier in the sentence or in the sentences immediately preceding. The pronoun must agree with the noun in number and gender. To best correct pronoun agreement errors, consider the following:

- Identify pronouns and then track them back to locate their corresponding nouns and make sure that they agree.

- In case you don't find the noun to which the pronoun refers, either insert a noun to make a referent or change the pronoun to a noun.
- Be aware that some pronouns (e.g., "each", "everybody", and "everyone") are treated as singular.
- To avoid gender bias, sometimes plural pronouns are used instead of singular to refer to singular nouns: "The writer needs to make *their* sentences concise and clear." Although this may be acceptable to avoid gender bias, it is, in fact, a matter of convenience, not of accuracy. Accuracy demands that singular pronouns be matched with singular nouns: "The writer needs to make his or her sentences concise and clear."

Spelling and typographical errors

Catching spelling mistakes in a lengthy piece of writing is a challenge that almost all writers have to grapple with. The best way to handle spelling errors is (1) to be aware of the most common types of spelling errors (there are lists of common spelling errors available on websites), and (2) to be aware of those mistakes typical of your own spelling. Awareness of the two types makes it much easier for you to detect your mistakes and correct them in a short time. (For lists of the most common spelling errors, see appendix 2.)

Apart from incorrect spelling, you might occasionally omit words from your sentences by mistake. In this case, spell checking is of no use. The best way to check for omitted words is to read through your paper carefully, paying attention to the meanings of sentences. If you feel that the meaning of a sentence does not seem right, it is quite possible that a word is missing that renders the sentence unclear.

16.2.2.2. *Checking for punctuation errors: comma errors*

Commas come after introductory words and phrases, and are also used with dependent clauses. To make sure that commas are in place with these phrases and clauses, check the following:

- For introductory words and phrases, read the first two words of each sentence to see if the sentence has an introductory word or phrase.
- Introductory words and phrases are elements that introduce a sentence by referring to time (e.g., "first", "finally") or condition (e.g., "additionally", "essentially"). They can be words, phrases, or clauses.
- Once you have the first few words of a sentence, you will be able to establish whether the sentence needs a comma or not.
- In case the sentence is composed of two independent clauses, make sure to join the two with both a comma and a coordinating conjunction; otherwise, the sentence will be a run-on sentence.
- Coordinating conjunctions ("and", "but", "or", "so", "nor", "for", "yet") combine independent clauses of equal weight to form compound sentences. Here both the comma and the conjunction are required in the compound sentence.

16.2.2.3. *Checking for style, diction, and vocabulary errors*

Sentence fragment errors

Sentence fragments are ungrammatical sentences because they lack a subject, verb, or meaning and are improperly punctuated. The following tips will help you identify and correct sentence fragments:

- Go over your sentences to make sure that every sentence contains a subject and a verb, and has a complete meaning.
- While checking, pay attention to sentences containing "signal words" (e.g., "first", "second", "additionally") and clarifications (e.g., "for example", "such as", "like"). These constructions often lead to sentence fragments because writers forget to include either a subject or verb.
- Because sentence fragments are only parts and are not complete sentences, pay special attention to compound and complex sentences joined by conjunctions (e.g., "and", "but", "so", "because", "although", "before", "as soon as"). Also check sentences signalled by sequence words ("first", "second", "finally"). Sentences containing these constructions are more likely to include sentence fragments.
- In all cases, always be sensitive to the types of errors typical of your writing—in this case, the types of sentence fragments you usually make (Child 1999).

Comma splice errors

A comma splice occurs when two independent clauses (sentences) are joined together by only a comma; it results in a type of ungrammatical sentence because of improper punctuation. The following may help you identify and correct comma splice errors:

- Locate sentences in your paper that have commas, and make sure they are used properly.
- If you find that the comma joins two independent clauses (sentences), then this is a comma splice and must be corrected.
- To correct a comma splice, you can choose to separate the two clauses with a full stop, making them two separate sentences. This option gives equal emphasis to the agents in each sentence.

- Alternatively, you can opt for one sentence with a comma and coordinating conjunction ("and", "but", "so", "or", "yet" etc.). Choose this option if you want to retain the special relationship between the two agents in the sentence (Kilborn 2004).

Errors with parallel structures

Parallel structure refers to items in sentences being written in a consistent manner using one grammatical form or another; that is, if you use nouns, then you have to use nouns consistently, or if you use infinitives or gerunds, you should also be consistent throughout with that particular form. To detect sentences with improper parallelism, consider the following:

- Read through your paper, pausing whenever you sense something is not quite right with the flow and rhythm of your sentences. Quite often, an unparalleled structure will sound awkward, and the rhythm will be broken.
- Since parallels are used more frequently in lists and series, check any lists that you may have written, making sure that items in your lists are parallel.
- When you spot unparallel forms, correct them for conformity to follow one specific grammatical form (e.g., nouns, adjectives, infinitives, or gerunds).
- If you can't make them parallel, rewrite your sentences to avoid the need for parallelism. (Wells et al. 2016)

16.3. Strategies for editing and revising by computer

Computers provide a number of useful facilities which writers can use to help edit and revise many errors. Spell checkers, grammar checkers, and find-and-replace are only a few of the many useful features a computer can offer towards revising and editing your paper.

However, the computer should be used with care, since it cannot check for all types of errors simply because the computer's electronic memory is fed only a limited set of rules to work on. Computers don't have the same social intelligence as people. It is only your human brain that has the ability to choose from an infinite number of possibilities. The computer has the ability to assist you by checking for and eliminating the obvious errors it can detect, thereby helping you to limit your revision to those "elusive" parts that only natural human intelligence can detect. The computer will tag as correct errors that only a rational human intelligence can detect as wrong.

Examples

>Elephants in the wild may consume up to three hundred kilos of grease per day.

>The barber cuts the man's head closely and finely.

The computer will always tag errors like those above as correct, which only rational thinking can see are wrong. A rational being understands that an elephant in the wild has no access to grease to consume, and consuming that amount would have long made all wild elephants extinct. Obviously, the intended word is "grass". In the second example, barbers who cut clients' heads will have been placed in jail and never again permitted to practise their trade. The intended word is "shave", not "cut".

16.3.1. Using the computer to check spelling

Computer spell checkers are one of the most useful tools for writing generally; they save a lot of valuable time that would otherwise be spent in looking up spellings in print dictionaries. English spelling, however, is problematic in a number of ways. First, the English language is not one, but many, and accordingly, spelling differs from one type of English to another; there is British English, American English, Australian (New Zealand) English, (South) African English, and Jamaican English. The diversity of English poses a challenge for writers as to which type of spelling to follow, and this is further complicated by the various forms of standard, colloquial, slang, and pidgin English. Indeed, many words that may be electronically tagged as wrong are, in fact, correct. Another major issue with English spelling is the obvious mismatch between pronunciation and spelling of many words that makes spelling a persistent problem with the English language even for native speakers. English is replete with words of similar pronunciation but different spelling (e.g., "right", "write", and "rite"), and many more of the same phonetic pronunciation but different spellings (e.g., "tough"/"puff"; "draught"/"brought" "wrought; butter/butcher/burner; stomach/church/headache).

Be aware that you cannot rely completely on the computer to do the spell checking. The computer will certainly pass many words as correctly spelt when in fact they are wrong in the given context. Consider the following example:

> The doctor asked the patient to swallow three tables
> a day after meals.

The world "tables" is correctly spelt, and the computer will pass it as such, when in fact it is the wrong word in the context, with only a missing *t* needed to form the correct word, "tablets", to correct the meaning. Such mistakes would send your reader laughing about how the computer could have overlooked such silly mistakes. But the computer is hardly to blame, as it is allowed to run the spelling check all alone, unaided by intuitive human knowledge. Bearing these considerations in mind, the best way for writers to benefit from the computer is to

- separate each individual word the computer identifies and then correct it if the word is obviously misspelt, or
- evaluate the word according to context and insert the correct one.

16.3.2. Using the computer to check grammar

Checking grammar by computer is much more complicated and unreliable than spell checking. Rules governing the grammar of natural language are infinitely varied; systematizing them for artificial intelligence devices, such as computer software, is extremely complex and costly. A score of grammarians and specialists in the field have pointed out that existing grammar checkers can be very unreliable and may sometimes be counterproductive.

16.3.3. Criticism levelled against grammar checkers

Grammar checkers are considered a type of "foreign language aid" especially designed to help non-native speakers check and proofread their writing. However, like other digital artificial intelligence technologies, grammar checkers are criticized for failing to identify errors, incorrectly flagging correct text as erroneous, and creating new errors. The linguist Geoffrey Pullum (author of the *Cambridge Grammar of the English Language*) has argued that grammar checkers are generally so inaccurate that in fact they do more harm than good: "… for the most part, accepting the advice of a computer grammar checker on your prose will make it **much** worse, sometimes hilariously incoherent" (Wikipedia [n.d.], "Editing Grammar Checker").

It has also been noted that the promise to deliver good and perfect grammar checkers by computer software companies has not been fulfilled. It has been argued that such claims are unrealistic and linguistically impossible. For example, spell checkers fail to flag contextual spelling errors, errors regarding compound modifiers that require hyphenation, and patterns of wordiness. This is simply because the number of grammatical alternatives open to users is infinitely varied and complex, rendering it practically impossible to exhaust them under any limited number of rules required in computerization. The problem is simply that no computer program can find and correct all such errors, because there are no general rules, and no inbuilt digital computing configuration can conceivably do so.

Most writers are pleased when grammar checkers spot mistakes in their writing. However, writers are many times not aware that checkers often fail to check correctly in three areas; they (1) overlook common or obvious mistakes, (2) falsely flag correct text as erroneous, and (3) offer new mistakes as corrections.

In a wide study designed to assess the effectiveness of a popular grammar and style checker, Grammatik V, based on empirical evidence, researchers identified two sets of problems: (1) mechanical and spelling problems and (2) grammatical errors. They divided the first set into mechanical problems (capitalization, punctuation, infinitive forms, number style), and spelling problems. In the list below, they revealed the inconsistencies found. Spelling errors have been separated from the others in order to highlight specific issues and to avoid misleading conclusions.

1. Mechanical problems

   The program spotted and commented on 142 mechanical errors, out of which 92 were correctly identified and 50 were undetected. The accuracy rate for capitalization was 26 per cent correctly detected, compared to 74 per cent undetected. For quotation marks, there was 50/50 accuracy. For punctuation, the program correctly detected 81 per cent of errors, compared to 19 per cent undetected (Wei and Davies 2011).

2. Grammatical errors

   For grammar, the program was fairly well able to detect errors like subject-verb agreement in simple sentences. However, it failed to identify the same types of mistakes in longer and more complex sentences, especially where the subject and verb were placed further apart from each other. The results of the two case studies revealed that the program was more efficient in detecting problems at the lower mechanical levels but was much less effective in dealing with problems at a more sophisticated level, such as dealing with semantic issues (Ibid.).

It is not surprising, therefore, to find that established editors and proofreaders often get dismayed when clients come to them stating that they did not do their job properly (perhaps also implying that they obtained money undeservedly). The general culture believes that computers are more perfect than the human brain. Gina de Miranda is an example of a seasoned editor who was "absolutely devastated" by computer checkers straining her relationships with clients. She complained that people frequently confronted her with the "evidence" that she had not checked their work properly, showing the "little green lines on the Damn MS Word checker". And when she tried to show them that the computer was actually wrong, she was ridiculed. (Miranda 2014)

16.3.4. Using the search-and-replace computer facility

The search-and-replace facility is one of the most useful computer features to help you fix a wide array of language problems efficiently and in a short time. This function offers you the convenience of scanning your entire document for specific words, phrases, names, acronyms, misused words, paddings, punctuation, or any other type of issue you want to correct. You can use the search-and-replace facility to detect and correct various types of errors, as outlined below:

- to scan for commonly misused words or phrases

  If you have a typical pattern of misusing or confusing some words, you can use this facility to check your entire paper for those problematic words and correct them. For example, if you consistently confuse "affluence" with "influence" and vice versa, you can make use of the search-and-replace facility to check your entire document for those two words and correct accordingly.

- to scan for your typical punctuation errors

Again, the *search-and-replace* facility offers a convenient tool to check and correct erroneous punctuation. Incorrect punctuation may include errors typical to your punctuation writing or those that you insert by mistake in certain sentence parts and need to be corrected. If, for example, you persistently use a comma when you are supposed to use a full stop or semicolon, use this facility to find all commas in the document, and correct those that need correction. The facility can also be applied to correct punctuation attached to sentence fragments, fused sentences, run-on sentences, and different types of clauses. Apply the facility to detect those incorrect constructions typical of yours, which will enable you to see and correct the punctuation errors in your work.

- to scan for your wordiness patterns

Repetitions, paddings, and filler words and phrases are examples of wordiness and unnecessary superfluous language to be discarded from writing because they blur the meaning. Writers have their typical wordiness patterns, which they need to be aware of and to know how to correct.

- to locate misspelt proper names or acronyms

The search-and-replace facility helps you locate proper names and acronyms you want to change. Enter the name or acronym you want changed (e.g., *The Republic*), and then run the document through, and all similar names in the whole document will be changed.

- to highlight technical terms and specific data

After you have finished with all essential editing and revision, you might need, for further refining, to check the accuracy of various important data and key terms that may need further clarification for the benefit of your audience. The search to locate function gives you the chance to reconsider those key technical terms that may require definition, or important data that may need to be explained. You may opt to include such explanatory items in the text itself, in appendices, or in a glossary.

Chapter References

Bailey, Stephen (2015). *Academic Writing: a Handbook for International Students*. 4th ed. Oxford: Routledge.

Child, Robert (1999). "Editing and Proofreading Strategies for Specific Sentence-Level Errors". Purdue University. Rev. by Judith Kilborn for the Write Place, St. Cloud State University. Last updated 26 March 1999. Accessed 10 November 2016.

"Common Misspellings" (n.d.). Oxford English Corpus. Oxford Dictionaries.com. https://en.oxforddictionaries.com/spelling/common-misspellings. Accessed 10 November 2016.

"Editing and proofreading" (2014). University of North Carolina, the Writing Center at UNC Chapel Hill. Licensed under a Creative Commons Attribution-Non-Commercial-NoDerivs 2.5 License. Accessed 14 November 2016.

"Gender-Inclusive Language" (2014). The Writing Centre at UNC–Chapel Hill. Under a Creative Commons Attribution-NonCommercial-NoDerivs 2.5 License. Accessed 20 February 2017. http://writingcenter.unc.edu/handouts/gender-inclusive-language/.

Miranda, de Gina (2014). Editor Software. Retrieved from http://www.editorsoftware.com/wordpress/does-grammar-checkers-work.

Kilborn, Judith (2004). "Avoiding Comma Splices, Fused Sentences, and Run-Ons". The Write Place. St. Cloud State University. Last updated 15 November 2004. http://leo.stcloudstate.edu/punct/avcsfsro.html.

Jacobs, G. and C. Rodgers (1999). "Treacherous Allies: Foreign Language Grammar Checkers". *CALICO Journal* vol. 16, no.4, 509–530.

Tate, Thomas (2000). "General Strategies for Revising and Editing on Computers". The Write Place. St. Cloud State University. Last updated 25 May 2000.

Tschichold, C. (1999). "Intelligent Grammar Checking for CALL", in Schulze M., M-J. Hamel and Thompson, eds. *Language Processing in CALL, Special Issue of ReCALL*. Hull: CTICML, University of Hull.

Wei, Yu Hong and Graham Davies (2011). *"Do Grammar Checkers Work? A report on Research into the Effectiveness of Grammatik V based on Samples of Authentic Essays by EFL Students*. Paper presented at EUROCALL 96, Dániel Berszenyi College, Hungary. Updated 12 October 2011.

Wells, Jaclyn M., Morgan Sousa, Mia Martini, Allen Brizee, and Ashley Velázquez (2016). "Proofreading Strategies to Try". The Writing Lab & the OWL at Purdue and Purdue University. Last edited 9 February 2016. Accessed 3 December 2016. https://owl.english.purdue.edu/owl/resource/561/01/.

Wikipedia (n.d.). "Editing Grammar Checker". Under the Creative Commons license. Accessed 9 January 2017. https://en.wikipedia.org/w/index.php?title=Grammar_checker&action=edit&section=3.

CHAPTER 17

Formatting and Submission

Abstract: A final general look is necessary to make sure that the final document satisfies the requisite academic research standards and that all the necessary sections are included in the proper format and style. This chapter provides the researcher with a checklist of the important sections the paper should have. These include the title page, acknowledgements, table of contents, body of the paper, graphics, conclusion, references, and appendices. The chapter gives useful guidelines on important formatting requirements to check before final submission. These include the main sections of the paper, general layout, margins, font size and line spacing, page numbers, headers and footers, paragraph indentation, headings and subheadings, and labelling of tables, graphics, and illustrations. Formatting requirements are presented in three different formats, illustrating the three major referencing styles: the APA, Harvard, and MLA formats. When finally the researcher is satisfied that all the necessary formatting requirements are included, she or he needs to incorporate the corrections and proofreading comments to produce the final draft. A further look should be made to ensure the inclusion of a list of tables, acknowledgements, an abstract, appendices, a glossary, and an index before preparing the final copy for binding and submission.

Keywords: title page; formatting guidelines of APA, Harvard, and MLA styles; final draft; final copy; binding; margins; font size and line spacing; page numbers; headers and footers; paragraph indentation; headings and subheadings; labelling of tables and graphics

At this stage, you have finished writing, editing, and proofreading your research. This is your final draft, which you are going to submit to your supervisor or publisher. Before final submission, there are a few last touches you need to make. These are meant to be final checks to ensure that everything is in place. Below is a checklist of the elements you will check in your last copy to get ready for binding and final submission.

17.1. General checklist of paper sections

- cover page
- acknowledgements
- table of contents
- introduction
- topic sentence and hook
- background
- thesis statement
- main body paragraphs
- topic sentences (each paragraph should have one)
- supporting details
- concluding sentence
- relation of body paragraphs to the main topic
- conclusion
- references
- appendices

It is also important to look up the following features and make sure they meet required formats:

- cover page
- titles and subtitles
- abstract (purpose, methods, and main findings)
- contents (main chapters and sections)
- introduction (reasons for the work, and its organization)
- references (list of all the sources used in the paper)
- graphics and visuals (numbered, titled, and referenced)
- appendix (to add information you deem necessary)
- index

17.2. General notes on formatting a research paper

After the editing and proofreading have been completed satisfactorily, it is advisable to take a final look at the general format of the paper, which includes a number of important features required by different conventions. These include

- main sections of the paper;
- general layout;
- layout of the title page;
- margins, font size, and line spacing;
- page numbers;
- headers and footers;
- paragraph indentation;
- headings and subheadings; and
- labelling of tables, graphics, and illustrations.

Different referencing systems have different formatting requirements. Below is a summary of the most salient formatting features for the APA (American Psychological Association), Harvard, and MLA (Modern Language Association) styles, which are the most commonly used referencing and citation systems in academic writing.

17.3. General formatting guidelines for APA style

Formatting a Research Paper in APA Style

Formatting Features	Formatting Method
Main sections of paper and layout	APA requires that a research paper should have at least four main sections: title page, abstract, main body, and references.

ACADEMIC RESEARCH WRITING

Layout of the title page

The title page contains three basic pieces of information: the paper title, the author name, and the institutional affiliation. Both capital and small letters are used to write the title, double-spaced and centred in the upper half of the title page, without abbreviating any words in the title, which may take up one or two lines. Below the title should be written the author's name, starting with the first name, followed by any middle names (or initials) and family name, with no titles (e.g., Prof., Eng., Dr, Mr) attached. Finally there should appear the name of the institution to which the author belongs or under the auspices of which she or he is conducting the research. The title should be typed in upper case and lower case letters, centred on the upper half of the page (APA Manual 2009, p. 23). Below is a sample title page in APA style:

Running head: ACADEMIC RESEARCH WRITING 1

Academic Research Writing
Methods, Concepts, Writing Process,
Language, Style, Punctuation, Common
Errors, Citations, Referencing, Editing,
Proofreading, and Submission
Ahmed Hamoda H. Fadlalla
English Language Institute of
the Royal Commission

Margin, font size, and line spacing	APA uses a 1" margin on both right and left and a twelve-point Times New Roman font, double-spaced and typed.
Page numbers, headers, and footers	APA uses a header for page numbering located in the upper right-hand corner, and a running head after the title page that runs throughout the whole document. The running head, located in the upper left-hand corner, should be a shortened version of the paper title, not exceeding fifty letters, in all capital letters (e.g., EYPYTIANOICS).
Paragraph indentation	
	APA style recommends a formatting arrangement according to the number of levels of subordination as follows:

Level 1	Centered, Boldface, Uppercase and Lowercase Heading
Level 2	Flush left, Boldface, Uppercase and Lowercase Heading
Level 3	Indented, boldface, lowercase paragraph heading ending with a period.
Level 4	indented, boldface, italicized lowercase paragraph heading ending with a period.
Level 5	*indented, italicized lowercase paragraph heading ending with a period.*

Headings and subheadings

(APA 2009, p. 62)

Tables are numbered in Arabic numerals (e.g., "Table 1"), and so are figures, labelled numerically (e.g., "Figure 1").

Tables are titled on top but are referenced underneath.

Example

Table 3

Infant Mortality Rates in Selected European and Asian Countries (2000 – 2015)

Labelling of tables, graphics and illustrations

	2000	2005	2010	2015
European				
Netherland		00.00	00.00	00.00
Germany		00.00	00.00	00.00
Belgium		00.00	00.00	00.00
Asian				
India		00.00	00.00	00.00
Pakistan		00.00	00.00	00.00
Singapore		00.00	00.00	00.00

(Eurostat 2016)

Figures, on the other hand, are titled and referenced underneath.

Creating a list of references in APA style

A reference list (but not a bibliography) at the end of the paper should include only the sources the author has actually cited in the document body. Personal communications may be cited in the body but should not be included in the reference list. Follow the general guidelines below for creating your reference list in APA style:

- Title your list "References", with the title centred on the page (APA 2010, p. 37).
- Start your reference list on a new page (APA 2010, p. 37).
- Arrange the list alphabetically by the authors' last names (APA 2010, p. 181).

- All reference entries are double-spaced, with the second line of the entry and every line after that in a hanging indent.
- Include only the references actually cited in the body of the paper (APA 2010, p. 180). In the reference list, single authors are listed before multiple authors when one same author is involved (APA 2010, p. 182). For example, "Fowler, H. W. (1965). *Modern English Usage*" is to be listed before "Fowler, H. W., and Fowler, F. (1906). *The King's English*. Oxford."

Sample Reference Entry in APA Style
American Psychological Association. (2010). *Publication Manual of the American Psychological Association* (6th ed.). Washington, DC: American Psychological Association.

17.4. General formatting guidelines for Harvard style

Formatting a Research Paper in Harvard Style

Formatting features	Formatting method
Main sections of paper and layout	Harvard requires that a research paper have at least four main sections: title page, introduction paragraph, main body, conclusion, and references or bibliography. A bibliography is a comprehensive list of sources including those that have been cited and those that have not but that the writer has consulted for the work. The List of references is an alphabetical listing according to authors' last names of all the sources actually referred to in the in-text citations in the body. References are double spaced with a hanging indent; the first line of each entry is flush left, while the following lines are indented one-half inch.

Layout of the title page

The Harvard system requires that the paper title be located halfway down the title page, written all in capital letters. This is followed three lines below by the author's name, then four lines down comes the name of the class, the name of the supervisor in the line after, and in the following line is the name of the institution. This is followed by the city and state of publication, and, finally the date. Below is a sample title page in Harvard Style:

ACADEMIC RESEARCH WRITING
Methods, Concepts, Writing Process, Language, Style, Punctuation, Common Errors, Citations, Referencing, Editing, Proofreading, and Submission

Ahmed Hamoda H. Fadlalla

English Language Institute of the Royal Commission
Jubail Industrial City, Kingdom of Saudi Arabia
March 2017

Margin, font size, and line spacing

Margins should be 1" on all four sides of the paper (top, bottom, right and left) straight aligned on the left and jagged on the right. Harvard uses a twelve-point font of one of the standard scripts, such as Times New Roman, Arial, or Courier New, with no colours, fanciful scripts or too much underlining, boldface or italics. Lines are double-spaced. A standard size 8½" × 11" paper is used.

- The entire document is double-spaced, including the reference list.
- Allow 2.5 cm margins on all sides of the page.
- Suggested fonts: Times New Roman, Arial, and Courier New for Windows; Times New Roman, Helvetica, and Courier for Mac. Twelve point size. Ensure that all Harvard citations are in the same font as the rest of the work.

	Harvard uses a header that carries simultaneously both a page number and a running head for the whole document. The running head is a shortened summary of the paper title and is right-aligned and not all in capital letters. Exactly five spaces separates the page number from the running head. It looks like this: Globalization 1
	To access the header in Microsoft Word, go to the top of any page in the document and double click.
Page numbers, headers, and footers	A blue dotted line appears with a small box on the lower left-hand corner that reads "Header", and above this is your cursor. A box will drop down simultaneously. Click the page number box and follow these directions. Click on the first option: "Top of the Page." Then click the one that reads "Plain Number 3." A number corresponding to the page you are on will appear on the right-hand side of the header. The cursor is now on the left side of the number. Type your partial title and then press the space bar exactly five times. Now double click anywhere in the body of the main document, and the page number header is set.
Paragraph indentation	The first paragraph of the paper is an introductory one that introduces the topic and attracts the reader with a hook and some background information about the topic, ending with a thesis statement—a one-sentence statement that focuses the topic and leads the reader to what follows in the body paragraph. The first sentence in each paragraph is indented and introduces the topic and main idea of the paragraph, followed by supporting details. Allow ½" indentation for every new paragraph (press the Tab key)
Headings and subheadings	In shorter essays, subheadings are italicized and left-aligned. For longer papers, headings are centred to break the body into major sections.

ACADEMIC RESEARCH WRITING

Tables, charts, diagrams, and other visuals should be titled and referenced if used in full or in part. If partial information is used from visual illustrations, cite it as a secondary source in the body text.

Example

in the table below, the figures reveal a slow but steady increase in oil prices in the last quarter (the Saudi National Statistics Office 2016, p. 283).

Labelling of tables, graphics, and illustrations

If the entire table is reproduced, it should be replicated and referenced below to acknowledge its sources.

Example

	October	November	December
Last quarter	65 SR/ liter	80 SR/ liter	95 SR/ liter

Source: Saudi National Statistics Office (2016)

Finally, the source should be entered in full in the reference list:

Example

Saudi National Statistics Office (2016). Chapter 3: "Oil Prices". Riyadh, KSA.

- For a heading, title your list "Reference List", "Works Cited" or simply "References" on a new page at the end of your document.
- General formatting should be in line with the rest of your work.

Creating a list of references in Harvard style

- Your reference list pages in Harvard style should include a header on the upper right-hand corner that contains a shortened version of the title and the page number.
- The entire document is double-spaced, including the reference list.
- Arrange the list in alphabetical order by the authors' last names.
- Titles with no author are alphabetized according to the work's title.

373

- Two or more sources by the same author should be listed in chronological order by the year of publication.
- When there are several works from one author or source, they should be listed together in date order, with the earliest work listed first.
- Italicize titles of books, reports, conference proceedings, etc. For journal articles, the title of the journal should be printed in italics rather than the title of the journal article.
- Capitalize the first letter of the publication title, the first letters of all main words in the title of a journal, and all first letters of a place name and publisher.

Sample Reference List Entries in Harvard Style:
Adler, P. A., and Adler, P. 1994. "Observation Techniques", in Norman K. Denzin and Yvonna S. Lincoln (eds.), *Handbook of Qualitative Research*. Thousand Oaks, California: Sage. Carlson, John W. 2012. *Words of Wisdom: A Philosophical Dictionary for the Perennial Tradition*. Amazon Paperback Books. https://www.amazon.com/Words-Wisdom-Philosophical-Dictionary-Perennial/dp/0268023700.

17.5. General formatting guidelines for MLA style

Formatting a Research Paper in MLA Style

Formatting features	Formatting method
Main sections of paper and layout	MLA style requires that a research paper should have main sections of paper and lay out.

Academic Research Writing

Layout of the title page

MLA style does not require a title page, as APA and Harvard do. It is optional. Instead, four elements (writer's name, supervisor, course, and date) are required to be inserted, each on a separate line and double-spaced, starting from the first page and flush with the left margin. This is followed with the paper title, double-spaced and centred on a new line. The title should not be italicized, capitalized, underlined, boldfaced, or inserted within quotation marks. Below is an illustration:

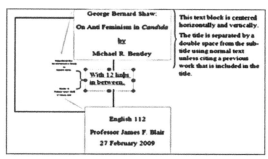

Figure 1: An example of a title page in MLA style.

Below is a sample first page in MLA style.

First page layout

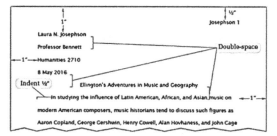

Figure 2: The top of the first page of a research paper.

375

Margin, font size, and line spacing	MLA uses a 1" margin on all four sides of paper (top, bottom, right and left), an easily readable typeface (e.g., Times New Roman) whose regular script contrasts clearly with the italic, set to a standard size (e.g., twelve point), double-spaced throughout the entire paper, including quotations, notes, and the list of works cited.
Page numbers, headers, and footers	MLA style uses a header for page numbering that runs consecutively throughout the whole paper, but a running head is optional. The page number is located on the top right-hand corner, ½" from the top, aligned right. The writer's last name is written followed by a single space before entering the page number (see example below). Page numbers appear in Arabic numerals without the abbreviation "p.", and no full stops, hyphens, or any other marks or symbols are to be added to page numbers.

Figure 3: The running head of a research paper.

Paragraph indentation	The first line of a paragraph is indented half an inch from the left margin; the rest of the paragraph runs immediately at the left margin. Long quotations are indented half an inch from the margin as well.
Sections, headings, and subheadings	Sections, headings, and subheadings are numbered in Arabic numerals, with the numbers followed by a full stop (.), a space, and then the name of the section. Headings and subheadings in the paper are not followed by periods.

Tables, graphics, and illustrations should be placed as close as possible to the text they describe. These should be labelled, numbered in Arabic numerals, and titled. Tables are labelled "Table" and given a number written on a separate line aligned left above the table. The title follows on a separate line, with the first letters of all important words capitalized (see example below). Below the table is given the source and any other relevant information to clarify the table. Title, source, and notes should all be double-spaced. All other visual illustrations, including figures, charts, maps, and photos, should be labelled "Figure" (this may be abbreviated "Fig."), numbered with Arabic numerals, and given a caption: "Fig. 1. Migrant Mother 1939, by Dorothea Lange". Unlike tables, captions of other visual illustrations appear directly below the figure, chart or map and are double-spaced with 1" margins like the rest of the text in the paper.

Labelling of tables, graphics, and illustrations

MLA requires that every parenthetical citation in the body of the paper must have a corresponding entry in the works cited list, giving full bibliographical details of the source. Here are some rules on how to format a list of works cited in MLA style:

- Title your list "Works Cited" at the top of the page.
- Include only the sources you have actually cited in the body of the document.
- Place the second line of the entry and every line after that in a hanging indent.
- Each page should be indented by 1" on both the left and right of the page.
- All entries should be in hanging indent. Entries that have more than one line should have an additional ½" margin from the left.

- Consider the place of commas, periods, colons, etc.
- All pages of MLA lists of works cited should include a header on the upper right-hand corner that contains the last name of the author and the page number.
- All MLA citations in your list of works cited should be double spaced.
- All entries in your list should be alphabetized according to the author's last name. If no author is cited, use the title of the source instead.
- End each entry of the list with a full stop to indicate the end of the entry.
- Titles of books and journals should be italicized.
- Titles of articles, book chapters, essays, and short stories should be written within quotation marks.
- In case more than one author shares a source, start the entry with the first author's last name, then list the first name. List the other authors normally, starting with their first names.
- Entries of sources taken from electronic database (ProQuest, EBSCOhost), should include the database title and the web medium.
- Websites URLs should be included in the body citations only if they do not lead clearly to their corresponding references in the list of works cited.

Creating a list of works cited in MLA style

Below is the top part of a sample illustration for a list of works cited in MLA style:

Copeland, Edward. "Money." *The Cambridge Companion to Jane Austen*. Edited by Copeland and Juliet McMaster. Cambridge: UP, 1997, pp. 131–48.

(MLA Style Center 2016a, MLA Style Center 2016b, MLA Style Center 2016c, MLA Style Center 2016d).

17.6. Final draft

The final draft of your paper should include the main sections in addition to incorporating the required corrections and editorial comments suggested by proofreaders. Additionally, make sure that your paper satisfies the requisite academic conventions. In case you have coloured illustrations and drawings, get them ready, but do not insert them as yet. Leave spaces for such illustrations to insert them later (or scan them into the document).

17.7. Final copy for binding and submission

Make sure to add the following parts before preparing the final copy for binding and submission:

- Write the table of contents, with the main headings and corresponding page numbers, so readers can easily find what they look for. The table of contents (TOC) goes at the beginning of your paper.
- Number your list of tables consecutively.
- Also prepare your appendices and put them in a list.
- Add a glossary and index, if you are including them.
- Arrange your list of references and check it thoroughly for bibliographical details.
- Write your acknowledgments and place them at the beginning.
- Write an abstract and place it at the beginning.
- Check that the cover page is properly formatted in the style you are writing in.
- Give a final quick look for small spelling and grammar mistakes, punctuation, line spacing, and consistency in font size, page numbers, and general format.

When all has been done, and the document is carefully checked, you have your final copy ready for biding and submission. Take your completed academic work to the stationery shop for binding. There are various types of binding available from which you can choose the one that suits your paper. Graduating students' research projects are usually bound with spiral rings with a transparent front and coloured paper back. Graduate students' longer theses, such as PhD and MA dissertations, are bound in hardback. Your final bound work should have an inviting good look since it is the first thing that the reader sees and touches, so bring it out to impress.

Chapter References

Harvard Formatting and Style Guide: Cover Page (n.d.). Retrieved 22 January 2017. *https://www.uvocorp.com/dl/Harvard%20Guide.pdf*

Harvard Writing Style Format (n.d.). EBSCOhost Complete. Retrieved 22 January 2017. https://www.uvocorp.com/dl/Harvard%20Guide.pdf.

MLA Style Center (2016a). "Formatting a Research Paper". Modern Language Association of America Style Center.

——— (2016b). "Understanding and Writing in MLA Format Style". Modern Language Association of America Style Center.

——— (2016c). "Formatting a Research Paper". Modern Language Association of America Style Center.

——— (2016d). "MLA Works Cited: The Guidelines". Modern Language Association of America Style Center.

University of North South West Sydney (2016). "The American Psychological Association (APA) Referencing System (a Guide)". Last updated 28 June 2016. Accessed 17 September 2016. DOI: H:\Guide to Academic Writing Files\UNSW Current Students.html.

CHAPTER 18

Samples and Illustrations

Sample Descriptive Essay

How to Eat a Guava

There are guavas at the *Shop and Save.* I pick one the size of a tennis ball and finger the prickly stem end. It feels familiarly bumpy and firm. The guava is not quite ripe; the skin is still a dark green. I smell it and imagine a pale pink center, the seeds tightly embedded in the flesh.

A ripe guava is yellow, although some varieties have a pink tinge. The skin is thick, firm, and sweet. Its heart is bright pink and almost solid with seeds. The most delicious part of the guava surrounds the tiny seeds. If you don't know how to eat a guava, the seeds end up in the crevices between your teeth.

When you bite into a ripe guava, your teeth must grip the bumpy surface and sink into the thick edible skin without hitting the center. It takes experience to do this, as it's quite tricky to determine how far beyond the skin the seeds begin.

Some years, when the rains have been plentiful and the nights cool, you can bite into a guava and not find many seeds. The guava bushes grow close to the ground, their branches laden with green then yellow fruit that seem to ripen overnight. These guavas are large and juicy, almost seedless, their roundness enticing you to have one more, just one more, because next year the rains may not come.

As children, we didn't always wait for the fruit to ripen. We raided the bushes as soon as the guavas were large enough to bend the branch.

A green guava is sour and hard. You bite into it at its widest point, because it's easier to grasp with your teeth. You hear the skin, meat, and seeds crunching inside your head, while the inside of your mouth explodes in little spurts of sour. You grimace, your eyes water, and your cheeks disappear as your lips purse into a tight O. But you have another and then another, enjoying the crunchy sounds, the acid taste, the gritty texture of the unripe center. At night, your mother makes you drink castor oil[1], which she says tastes better than a green guava. That's when you know for sure that you're a child and she has stopped being one.

I had my last guava the day we left Puerto Rico. It was large and juicy, almost red in the center, and so fragrant that I didn't want to eat it because I would lose the smell. All the way to the airport I scratched at it with my teeth, making little dents in the skin, chewing small pieces with my front teeth, so that I could feel the texture against my tongue, the tiny pink pellets of sweet.

Today, I stand before a stack of dark green guavas, each perfectly round and hard, each $1.59. The one in my hand is tempting. It smells faintly of late summer afternoons and hopscotch under the mango tree. But this is autumn in New York, and I'm no longer a child.

The guava joins its sisters under the harsh fluorescent lights of the exotic fruit display. I push my cart away, toward the apples and pears of my adulthood, their nearly seedless ripeness predictable and bitter sweet.

(from: *When I Was Puerto Rican*, by Esmeralda Santiago)

Sample Definition Essay

E-Commerce (Electronic Commerce, or EC)

E-commerce (electronic commerce, or EC) is the transmission of business transactions, such as exchanges of goods and services, exchanges of business information, transfers of funds, and other business operations through electronic means. E-commerce is now widely used in business worldwide, and it is estimated that the volume of retail e-commerce sales—including both products and services conducted through electronic channels—will reach $1.915 trillion in 2016, accounting for 8.7% of total world retail business. Projections estimate an increase of $4.058 trillion in 2020, making up 14.6% of total retail spending that year. The unprecedented expansion of e-commerce in a short period of time reflects the ease and convenience of conducting business for both parties involved in a business transaction, with a virtual elimination of the constraints of time and distance.

E-commerce is conducted in various forms of business operations, including three distinct types: business to consumer (B2C), business to business (B2B), and consumer to consumer (C2C).

The first type, business to consumer (B2C), involves conducting deals with a business and its customers via the internet for payment and delivery arrangements. B2C is the most common type of e-commerce. One of the most prominent examples of B2C is that involving smartphone businesses and their customers. By 2015, smartphone audiences in Brazil and Mexico, for example, reached 48.6 and 34.2 million, respectively, with a stunning majority of eighteen- to thirty-four-year-olds representing a staggering 88% of smartphone buyers in Mexico. In 2014, a poll revealed that 34% of adult digital buyers in Brazil and 46% of those in Mexico said they had completed at least one purchase via smartphone in the past twelve months. It is estimated that in Latin America alone, business-to-consumer ecommerce sales will rise to 24.2% this year, accounting for $88.3 billion. Growth rates are expected to remain in the double-digits zone through 2018, with a projected volume of sales of $140.9 billion. In Latin America, Brazil and Mexico continue to be the leading contributors in the region, with sales of $31.9 and $17.5 billion respectively in 2015. Another example of B2C is Souq. com, one of the most popular e-commerce sites in the Middle East. Founded in 2016 in the United Arab Emirates, Souq.com connects businesses and merchants in the UAE with retailers and individual consumers in the wider Middle East market. Souq is the leading business-to-consumer (B2C) e-commerce platform in the region, used by 74% of total internet users.

The second type, business to business (B2B), is the type of transaction conducted among and between firms via the internet and other digital platforms. B2B is not keeping pace with the rate of growth achieved by B2C. The B2B e-commerce market is growing, but it's still in its infancy. For example, in USA in 2015, few companies offered an online website as a purchasing channel to B2B buyers. Companies are becoming more and more sophisticated, making efforts to offer clients digital platforms for conducting business transactions. A survey of the websites of seventy-eight B2B wholesale distributors and brand manufacturers in the USA in 2016 revealed that companies are making efforts to improve their websites. They are starting to offer click-to-chat digital features to enable smoother business deals, reaching in 2016 up to 45% of the total business websites, with a 24% increase from that in 2015. By 2020, B2B e-commerce total sales are projected to reach $6.7 trillion worldwide, contributing 27% of all B2B sales.

The third type, consumer to consumer (C2C), is the type of transaction in which deals are conducted on a personal individual level between customers, especially through social networks, such as Facebook, Instagram, and Pinterest. This explains why this type of e-commerce is sometimes referred to as social commerce. Social networks have indeed doubled their efforts to make their sites a rendezvous where users can exchange goods and services conveniently. Social networks are now adding click-to-buy digital features. One of the most vibrant C2C e-commerce markets is found in South East Asia. Social commerce is already making big leaps here, with a volume of sales estimated to account for about 30% of total digital sales in the region in 2017, conducted chiefly through social networks. The South East Asian market is particularly suited to this type of ecommerce, with its high percentage of young people vying for using modern technology such as smartphones, social networks, and the internet. For example, in markets like Indonesia, users have relied on Facebook for years to facilitate consumer-to-consumer (C2C) e-commerce transactions by posting items for sale and soliciting offers from friend networks. Facebook has clearly taken note of these social-relations types of business by creating tools to facilitate the smooth exchange of goods and services between its users in both C2C and business-to-consumer (B2C) transactions on its platform. As a result, Facebook has launched a new feature called "shop" to invite its users to try out the new applications and services it offers.

E-commerce business transactions are conducted mainly through electronic channels, and there are three main types of such transactions: business to consumer (B2C), business to business (B2B), and consumer to consumer (C2C). E-commerce has gained popularity among businesses everywhere in the world and has sliced a considerable share from the total sales market. This popularity and rapid expansion have been mainly due to the ease and convenience with which business deals can be done via e-commerce, with around-the-clock availability, rapid access, a wide availability of goods and services for the consumer, ease of accessibility, and international reach.

Sample Classification / Partition Essay

Parts and Functions of the Eye

The eye is the most valued of the five human senses—sight, hearing, smell, touch, and taste—and when people are asked to value their senses, they consistently rate their eyesight as the most valued and the one they fear losing most. Nature has it that the eye is composed of different parts. Each part is carefully enclosed in a protective shield to enable proper lifelong functioning for the overall complex vision process. The eye functions like a camera in that it takes in light and depicts objects around us in exactly the same shapes, colours, and details as they appear in nature, and sends the images through the optic nerve to the brain, where they are interpreted to enable people to make informed decisions about them. There are several parts of the eye consisting of physical and chemical elements; each carries out its function in harmony with the other parts to make up the overall perceptual process.

Following the vision process, which resembles that of a digital camera, the first part that takes in light is the cornea. The cornea is a clear outer covering of the eye that functions exactly like a camera's lens. The cornea's clear and transparent covering that allows in light is in fact a composite of several layers of tissue shaped like a dome, which make a tough protective shield for additional protection of the inner parts of the eye. The essential function of the cornea is to take in light and focus images clearly and effectively. Another important function of the cornea is the continuous cleansing of the eye through a process of continuous regeneration of the cornea's protective tissue, which helps eliminate any damage that might occur.

Next comes the iris, which receives the light passed from the cornea. The iris contains the pigment which gives the eye its distinctive colour. This area surrounds the pupil and uses the dilator pupillary muscles to widen or narrow the pupil. The iris controls the amount of light that passes to the back of the eye, at the same time adjusting the size of the pupil to allow just the right amount of light pass through. This makes the iris function exactly like the aperture of a camera that opens and closes automatically to adjust the amount of light that passes through. It allows the eye to take in more or less light depending on how bright the surrounding area is. If it is too bright, the iris will shrink the pupil so the eye can focus more effectively.

An essential part is the eye's lens. The lens is composed of a crystalline tissue that sits directly behind the pupil. The function of the lens is to sharpen the focus of light taken in through the pupil. The lens and pupil work in coordination. The pupil, which appears like a black dot in the middle of the eye, is in fact a hole that allows light to pass through. Then the lens takes the light passed through the pupil and focusses it more sharply. The lens allows the eye to focus on the objects it perceives and adjusts the amount of light, depending on the distance, to allow for a better view, just like a camera's lens.

The final stage of forming the image occurs when the light reaches the retina after being passed from the cornea through the pupil and lens, and adjusted by the iris. The retina is a delicate tissue that is sensitive to the incoming light, located at the back of the eye. The retina is made up of rods arranged in a number of layers that convert light into chemical and electrical pulses to be transmitted to the brain. It is connected to the brain by the optic nerves. It transmits the images through the optic nerves to the visual cortex of the brain, where they are interpreted. Thus the retina functions just like the automatic image sensor of a camera; it transforms optical images into electronic signals that reach the brain for final interpretation.

Sample Cause-and-Effect Essay

The Effects of Weather on People's Lives

Although weather forecasting has helped us better understand turbulence in frequently changing weather conditions, weather still remains an element of nature that continues to have a tremendous impact on human life. Weather affects our daily lives by influencing our normal decisions, such as going out on a picnic or staying at home. It affects our moods with the passage of seasons. It may even affect decisions involving big political matters, such as wars that leave their marks in the chronicles of history.

In routine working life, people may commute to work every day, and favourable weather conditions are always a blessing. Sometimes, however, when conditions are turbulent, with storms, rain, or snow, the effects on commuters can be dismaying. Instead of the usual fifteen-minute drive to work, commuters may need much more time to arrive at work. Much stress can arise in such situations, owing to the increased risk of the unexpected, sometimes with an added unwelcome retort from the manager for tardiness. On a beautiful sunny morning, your family may decide to go on a picnic to enjoy the fine weather, but a sudden change can bring a thunderstorm with strong winds and heavy rains, forcing you to pack quickly to return home, only to get stuck in the middle of a dangerously flooded valley, leaving you feeling luckily to reach home after spending several hours wet, cold, and hungry.

The changes in weather that are typically associated with the passage of seasons are found to trigger strong changes in people's moods and health conditions. During the wet rainy season in autumn, moods may become low, and some people feel down and blue. This is partly because of the long period of murky and dull conditions in the absence of moderating sunshine. In spring, on the other hand, people feel cheerful and may be imbued with a catchy, buoyant mood. In the cold winter months, people may feel unhappy and depressed. In summer, people feel more active and energetic, with high sporty and courtly moods. Extreme heat and extreme cold can have strong negative impacts on people's health, ranging from simple colds and flu in winter to sun stroke and skin cancer in long, hot summers.

The strong mood swings associated with the seasonal cycle are also found to be caused by changes in the body chemicals that bear strongly on our emotional well-being. Prolonged periods of dark weather and lack of sunlight brought about by seasonal changes or extended periods of unfavourable weather are found to reduce the levels of vitamin D in the body. Low levels of vitamin D in the body can cause fatigue and tiredness. Lower levels of this vitamin are also associated with reduced levels of serotonin, a brain chemical that influences a person's moods; high levels of serotonin are associated with happy, joyful moods, and reduced levels can cause severe states of depression in certain people. The seasonal cycles affect many people's moods in various ways in what is known as seasonal affective disorder (SAD), a psychological emotional state characterized by low moods and low productivity.

On yet another grander plane, weather has indeed caused world history to radically shift in important ways that are still felt today. Numerous examples from world history document the long-term effects of weather in the formation of cultures and nations. One notable example is that of the Mongol leader Kublai Khan, who ruled in the thirteenth century over the vast Mongol empire that spanned from present-day Siberia in the north to Afghanistan in the south, and from the Pacific Ocean in the east to the Black Sea in the west. To expand his reign further, Kublai Khan mounted two invasions of Japan. Two monsoons, however, caused him to end his attacks.

Delgado (2008) describes legendary accounts of this event: "The legend, oft repeated in countless history books, speaks of gigantic ships, numbering into the thousands, crewed by indomitable Mongol warriors, and of casualties on a massive scale, with more than 100,000 lives lost in the final invasion attempt of 1281" (p. 4). Because of this unexpected defeat, Kublai Khan decided to stage a third invasion of Japan, but he died before he could fulfil this ambition. Without these monsoons, Japan might have been defeated by the Mongols and thus lost its identity as a unique culture, with far-reaching consequences for Asian and world history.

These examples clearly illustrate the powerful impact of weather on human life both on a day-to-day basis and in long-term far-reaching historical events that have left their indelible marks until today. It is also evident that the range of effects the weather has on our lives can be infinite and unpredictable.

Sample Comparison/ Contrast Essay

Essay Comparing Ancient Roman and Greek Architecture

Ancient Greek architecture is featured by two main orders, namely the Doric and the Ionic. Greeks effectively applied these architectural styles in constructing buildings, theatres, and temples. The Doric style was predominantly applied in mainland Greece, with a further spread to the Greek settlements in Italy. The Ionic style was applied in Ionia and the Aegean islands. The Doric style was more austere and formal, whereas the Ionic was more decorative and relaxed.

The styles are mostly reflected in the three orders of column capitals, which bear different decoration and design features. Some examples of the Doric order are the Temple of Hephaestus and the Parthenon in Athens. In turn, the Ionic masterpieces include the temple of Athena Nike on the Acropolis and the Erechtheum. The Ionic order gained dominance during the Hellenistic period; however, it was prone to a great deal of resistance by many Greek states.

In their architectural constructions and designs, the ancient Greeks used wood for roof beams; plaster for bathtubs; brick for walls; marble and limestone for walls, columns, and upper portions of public buildings and temples; terracotta for ornaments and roof tiles; and metals for decorative details to construct civic, religious, domestic, recreational, and funerary buildings.

The commonest form of Greek public architecture was the temple, with an altar standing under the open sky in the sacred, or temenos, fane before the temple. Temples were closely associated with the cults of gods. Palaestra (gymnasiums) served as the social centre for males, providing a space for physical exercises and athletic contests.

Council chambers in Greek cities served the functions of a meeting place for the town council and courthouses. In contrast to ancient Romans, Greeks did not employ domes and arches, and therefore they could not build constructions with huge interior spaces. Theatres were the specific spots in all ancient Greek towns used either for public meetings or dramatic performances. Theatres were constructed in semicircular form, extending round the central performance area.

Ancient Romans, on the other hand, developed their architecture on the basis of the standards of the classical Greek architecture. Arches and domes are regarded as the distinctive features of ancient Roman architecture. Roman buildings significantly differed from those of the Greeks, and so a new architectural style was created. Mainly because of high population densities and wealth in the cities, the ancient Romans discovered their own architectural solutions. In particular, they applied arches and vaults, as well as building materials that enabled them to attain unprecedented progress in the construction of public structures. The Colosseum, the basilicas, the Baths of Caracalla and the Baths of Diocletian, the aqueducts of Rome, and the Pantheon are all relevant proofs of genuinely Roman architectural innovations. These impressive buildings all served important public functions. In contrast to Greek aesthetic concerns, these objectives were attained with a wide vision regarding public effect.

As well as this, Roman architecture was influenced by the worship needs of the Roman religion. The Pantheon, for example, is an amazing engineering construction created to serve purely religious purposes.

Sample Process Essay

The Process of Oil Refining

Oil refining is a chemical engineering process used in petroleum refineries to convert crude oil into useful products. Crude oil is not extracted from underground in its final, useable form. It goes through a lengthy process: first it is transported to a refinery, processed, and treated so that its components can be used as final usable products, such as liquid gas, diesel oil, kerosene, jet fuel, butane, petrol, and fuel oils. Crude oil undergoes several processes at oil refineries, usually including three distinct phases: separation (or distillation), conversion, and treatment.

Separation (or Distillation)

In its basic form, crude oil contains a mixture of hydrocarbons of different length chains when it is extracted from underground wells. Then it goes into the initial stage of processing, which is separation, or distillation. Crude oil is first transported into a special tower called a "crude oil distillation unit (CDU), where it is heated under controlled pressure. The CDU distils the incoming crude oil into various fractions of different boiling ranges, and it is separated into its various components through the process of fractional distillation. Fractional distillation is the process of using differences in boiling temperature to separate different gases in a refinery. Essentially, it involves heating up the crude oil, letting it vaporize, and then condensing it. The crude oil is heated at the bottom of a sixty-metre distillation column at a temperature of 350 to 400°C, causing it to vaporize. The vapours rise inside the column, while the heaviest molecules, or residuals, remain at the bottom, with lighter substances such as petrol collecting at the cooler top of the tower while the heaviest components collect at the bottom. The condensation process requires an exchange of heating and cooling temperatures in the distillation tower. This necessary exchange is provided partially by exchanging heat with the incoming crude oil, and partially by either an air-cooled or water-cooled condenser. Additional heat is removed from the distillation column by a pump-around system.

Conversion

After the first separation phase, there are still many heavy hydrocarbons—organic compounds consisting of carbon and hydrogen. Hydrocarbons are the principal constituents of crude oil, natural gas, and petroleum products remaining after the separation process. To meet demand for lighter products, the heavy molecules are "cracked" into two or more lighter ones. The conversion process, which is carried out at 500°C, is also known as catalytic cracking because it uses a substance called a catalyst to speed up the chemical reaction. This process converts 75 per cent of the heavy products into gas, petrol, and diesel. The yield can be increased further by adding hydrogen—the simplest and lightest atom, and the most abundant element in the universe—in a process called hydrocracking. It is a refining process that converts heavy hydrocarbons into lighter, low-sulphur products in the presence of hydrogen, or by using deep conversion to remove carbon. The more complex the operation, the more it costs and the more energy it uses. The refining industry's ongoing objective is to find a balance between yield and the cost of conversion.

Treatment

"Treatment" refers to all of the refining processes intended to remove unwanted compounds (contaminants). It involves removing or significantly reducing molecules that are corrosive or cause air pollution—especially sulphur. The European Union's sulphur emission standards are very stringent. Since January 1, 2009, petrol and diesel sold in Europe cannot contain more than ten parts per million (ppm). The purpose of these measures is to improve air quality and optimize the effectiveness of catalytic converters used to treat exhaust gas. For diesel, desulfurization, an operation that removes most of the sulphur from gas, smoke, sour natural gas, and refined petroleum products, is performed at 370°C at a pressure of 60 bars. The hydrogen used in the process combines with the sulphur to form hydrogen sulphide (H_2S), which is then treated to remove the sulphur, which is used in industry. Kerosene, butane, and propane are washed in a caustic soda (sodium hydroxide) solution to remove thiols, also known as mercaptans. This process is called sweetening. The octane rating measures a fuel's resistance to detonation, which causes engine knocking.

Sample Opinion / Argument Essay

Exploring Unknown Space while 95 Per Cent of the Earth's Oceans Remain Unexplored

It is ironic that billions of dollars are spent each year on trying to explore unknown space while more than twice as much area as the earth's inhabited land remains unexplored—namely, the mysterious ocean floor. More precisely, 29% of the earth's surface is land, while 71% is water. Only about 5% of the ocean floor has been explored; 95% remains a mystery for humans to discover what potentialities and opportunities it holds for the future of humankind. Indeed, we know very little about the deep ocean and the resources that lie hidden in its floor. Therefore, it is legitimate to question the wisdom of the massive spending on exploring unknown outer space while 95% of the ocean floor remains unknown to humans right here on Earth.

When examining the spending on the world space exploration programme, it is worth looking into the expenditures of countries which have space agencies involved in human space flight. These include the US (NASA), Russia, the European Union (ESA), China, Canada, Japan, and India. Only the United States, Russia, and China have successfully and independently managed to put astronauts in space. India and Japan are vying to do so in the near future, while astronauts from the EU countries and Canada work closely with American, Russian, and international space stations.

In 2005, total spending on the world space programme came to about $25 billion. This means a cost of $3.90 to be incurred on every person worldwide. The total spending on space constitutes about 0.05% of global gross domestic product (GDP). In 2014, NASA's budget was $17.6 billion; the European Space Agency was earmarked €4.3 billion (equivalent to $5.51 billion); the Russian Federal Space Agency was allocated $5.6 billion; Japan's space agency's, JAXA's, funding was $2.03 billion; the China National Space Administration (CNSA) spending was $1.3 billion, and the Indian Space Research

Organization had a budget of $1.1 billion. This brings the total spending on the world space programme in 2014 to about $33.14 billion.

Numerous questions need to be asked: Is the money spent on the world space programme worth spending? And with what results? Could this money have been better spent here on Earth to improve human conditions? And more specifically, why is this money not being spent on exploring the depths of the oceans to discover the potentialities and resources that could be more easily and cheaply utilized to improve human conditions than to attempt exploring unknown outer space? What is the world's agenda behind the competition between powerful nations to explore the outer space?

Ocean exploration needs to be put on the high-priority agendas of governments and international organizations. The benefits that can be derived from exploring the ocean floor could yield far more results than those gained by exploring space. Apart from the vital role the oceans play in regulating weather and global climatic conditions, nearly 95% of deep ocean resources and treasures remain virtually unknown to humans, who live on land adjacent to the ocean's floor, which lies only three and half kilometres deep. (The average ocean depth is 12,080 feet, while the deepest point, the Challenger Deep, is 36,200 feet deep). The limited knowledge that we have of the 5% of the ocean we have explored has mainly been obtained from the shallower waters. Vast unknown resources lie deep in the ocean, including some of the richest fisheries, offshore energy sources, and mining sites. The deep ocean waters may contain mysteries of yet undiscovered biotic species that may hold clues to scientific and medical discoveries, and cures for crippling and terminal diseases.

Ocean exploration, therefore, should be given the attention it deserves as one of the top world priorities in research and scientific discovery. Doing so will enable the search for things that are yet unknown, unusual, and unexpected, which will advance human knowledge and add to the prosperity and future well-being of people here on earth.

Academic Research Writing

Sample Survey Form

Course Evaluation Survey Form

Thank you for participating in this course evaluation survey. Please provide your responses by ticking (√) the appropriate boxes below. (*Note on Ethical Conduct*: Your identity and the information you provide will remain strictly confidential and will be used only for the purposes of this survey.)

Your name:

Your department:

Specify the course(s) you have already attended:

Choose the best response for each of the questions and statements below.

1. Do you think the instructors delivered the course materials clearly?
   - ○ Strongly agree
   - ○ Agree
   - ○ Neutral
   - ○ Disagree
   - ○ Strongly disagree

2. I fully understand the course contents.
   - ○ Strongly agree
   - ○ Agree
   - ○ Neutral
   - ○ Disagree
   - ○ Strongly disagree

3. This course helped me improve my skills:
   - ○ Strongly agree
   - ○ Agree

399

- ○ Neutral
- ○ Disagree
- ○ Strongly disagree

4. This course was not a waste of time.
   - ○ Strongly agree
   - ○ Agree
   - ○ Neutral
   - ○ Disagree
   - ○ Strongly disagree

5. I find it easy to apply what I've learnt.
   - ○ Strongly agree
   - ○ Agree
   - ○ Neutral
   - ○ Disagree
   - ○ Strongly disagree

6. Did you find the course too difficult for the amount of material it covered?
   - ○ Too difficult
   - ○ Difficult
   - ○ Average
   - ○ Easy
   - ○ Too easy

7. Did you find this course long enough for the amount of material it covered?
   - ○ Too long
   - ○ Long
   - ○ Average
   - ○ Short
   - ○ Too short

8. Would you recommend this course to a co-worker or colleague?
   - ○ Very likely
   - ○ Likely
   - ○ Neutral
   - ○ Unlikely
   - ○ Very unlikely

9. How pleased were you with this training course?
   - ○ Very satisfied
   - ○ Satisfied
   - ○ Neutral
   - ○ Dissatisfied
   - ○ Very dissatisfied

10. Check some other courses you still need to attend:
    - ○ Reading skills
    - ○ Cultural diversity
    - ○ Business ethics
    - ○ Critical thinking
    - ○ Management information systems
    - ○ Communications skills

Please add any comments or suggestions you deem important.

Verification

Submit

Sample Reference Page in APA Style

American Psychological Association (2010). *Publication Manual of the American Psychological Association* (6th ed.). Washington, DC: American Psychological Association.

Bjork, R. A. (1989). "Retrieval inhibition as an adaptive mechanism in human memory", In H. L. Roediger and F. I. M. Craik (eds.), *Varieties of memory and consciousness* (pp. 309–30). Hillsdale, New Jersey: Erlbaum.

Fischer, K., Demetriou, A., and Dawson, T. L. (1992). *The Development of Mental Processing:*

Efficiency, Working Memory and Thinking. Boston: Blackwell Publishing.

Sternberg, R. J. (1993). *The psychologist's companion* (2nd ed.). Cambridge: Cambridge University Press.

ACADEMIC RESEARCH WRITING

Sample Reference Page in Harvard Style

Adair, J. (1988). *Effective Time Management: How to Save Time and Spend It Wisely.* London: Pan Books.

Barnes, R. (1995) *Successful Study for Degrees.* 2nd edition. London: Routledge.

Berkowitz, P. (1995). "Sussy's gravestone". Mark Twain Forum [Online]. 3 April. Available email: TWAIN-L@yorkvm2.bitnet.

Byrne, J. (1995) "Disabilities in tertiary education", in Rowan, L. and McNamee, J. (eds.), *Voices of a Margin.* Rockhampton: CQU Press.

Cumming, F. (1999) "Tax-free savings push". *Sunday Mail.* 4 April, p. 1.

Department for Education and Employment (DfEE) (2001). *Skills for life: The National Strategy for Improving Adult Literacy and Numeracy Skills.* Nottingham: DfEE Publications.

Hart, G., Albrecht, M., Bull, R., and Marshall, L. (1992). "Peer consultation: A professional development opportunity for nurses employed in rural settings". *In front Outback–Conference Proceedings.* Australian Rural Health Conference, Toowoomba. pp. 143–48.

McCarthy, P. and Hatcher, C. (1996). *Speaking Persuasively: Making the Most of Your Presentations.* Sydney: Allen and Unwin.

Muller, V. (1994). "Trapped in the body: Transsexualism, the law, sexual identity". *The Australian Feminist Law Journal* vol. 3. August, pp. 103–107.

Napier, A. (1993a). *Fatal Storm.* Sydney: Allen and Unwin.

Napier, A. (1993b) *Survival at Sea.* Sydney: Allen and Unwin.

Skargren, E. I., and Oberg, B. (1998). "Predictive factors for 1-year outcome of low-back and neck pain in patients treated in primary care: Comparison between the treatment strategies chiropractic and physiotherapy". *Pain* [Electronic], vol. 77, no. 2. pp. 201–8. Available: Elsevier/ScienceDirect/ O304-3959(98)00101-8 [8 February 1999].

The University Encyclopedia (1985). London: Roydon.

Young, C. (2001). *English Heritage Position Statement on the Valletta Convention* [Online]. Available: http://www.archaeol.freeuk.com/EHPostionStatement.htm [24 August 2001].

Whiteley, B. C. (1979). "Emotional Response", *Brain Talk* vol. 2, no. 12. pp. 234–35.

ACADEMIC RESEARCH WRITING

Sample list of works cited in MLA Style

Hymowirz, Kay S. "The Incredible Shrinking Father." *City Journal*, spring 2007. www.city-jounal.org/html/17_2_artificial_insemination.html.

Marcotty, Josephine, and Chen May Yee. "New World of fertility Medicine Is a Big-Money Marketplace." Seacostonline. com. 30 October 2007. www.seacostonline.com/article/20071030/PARENTS/71029007.

"Mother's Eggs Could Mean Daughter Gives Birth to Sibling." *Herald Scotland*. Herald and Times Group. 3 July 2007. www.heraldscotland.com/news/12775922.Mother_apos_s_eggs_could_mean_daughter_gives_birth_to_sibling/.

Samples of Graphics and Visuals

Different types of visuals and their uses

Tables

A table is an arrangement of data in rows and columns, or possibly in a more complex structure. Tables are widely used in communication, research, and data analysis. Tables appear in print media, handwritten notes, computer software, architectural ornamentation, traffic signs, and many other places. Moreover, tables differ significantly in variety, structure, flexibility, notation, representation, and use.

Simple tables

The following illustrates a simple table with three columns and seven rows. The first row is not counted, because it is used only to display the column names. This is called a "header row".

Age Table

First name	Last Name	Age
Huessin	Tunde	14
Amara	Dungus	25
Abdul Karim	Bin Adam	16
Biko	Mamako	22
Alfred	Wilde	22
Ibrahim	Yabagi	22
Aaqib	Hamoda	22
Tasneem	Farah	15
Sultan	Otaibi	11

Any simple table can be represented as a multidimensional table by normalizing the data values into ordered hierarchies.

Multidimensional tables

Faculty Information

Faculty ID	Faculty Name	Faculty Hire Date	Faculty Course Code
388	Dr. Sultana	11 March 2006	IT 202
437	Dr. Tunde	21 September 2011	MIS 301
802	Dr. Peterson	18 February 2012	ENG 205
916	Dr. Bubakar	28 August 2008	ME 401
			???
541	Dr. Ali	9 June 2014	

The table above is a multidimensional table that includes an insertion anomaly, illustrating the status of the new faculty member, Dr. Ali, who is assigned to teach at least one course. His details cannot be recorded in the main table. The information can be expressed in multiple rows. Each record contains a faculty member's ID, name, and the courses she or he teaches.

Multiplication tables

In multidimensional tables, each cell in the body of the table (and the value of that cell) relates to the values at the beginnings of the column (i.e., the header) and row (and other structures in more complex tables). This is an injective relation; each combination of the values of the header row and the header column is related to a unique cell in the table. For example,

- column 1 and row 1 will only correspond to cell (1,1);
- column 1 and row 2 will only correspond to cell (2, 1), etc.

The traditional rote learning of multiplication was based on memorization of columns in a table up to 12×12.

<u>Spreadsheets</u>

No	Name	Quiz 1	Mid-term	Quiz 2	Final	Grade
1	Marhoon, G.	7.5	17	8	33	B +
2	Ali, A.	9	18	7	32	B +
3	Sami, B.	8	16.5	6.5	38	B +
4	Hussein, K.	8.5	15	7.5	30	B
5	Fahad, J.	8.5	15.5	8	35	B +
6	Coni, S.	7	16	6.5	31	C +
7	Arnel, E.	8	18.5	9	29	B
8	Farah, M.	9	17	8	37.5	A
9	Alateef, F.	9.5	18	8	38	A +
10	Kahlid, M.	7	14	7.5	31	C

Figure 1: Students Exam Results

A spreadsheet consists of a table of cells arranged into rows and columns referred to by X.

Charts

A chart, also called a graph, is a graphical representation of data in which the data are represented by symbols, such as bars in a bar chart, lines in a line chart, or slices in a pie chart. A chart can represent tabular numeric data, functions, or qualitative structures, and it provides various types of information. Charts are often used to ease understanding of large quantities of data and the relationships between parts of the data. Charts can usually be read more quickly than the raw data.

Column chart/graph

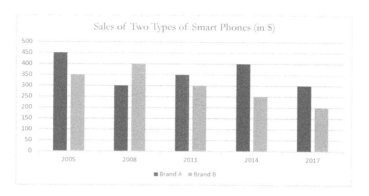

Bar chart or bar graph

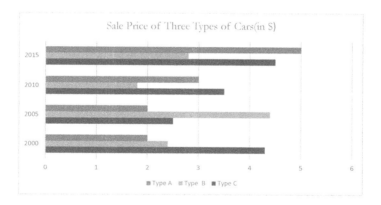

Both column and bar charts or graphs are charts or graphs that present categorical data with rectangular bars having heights or lengths proportional to the values that they represent. The bars can be plotted vertically or horizontally. A bar graph shows comparisons among discrete categories. One axis of the chart shows the specific categories being compared, and the other axis represents a measured value. Some bar graphs present bars clustered in groups of more than one, showing the values of more than one measured variable.

Line graph/chart

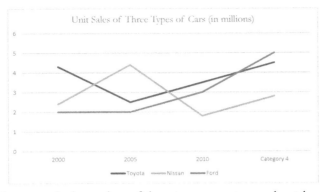

The above graph shows data of three items over intervals with upward and downward movements of lines.

A line chart, or line graph, is a type of chart which displays information as a series of data points called "markers" that are connected by straight line segments. It is a basic type of chart common in many fields. A line chart is often used to visualize a trend in data over intervals of time—a time series—thus the line is often drawn chronologically. In these cases, they are known as run charts.

Pie chart

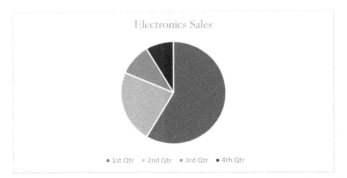

A pie chart (or a circle chart) is a circular statistical graphic which is divided into slices to illustrate numerical proportions. In a pie chart, the arc length of each slice is proportional to the quantity it represents. While it is named for its resemblance to a pie which has been sliced, there are variations on the way it is presented. The earliest known pie chart is generally credited to William Playfair's *Statistical Breviary* of 1801.

Pie charts are very widely used in the business world and the mass media. However, they have been criticized, and many experts recommend avoiding them, pointing out that research has shown it is difficult to compare different sections of a given pie chart, or to compare data across different pie charts. Pie charts can be replaced in most cases by other plots, such as the bar chart, box plot, or dot plot.

Flowchart

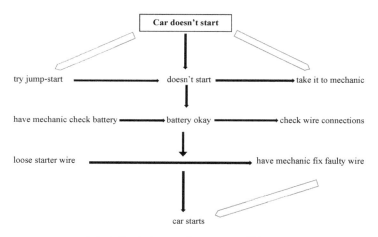

A simple flowchart representing a process of fixing a car.

A flowchart is a type of diagram that represents an algorithm, workflow, or process, showing the steps as boxes of various kinds and their order by connecting them with arrows. This diagrammatic representation illustrates a solution model to a given problem. Flowcharts are used in analysing, designing, documenting, or managing a process or programme in various fields.

Graphic Organizers

Venn diagram

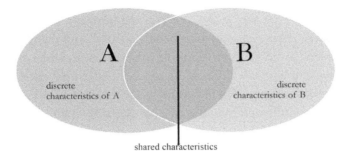

A Venn diagram is used to display information relating to two or more objects in overlapping circles or ovals. The peripheral information contained in each circle represents the discrete characteristics of that object, whereas the information contained inside the overlapping area represents shared characteristics common to all the items in the diagram.

Concept map

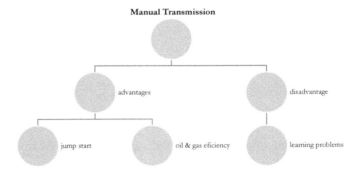

A concept map or conceptual diagram is a diagram that depicts suggested relationships between concepts. It is a graphical tool that instructional designers, engineers, technical writers, and others use to organize and structure knowledge.

Cause-and-effect chain

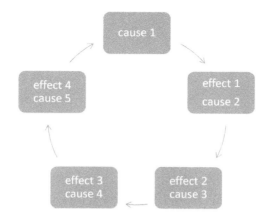

This graphic organizer helps in identifying, understanding, and remembering a cause leading to an effect, which itself becomes a cause, leading to another effect, and so the chain goes in a circle—thus the term "causal chain".

Hierarchy chart

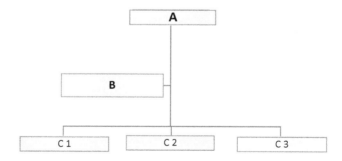

This graphic organizer is useful in concept-based instruction. It allows one to see the big picture—the main concept at the top—as well as the main topics and supporting details branching underneath. It helps to see the relationships between the different levels of ideas at a glance.

Maps

World Map 1689, Amsterdam (Wikipedia)

A map is a symbolic depiction emphasizing relationships between elements of a space, such as objects, regions, or themes. Many maps are static, fixed to paper or some other durable medium, while others are dynamic or interactive. Although most commonly used to depict geography, maps may represent any space, real or imagined, without regard to context or scale, such as in brain mapping, DNA mapping, and computer network topology mapping. The space being mapped may be two dimensional, such as the surface of the earth; three dimensional, such as the interior of the earth; or even more abstract spaces of any dimension, such as those that arise in modelling phenomena, having many independent variables.

APPENDIX 1

List of Commonly Misused English Words

This list of commonly misused English words is not exhaustive and includes only words with uses that do not follow standard usage and those that are used mistakenly for meanings other than their actual linguistic or semantic meanings.

a lot and **allot:** "A lot" (adv. of quantity) means "many"; "allot" (trans. verb) means "to distribute something".

accept and **except:** While they sound similar (or even identical), "except" is a preposition that means "apart from", while "accept" is a verb that means "agree with".

affect and **effect:** The verb "affect" means "to influence something", but the noun effect means "the result of". "Effect" can also be a verb that means "to cause [something] to be", while "affect" as a noun has technical meanings in psychology and music.

allusion, hallucination, and **illusion:** An allusion is an indirect or metaphorical reference to something, an illusion is a false picture of something that is there, and a hallucination is the seeing of something that is not there.

alternately and **alternatively:** "Alternately" is an adverb that means "in turn; one after the other". "Alternatively" is an adverb that means "on the other hand; one or the other".

ascent and **assent. ascent** and **assent:** To assent is to agree. To ascend means to go up or advance from an original position.

assure, ensure, and **insure:** In American English, to assure is purely to intend to give the listener confidence, to ensure is to make certain of, and to insure is to purchase insurance.

bacteria, criteria, media, and **phenomena:** Are of these words are plurals and should be used as such, regardless of their widespread misuse.

barter, haggle and **banter:** To barter is to exchange goods rather than carrying out commercial transactions using money. To haggle is to negotiate a price. "Banter" is a noun meaning "a friendly or good-natured exchange of remarks".

born and **borne:** "Born" refers to a living creature entering the world through the birthing process. "Borne" is a past tense form of "bear", which means "to carry or realize something".

breath and **breathe:** A breath (noun) is the air that is inhaled or exhaled from the lungs. To breathe (verb) is to engage in the act of inhaling or exhaling.

buy and **by**

can't and **cant:** "Can't" is a contraction of "cannot"; "cant" has a number of different meanings, including "a slope or slant" and "a kind of slang or jargon spoken by a particular group of people".

canvas and **canvass:** Canvas is a type of fabric known for being tough and strong. Canvassing is a way to try to get people's support or find out where their support lies.

complementary and **complimentary**

complacency and **complaisance:** "Complacency" means "self-satisfaction", especially when accompanied by unawareness of actual dangers or deficiencies. "Complaisance" means "the willingness to comply with the wishes of others".

copy write and **copyright**

decimate and **devastate**

defuse and **diffuse:** To defuse is to remove the fuse from a bomb or, in general, to render a situation less dangerous, whereas to diffuse is to disperse randomly. Diffuse can also be used as an adjective, meaning "not concentrated".

desert and **dessert:** A desert is a barren or uninhabited place; an older meaning of the word is "what one deserves", as in the idiom "just deserts." A dessert is the last course of a meal.

disassemble and **dissemble:** To disassemble is to dismantle (e.g., to take a machine code program apart to see how it works); to dissemble is to tell lies.

disburse and **disperse:** "Disburse" means "to give out", especially money. "Disperse" means "to scatter".

discreet and **discrete:** "Discreet" means "circumspect". "Discrete" means "having separate parts", as opposed to "contiguous".

disinterested and **uninterested:** To be disinterested in something is to not be biased about something (e.g., to have no personal stake in a particular side of an issue). To be uninterested is to not be interested in or intrigued by something.

economic and **economical:** "Economic" means "having to do with the economy". "Economical" means "financially prudent; frugal" and also, figuratively, "sparing use" (of time, language, etc.)

either and **neither:** "Neither" is used to agree with a negative statement. "Either" indicates a similarity

emigration and **immigration:** Emigration is the process of leaving a country; immigration is the process of arriving in a country—in both cases, indefinitely.

eminent, immanent, imminent, and **preeminent:** "Eminent", originally meaning "emerging", means "illustrious or highly-regarded". "Preeminent" means "most highly regarded". "Imminent" means "about to occur". "Immanent" (less common than the other two, and often theological) means "indwelling; pervading".

exacerbate and **exasperate:** "Exacerbate" means "to make worse". "Exasperate" means "to exhaust"—usually someone's patience.

forego and **forgo:** "Forego" means "to go before". "Forgo" means "to give up or do without".

guarantee and **guaranty**

Hangar, hanger, and **hunger**

hay and **straw:** Hay is animal fodder made by cutting and drying a grassy plant. Straw is the dry stalk of a cereal plant (e.g., barley, oats, rice, or rye) after the grain or seed has been removed; it is used to line an animal's stall or for insulation.

hear and **here:** To hear is to detect a sound with one's ears. "Here" refers to one's immediate location.

hoard and **horde:** A hoard is a store or accumulation of things. A horde is a large group of people.

it's and **its:** "It's" is a contraction that replaces "it is" or "it has" (see "Apostrophe"). "Its" is the possessive determiner corresponding to it, meaning "belonging to it".

isle and **aisle:** An isle is an island. An aisle is a corridor through which one may pass from one place to another.

lay (lay, laid, laid, laying, lays) and **lie** (lie, lay, lain, lying, lies): These terms are often used synonymously. "Lay" is a transitive verb, meaning that it takes an object. To lay something is to place it.

loathe and **loath** or **loth:** "Loathe" is a verb meaning "to strongly dislike", and "loath" (or "loth") is an adjective meaning "unwilling" or "reluctant".

lose and **loose:** "Lose" can mean "fail to win", "misplace", or "cease to be in possession of". "Loose" can mean the opposite of "tight" or the opposite of "tighten". "Lose" is often misspelt as "loose", likely because "lose" has an irregular rhyme for the way it is spelt.

me, myself, and **I:** In a traditional prescriptive grammar, "I" is used only as a subject, "me" only as an object, and "myself" only as a reflexive object—that is to say, when the subject is "I" and the object would otherwise be "me". The word "myself" is often used incorrectly.

methodology: Methodology is the study or discussion of method. It is commonly and incorrectly used as a pretentious synonym for "method".

past and **passed:** "Past" refers to events that have previously occurred, while "passed" is the past tense of "to pass", whether in a congressional action or a physical occurrence.

perpetrate and **perpetuate:** To perpetrate something is to commit it, while to perpetuate something is to cause it to continue or to keep happening.

perspective and **prospective:** Perspective is a view with correct visual angles—for example, parallel railway tracks converging in the distance. "Prospective" is and adjective that refers to a future possibility or expectation.

pored and **poured:** The phrase "pored over" means "studied an item intently". However, sometimes seen incorrectly in its place is "poured over", which would correctly describe the act of tipping a substance onto something.

practice and **practise:** In most English dialects, "practice" is the noun and "practise" is the verb, although this distinction is not maintained in American English, which uses "practice" for both.

prescribe and **proscribe:** To prescribe something is to command or recommend it. To proscribe somebody or something is to outlaw him, her, or it.

rain, **reign,** and **rein:** A reign is the rule of a monarch. Reins are the straps used to control the movements of an animal (typically a horse). Thus, to "take the reins" means to assume control, and to have "free rein" means to be free of constraints.

regime, **regimen** and **regiment:** A regimen is a system of order, and the term may often refer to the systematic dosing of medication. A regiment is a military unit.

sensual and **sensuous:** Both words mean "to do with the senses". "Sensual" is more often applied to a pleasure or experience or to a person's character; "sensuous", to someone or something of enticing appearance.

suit and **suite:** "*Suit*" is a noun that refers to an article of clothing; it is also a verb that means "to make or be appropriate". "Suite" is a noun that means "a set of things forming a series or set".

their, there, they're, and **there're:** "There" refers to the location of something. "Their" means "belonging to them". They're is a contraction of "they are". "There're" is a contraction of "there are".

throe and **throw:** A throe is a spasm. "Throw" means "to pass an object through the air".

to and **too:** "Too" means "in excess" or "also". "To" is a preposition or is a part of an infinitive. At the end of a sentence, "to" may also refer to a dropped verb in the infinitive form.

who's and **whose:** "Whose" is a possessive interrogative ("Whose is this?") or a relative pronoun ("The people whose house you admired"); "who's" is a contraction for "who is" or "who has".

APPENDIX 2

List of Common Misspellings

Below is a list of the most common misspellings in English.

accidentaly	comming	enviroment	irresistable	sieze
accomodate	consious	existance	knowlege	seperate
acheive	critisize	feiry	later / latter	sheferd
acros	curiousity	finaly	led /lead	seige
agressive	deicive	foriegn	lose / loose	similer
apearance	definately	formarly	mariage	supercede
apparantly	discribe	freind	millenium, millenia	tommorrow
arguement	dispise	happend	mischeif	to/ too
assasination	devlop	harrassment	murmor	tounge
begining	dilema	humorus	neccessary	tragdey
beleive / belive	disapoint	hypocricy	noticable	truely
benifit	dissapear	idiosyncracy	occured	undoutedly
buisness	duel / dual	immediatly	paralel	untill
chalenge	ecstacy	incidentaly	peice	whereever
colleque	embarras	independant		

423

BIBLIOGRAPHY

Adams, George (2008). *Plagiarism in Higher Education Institutions: a Study on Students' Ethical Behavior at College and Future Ethical Behavior in the Workplace.*, Oxford: Oxford University Press.

Addressing the Limitations)pamphlet, 2010). Writing Tutorial Services, Indiana University–Bloomington., Centre for Innovative Teaching and Learning, Wells Library Learning Commons. Last updated 12 October 2010.

Adler, Patricia A., and Peter Adler (1994). "Observation Techniques", in Norman K. Denzin and Yvonna S. Lincoln (eds.). *Handbook of Qualitative Research.* Thousand Oaks, California: Sage, pp: 377–92.

Algis, Uzdavinys (2003). "Approach to Philosophy, Theology and Metaphysics: Frithjof Schuon and Neo-Platonic Tradition", in *Dialogue and Universalism* vol. 1, no. 2, pp. 139–47. *EBSCOCompleteFiles/PhilosophyTheologyandMetaphysics.pdf.*

American Psychological Association (2010). *The Publication Manual.* 6th ed. Washington, DC: American Psychological Association. ISBN-10: 1-4338-0559__6.

Angeli, E., J. Wagner, E. Lawrick, K. Moore, M. Anderson, L. Soderlund, and A. Brizee (2010). *"General format".* Retrieved from *http://owl.english.purdue.edu/owl/resource/560/01/.*

Anson, Chris M., and Robert A. Schwegler (2011). *The Longman Handbook for Writers and Readers.* 6th ed. Boston: Longman. ISBN 978-0-2005-74199-1.

Ascher, Allen (2006). *Think about Editing: An ESL Guide for the Harbrace Handbooks.* Boston, Wadsworth Cengage Learning.

Bagraim, Jeffrey, Suki Goodman, and Stephanie Pulker (2014). "Understanding Dishonest Academic Behaviour amongst Business Students__the Business Leaders of the Future". *Industry & Higher Education* vol. 28, no. 5, Oct. 2014, pp. 331–340. ResearchGate, *DOI: 10.5367/ihe.2014.0222.*

Bailey, Stephen (2015). *Academic Writing: a Handbook for International Students.* 4th ed. Oxford: Routledge.

Bairstow, Jeffrey (2012). "Good Writing is Clear Thinking Made Visible". *Laser Focus World 76. EBSCOFiles/ GoodWritingClearThinkingMadeVisible.pdf.*

Bălcescu, Nicolae (2013). "Writing Well__A Must in the Military Profession". Marioara PATEŞAN. *Social-Behavioral Sciences,* pp. 60–66. Revista Academemie Fortelor Terestre No. 1 (69), 2013; *EBSCOFiles/WRITINGWELLAMUST.pdf.*

Basturkme, Helen, Martin East, and John Bitchener (2014). "Supervisors' on-Script Feedback Comments on Drafts of Dissertations: Socializing Students into the Academic Discourse Community". *Teaching in Higher Education* vol. 19, no. 4, pp. 432–45. Routledge, Francis and Taylor Group. *http://dx.doi.org/10.1080/ 13562517.2012.752728.*

Bello, Iria (2016). Cognitive Implications of Nominalizations in the Advancement of Scientific Discourse, *International Journal of English Studies (IJES)* vol. 16, no. 2, pp. 1–23. *Accessed 28th Jan 2017* http://revistas.um.es/ijes. Accepted 10 August 2016. Servicio de Publicaciones, Universidad de Murcia, *IJES,* Print ISSN: 1578-7044. Online ISSN: 1989-6131.

BetterEvaluation. "Analyze Data". Accessed 7 December 2017. http:// betterevaluation.org/plan/describe/look_for_patterns.

_____ "Combine Qualitative and Quantitative Data". Accessed 7 December 2017. http://www.betterevaluation.org/en/plan/describe/ combining_qualitative_and_quantitative_*data*.

Blum, Christopher O. (2013). *A Fruitful Restraint: The Perennial Relevance of the Virtue of Studiousness.* Denver, Colorado. Augustine Institute. EBESCOCompleteFiles/ AFruitfulRestraintThePerennialRelevance.pdf.

Boyce, C., and P. Neale (2006). "Conducting in-Depth Interviews: A Guide for Designing and Conducting In-Depth Interviews". Pathfinder International Tool Series. *http://www2.pathfinder.org/site/ DocServer/m_e_tool_series_indepth_interviews.pdf*

Brew, Angela (2006). *Research and Teaching: Beyond the Divide.* Palgrave Publishing.

Brizee, Allen (2003). "Introductions, Body Paragraphs, and Conclusions for an Argument Paper". The Purdue OWL, Purdue University Writing Lab. Last updated 14 October 2003. https://owl. english.purdue.edu/owl/owlprint/724/.

_____ (2013). "Body Paragraphs: Moving from General to Specific Information", The Purdue OWL, Purdue University Writing Lab. Last updated 25 February 2013. https://owl.english.purdue.edu/owl/ resource/724/02/.

Brown, Gavin T. L., and Jennifer C. Marshall (2012). "The Impact of Training Students how to Write Introductions for Academic Essays: an Exploratory, Longitudinal Study". *Assessment and Evaluation in Higher Education* vol. 37, no. 6, September 2013, pp. 653–70.

Bryman, A., and Bell, E. (2007). *Business Research Methods.* 2nd edition. Oxford University Press.

Butler, Eugenia, Mary Ann Hickman, Patricia J. McAlexander, and Overby Lalla (1995). *Correct Writing.* 6th ed. Lexington, Massachusetts: Heath and Co.

Campbell, Anthony (2000). Review of *Style* by F. L. Lucas. EBSCOhost, accessed 2 January 2017. http://www.acampbell.org. uk/bookreviews/r/lucas.html.

Campion, M. A., J. E. Campion, and J. P. Hudson Jr. (1994). "Structured Interviewing: A Note on Incremental Validity and Alternative Question Types". *Journal of Applied Psychology* 79, pp. 998–1002.

Cargill, Margaret, and Patrick O'Connor (2009). *Writing Scientific Research Articles.* Wiley-Blackwell. ISBN 978-1-4051-8619-3.

Carlson, John W. (2012). *Words of Wisdom: A Philosophical Dictionary for the Perennial Tradition.* University of Notre Dame Press. *EBESCOCompleteFiles/WordsofWisdomAPhilosophical.pdf.*

Carr, David (1998). "Traditionalism and Progressivism: a Perennial Problematic of Educational Theory and Policy". *Westminster Studies in Education* vol. 21, pp. 47–55. 0140-6728/98/010047-0'J@ 1998 Catfax Publishing Ltd.

Cavaliere, Frank, J., Toni P. Mulvaney, and Marleen R. Swerdlow (2010). "Teaching Business Ethics after the Financial Meltdown: Is It Time for Ethics with a Sermon?" *Department of Accounting & Business Law Lamar University, Beaumont, Texas, Education* vol. 131, no. 1, pp. 3–17.

Charlton, Claire (2006). "Just a Click Away: Online Writing Labs at Universities Offer Free Help with Grammar, Style, Editing and Other Issues". Charlton, Claire (Kalmbach Publishing), 00439517, Sep 2006. Database: Academic Search Complete. http://search. ebscohost.com/?authtype=cookie,ip,uid.

Chernin, Eli (1988). "'The Harvard System': a Mystery Dispelled" *British Medical Journal* vol. 297, no. 22, October 1988.

Child, Robert (1999). "Editing and Proofreading Strategies for Specific Sentence-Level Errors". Purdue University. Revised by Judith Kilborn for the Write Place, St. Cloud State University. Last updated 26 March 1999. Accessed 10 November 2016.

Citation Producer (2012). (Blog). "Understanding and Writing in the MLA Format Style". Accessed 22 February 2017. *http://citationproducer.com/article/understanding-and-writing-in-the-mla-format-style/*

Clarke, Matthew, and Alex Moore (2013). "Professional Standards, Teacher Identities and an Ethics of Singularity". *Cambridge Journal of Education* vol. 43, no. 4, pp. 487–500.

Cogdill, Sharon, and Judith Kilborn (2004). "Comma Splices, Fused Sentences, and Run-ons". The Write Place. St. Cloud State University. Last updated 11 November 2004. Accessed 10 November 2016.

Colorado State University: the Writing Studio (2014). "Tips for Writing a Good Conclusion". http://writing.colostate.edu/files/classes/7998/file_b4a54838- fc40-1691-86bb6f50fa6b3141.pdf.

Connaway, L. S., and R. P. Powell (2010). "Basic Research Methods for Librarians". ABCCLIO.

Council of Writing Program Administrators (2003). *Defining and Avoiding Plagiarism: the WPA Statement on Best Practices.* January 2003. Accessed 21 November 2016. http://wpacouncil.org/files/wpa-plagiarism-statement.pdf. "Best Book Award". (Blog post). Retrieved from http://wpacouncil.org/node/7019.

_____ (2014).

Dafermos, M. (2016). "Critical Reflection on the Reception of Vygotsky's Theory on the International Academic Communities". *Cultural-Historical Psychology* vol. 12, no. 3, pp. 27–46.

Dale, Terry (2004). *An Introduction to Academic Discourse.* 3rd ed. Dhahran, Saudi Arabia: King Fahad University for Petroleum and Minerals.

Council of Writing Program Administrators (2003). *Defining and Avoiding Plagiarism: the WPA Statement on Best Practices.* January 2003. Accessed 21 November 2016. http://wpacouncil.org/files/wpa-plagiarism-statement.pdf.

Denscombe, M. (2004). *The Good Research Guide for Small-scale Social Research.* 2nd ed. Open University Press.

Denzin, Norman K., and Yvonna S. Lincoln, eds. (1994). *Handbook of Qualitative Research.* 2nd ed. Thousand Oaks, California: Sage.

DeWalt, Kathleen M., and Billie R. DeWalt (2002). *Participant Observation: a Guide for Fieldworkers.* Walnut Creek, California: AltaMira Press.

Dobson, Ian R. (2010). Review of *Academic Writing and Publishing: a Practical Handbook,* by James Hartley, and *Guide to Publishing a Scientific Paper,* by Ann M. Körner. *Journal of Higher Education Policy and Management.* February 2010, vol. 32, no. 1, pp. 111–113.

Donald L. McCabe, Linda Klebe Treviño, and Kenneth D. Butterfield (2001). "Cheating in Academic Institutions: A Decade of Research" in *ETHICS and BEHAVIOR* vol. 11, no. 3, pp. 219–32. Accessed 20 August 2015.

Driscoll, Dana Lynn (2013). "Parallel Structure", the Writing Lab and the OWL at Purdue and Purdue University. Last edited 22 March 2013. *https://owl.english.purdue.edu/owl/resource/623/01/.*

_____, and Allen Brizee (2010). "What is Primary Research and How Do I Get Started?". The Writing Lab & the OWL at Purdue and Purdue University. Last updated 17 April 2010. Accessed 18 November 2016.

_____ (2012). "Appropriate Language: Overview", The Writing Lab and the OWL at Purdue and Purdue University. Last updated 4 June 2012. Accessed 27 October 2016. *https://owl.english.purdue.edu/writinglab/*

_____ (2013). "Evaluating Sources: Overview". The Writing Lab and the OWL at Purdue and Purdue University. Accessed 19 November 2016.

D'Youville College Learning Center (2012). "Prepositions and Prepositional Phrases." The Purdue OWL, Purdue University Writing Lab *https://owl.english.purdue.edu/writinglab/*

Encyclopedia Britannica (2017). "Education and Plato's Parable of the Cave". Originally appeared in *Journal of Education* vol. 178, no. 3, 1996. (All original content on this website is licensed under a Creative Commons License). file/EncyclopediaBritannicaBritannica.com.html.

Escalas, Maggie (1999). *"Words That Confuse"*. The Write Place, St. Cloud State University. Last updated 5 October 1999. Accessed 10 November 2016.

_____ (2000). "Summary of Verb Tenses". The Write Place. St. Cloud State University. Last Updated 22 September 2000.

Foddy, Willam (1993). *Constructing Questions for Interviews*. Cambridge University Press.

Foster, Stuart, J. (1998). "Politics, Parallels, and Perennial Curriculum Questions: the Battle over School History in England and the United

States". *The Curriculum Journal* vol. 9, no. 2. Summer 1998, pp. 153–64. ISSN 09585176.

Fowler, H. W. (1965). *Modern English Usage*, 2nd ed. Revised by Ernest Dowers. Oxford University Press.

_____, and F. Fowler (1906). *The King's English*. Oxford: Clarendon Press.

Freedman, Leora, and Jerry Plotnick (n.d.). "Introductions and Conclusions". University College Writing Centre, University of Toronto. Accessed 15 March 2017. http://advice.writing.utoronto. ca/wp-content/uploads/sites/2/intros-and-conclusions.pdf.

Gal, Yoav (2015). "Knowledge Bias: Perceptions of Copying among Lecturers and Students of Education. Case Study of a Teaching College". https://www.researchgate.net/publication/275828944_ Knowledge_Bias_Perceptions_of_ Copying_among_Lecturers_ and_Students_of_Education_Case_Study_of_a_Teaching_college.

Galvan, Jose L. (1999). *Writing Literature Reviews: A Guide for Students of the Social and Behavioral Sciences*. Los Angeles: Pyrczak Publishing.

Geography Notes "Data Collection, Processing, and Analysis. Local Area Planning", Geography Notes (Web page). Accessed December 7 2017. http://www.nios.ac.in/media/documents/316courseE/E-JHA-31-10A.pdf.

George, Bill (2003). *Authentic Leadership: Rediscovering the Secrets to Creating Lasting Value*. John Wiley & Sons.

Gibaldi, Joseph (2003). Review of *MLA Handbook for Writers of Research Papers*. 6th ed. *Journal of Scholarly Publishing*, Vol. 57, No.2, pp. 179–83.

Gold, Raymond L. (1958). "Roles in Sociological Field Observations". *Social Forces* vol. 36, pp. 217–23.

Gomez, Heidi (2005). *Understanding and Decoding URLs*. (Document written for the Write Place, St. Cloud State University). Last updated 12 January 2005.

Hansen, William, et al. (2016). "Theory of Moral Development of Business Students: Case Studies in Brazil, North America and Morocco". *Academy of Management Learning and Education*, June 2016. *https://www.researchgate.net/publication/304009529. DOI: 10.5465/amle.2014.0312.*

Harding, Trevor S., Donald D. Carpenter, Cynthia J. Finelli, and Honor J. Passow (2004). "Does Academic Dishonesty Relate to Unethical Behavior in Professional Practice? An Explanatory Study". *SciEng Ethics* vol. 10, no. 2, April 2004, pp. 311–24. Accessed 16 August 2015. https://www.ncbi.nlm.nih.gov/pubmed/15152857.

Hartley, James (2008). *Academic Writing and Publishing: A Practical Guide*. New York: Routledge.

Harvard Formatting and Style Guide: Cover Page (n. d.). Harvard Guide.pdf https://www.uvocorp.com/dl/Harvard%20Guide.pdf, Retrieved 22 January 2017.

Harvard Writing Style Format (n.d.). EBSCOhost Complete. Retrieved 23 January 2017. http://www00.unibg.it/dati/corsi/8916/37567Harvard%20Style%20of%20Writing%20Format.pdf

Herbert, J. (1999). "Participant Observation in the Era of 'Ethnography'". *Journal of Contemporary Ethnography* vol. 28, no. 5, 540–48. http://www.betterevaluation.org/en/plan/describe/combining_qualitative_and_quantitative_data.

Hoffman, Rachel M. (2010). "Trustworthiness, Credibility, and Soundness: A Vision for Research". Editorial. *Journal of Mental Health Counseling* vol. 32, no. 4. October 2010, pp. 283–87.

Holowchak, M. (2013). "The Paradox of Public Service: Jefferson, Education, and the Problem of Plato's Cave". *Studies in Philosophy and Education* vol. 32, no. 1, pp. 73–86.

Howard, Rebecca Moore, and Laura J. Davies (2009). "Plagiarism in the Internet Age". *Literacy* vol. 66, no. 6, pp. 64–67.

Ibn Rajab al-Hanbali (736–795). Selections from Ibn Rajab al-Hanbali's Essay on the Hadith: "Scholars are Heirs of the Prophets". *SelectionsfromIbnRajabal-Hanabali'sstrongTheHeirsoftheProphet-strong.htm#virtue.*

Introduction to Harvard Referencing (n.d). EBSCOhost Login. Retrieved 17 September 2016. (CiteThisForMe web document). http://www.citethisforme.com/harvardreferencing.

Jackson, S. (2011). *Research Methods and Statistics: A Critical Approach.* 4th ed. Cengage Learning.

Jacobs, G., and C. Rodgers (1999). "Treacherous allies: Foreign Language Grammar Checkers". *CALICO Journal* vol. 16, no. 4, pp. 509–530.

Kanazawa, Satoshi (2010). "Why Liberals Are More Intelligent Than Conservatives". The Scientific Fundamentalist. Published 21 March 2010. Appeared in *Psychology Today.* Accessed 22 April 2013.

Kawulich, Barbara B. (2005). "Participant Observation as a Data Collection Method" *Forum Qualitative Sozialforschung / Forum: Qualitative Social Research* vol. 6, no. 2. http://nbn-resolving.de/urn:nbn:de:0114-fqs0502430.

Keats, John (2012) "Ode to a Nightingale" in *Romanticism: An Anthology*. 4th ed. Edited by Duncan Wu. Chickester, West Sussex: John Wiley & Sons, pp. 1464–66.

Kilborn, Judith (2004a). "Writing Abstracts". Written for the Writing Lab at Purdue University, and revised for LEO and the Write Place, St. Cloud State University.

_____ (2004b). "Avoiding Comma Splices, Fused Sentences, and Run-Ons". The Write Place, St. Cloud State University. Last updated 15 November 2004. http://leo.stcloudstate.edu/punct/avcsfsro.html.

_____ (2005). "Assessing the Credibility of Online Sources." Written for the Write Place and LEO, St. Cloud State University. Updated 7 January 2005.

Kirk, Elizabeth (1996). "Understanding and Decoding URLs" http://milton.mse.jhu.edu:8001/research/education/url.html. Updated 12 January 2005 by Heidi Gomez and Judith Kilborn for the Write Place, St. Cloud State University. http://leo.stcloudstate.edu/research/readingurls.html / leolink@stcloudstate.edu.

Koran, surah al-Alaq [the Clot] 96, verses 1–5.

Kvale, Steinar (1996). *Interviews: An Introduction to Qualitative Research Interviewing.* Sage Publications.

Lane, Janet, and Ellen Lange (2011). *Writing Clearly: Grammar for Editing.* 3rd ed. Boston: Heinle ELT.

Larson, Kelly A. (2004). "APA Documentation: Name and Year". The Purdue OWL, Purdue University Writing Lab. Updated 16 March 2004 by Judith Kilborn.

_____ (2004). "Fused Sentences". The Write Place, St. Cloud State University. Last updated 11 November 2004. Accessed 10 November 2016.

_____ (2004). "Using Paraphrases". Written for the Write Place, St. Cloud State University. Last updated 5 March 2004.

Lawrence, Joshua (2006). "Perennial Themes in Education". *Journal of Education* vol. 186, no. 1, pp. 87–95.

Leahy, Robert L. (2005). Review of *Authentic Happiness: Using the New Positive Psychology to Realize Your Potential for Lasting Fulfillment* by Martin E. P. Seligman. *Cognitive Behavioral Therapy Book Reviews* vol. 1, no. 8. http://www.CognitiveTherapyAssociation.org/cbtbr.aspx.

Leddy, Chuck (2007). "How to Be Your Own Editor: Reviews of Books of Kalmbach Publishing Co. **Database:** Academic Search Complete, http://search.ebscohost.com/?authtype=cookie,ip,uid

Levin, P. (2004). *Academic Essay Writing.* Booklet sponsored by the Australian Centre for Indigenous Knowledge and Education; Charles Darwin University.

_____ (2004). *Write Great Essays! Reading and Essay Writing for Undergraduates.* London: Open University Press.

Literary Devices (2016). "Definition and Examples of Literary Terms". (Blog post). Accessed 11 October 2016. *https://literarydevices.net/.*

Littlefield (2010). *Ethical Dilemmas in Education: Standing up for Honesty and Integrity.* ISBN-13: 978-157-88-6783-7.

Livengood, Stephanie Plank (1997). "An Evaluation Instrument of Internet Websites" (master's degree dissertation). Accessed 27 March 2017. https://ia601308.us.archive.org/7/items/ERIC_ED413899/ ERIC_ED413899.pdf.

Lourev, Jessica (2000). *"Punctuating Quotations"*. Written for the Write Place, St. Cloud State University. http://leo.stcloudstate.edu/research/puncquote.html.

Lucas, F. L. (1955). *Style.* 2nd ed. Rev. 1962. Cassell, London: Pan Books.

_____ (1968). "On the Fascination of Style". *Holiday,* March 1960. Reprinted in *The Odyssey Reader: Ideas and Style,* 1968, and in *Readings for Writers,* edited by Jo Ray McCuen and Anthony C. Winkler (2009). Accessed 2 January 2017. http://www.mrbauld.com/stylelc.html.

Marchant, Becky (2000). "Common Causes of Sentence Fragments". Revised by Jill Cadwell and Donella Westphal. Last updated 18 August 2000. http://leo.stcloudstate.edu/punct/fragmentcauses.html.

_____ (2000). "Parallelism". The Write Place, St. Cloud State University. Last updated 27 June 2000. Accessed 10 November 2016. http://leo.stcloudstate.edu/grammar/parallelism.html.

Marcia S. Freeman (2003). *Building a Writing Community: A Practical Guide.* Maupin House.

Marshall, Anne, and Batten, Suzanne (2004). "Researching Across Cultures: Issues of Ethics and Power". *Forum Qualitative Sozialforschung / Forum: Qualitative Social Research* vol. 5, no. 3. http://www.qualitativeresearch.net/fqs-texte/3-04/04-3-39-e.htm.

Marshall, Catherine, and Gretchen B. Rossman (1995). *Designing Qualitative Research.* Newbury Park, California: Sage.

Martin, Brian (1992). "Plagiarism by University Students: the Problem and Some Proposals". Published in *Tertangala* (a publication of the University of Wollongong Students' Representative Council). 20 July–3 August 1992, p. 20. DOI: I:\Philosophy of Education\ Plagiarism by university students the problem and proposals.mht.

Merriam, Sharan B. (1988). *Case Study Research in Education: A Qualitative Approach.* San Francisco: Jossey-Bass Publishers.

Mike, Grace Marie (2014). "Literature Reviews". The Writing Lab and The OWL at Purdue and Purdue University. Last updated on June 2014.

Minear, Richard H. (2004). "E. B. White Takes His Leave, or Does He? *The Elements of Style,* (5th Edn. 1918-2000)". *The Massachusetts Review*, pp. 51–71.

Miranda, Gina de (2014). Grammar Checkers (Blog post). http://www.editorsoftware.com/wordpress/does-grammar-checkers-work.

Modern Language Association. (n.d.)"MLA Style". *https://www.mla.org/MLA-Style*

Modern Language Association of America (2016). "Formatting a Research Paper". MLA Style Center. Retrieved 22 January 2017. https://MLA%20Style%20Center.htm.

_____ (2016). "Formatting a Research Paper/ Understanding and Writing in MLA Format Style / MLA Works Cited: the Guidelines". Accessed 24 March 2017. http://citationproducer.com/article/mla-works-cited-the-guidelines/.

_____ (2016). "What's New in the Eighth Edition". Accessed 21 January 2017. https://style.mla.org/.

_____ (2016). "In-Text Citations". The MLA Style Center. Accessed 20 January 2017. https://style.mla.org/.

_____ (2016). "Works Cited: A Quick Guide". Accessed 20 January 2017. https://style.mla.org/.

Mohammad, Adam Azzain (2008). *Scientific Research Methods in Social Sciences*. Khartoum: Public Administration and Federalism Studies Institute, University of Khartoum.

Monippally, Mathukutty M., and Badrinarayan Shankar Pawar (2010). *Academic Writing: a Guide for Management Students and Researchers*. California: Sage Publications. ISBN: 978-81-321-0441-4 (PB).

Murray, Rowena, and Sarah Moore (2006). *The Handbook of Academic Writing: A Fresh Approach*. New York: Open University Press.

Nesbitt-Johnston Writing Centre (2014). "Conclusions". The Trustees of Hamilton College, Hamilton College, Clinton, New York. Accessed 14 November 2016. *https://www.hamilton.edu/documents/Conclusions.pdf*

Nonis, Sarath A., and Cathy Owens Swift (2001). "An Examination of the Relationship between Academic Dishonesty and Workplace Dishonesty: A Multi-campus Investigation". *Journal of Education for Business* vol. 77, no. 2, pp. 69–77. ResearchGate. Accessed 21 April 2016. DOI: 10.1080/08832320109599052.

Ojogwu, C. N. (2008). "Ethical Crisis in the Nigerian Education System: A Challenge to Educational Administrators and Parents". *College Student Journal* vol. 42, no. 2.

Oliveira, Renato José (n.d). "Plato and Philosophy of Education." Universidade Federal do Rio de Janeiro. In *Stanford Encyclopedia of Philosophy of Education*. https://plato.stanford.edu/entries/education-philosophy/.

Oxford University Press (2016). "Common Misspellings". Accessed 10 November 2016. https://en.oxforddictionaries.com/spelling/common-misspellings.

_____ (2017a). "Punctuation". Accessed 20 February 2017. https://en.oxforddictionaries.com/theoxford-english-corpus// https://en.oxforddictionaries.com/punctuation.

_____ (2017b). "The Corpus and Oxford Dictionaries" Accessed 20 February 2017. https://en.oxforddictionaries.com/the-oxford-english-corpus.

Paiz, Joshua M., Elizabeth Angeli, Jodi Wagner, Elena Lawrick, Kristen Moore, Michael Anderson, Lars Soderlund, Allen Brizee, and Russell Keck (2016). *"APA General Format"*. The Writing Lab and the OWL at Purdue and Purdue University. Last edited 13 May 2016. Accessed 6 December 2016. https://owl.english.purdue.edu/owl/owlprint/560/.

Palmer, Richard (2002). *Write in Style: A Guide to Good English*. 2nd ed. Routledge.

Peersman, Greet (n. d.). "Methodological Briefs Impact Evaluation No. 10, Overview: Data Collection and Analysis Methods in Impact Evaluation." UNICEF Office of Research – Innicenti. Accessed 7 December 2017. https://www.unicefirc.org/publications/pdf/brief_10_data_collection_analysis_eng.pdf.

Perelman, Leslie C., James Paradis, and Edward Barret (1998). *The Mayfield Handbook of Technical Scientific Writing*. Mountain View, California: Mayfield Publishing Co. ISBN 1-55934-647-7.

Plato (n. d.). *The Republic*. Translated by Benjamin Jowett. Provided by the Internet Classics Archive. http://classics.mit.edu//Plato/republic.html.

Prinz, Aloys, and Björn Bünger (2009). "From 'Full Life' to 'Balanced Life': Extending Martin Seligman's Route to Happiness". Institute of Public Economics, University of Münster. CAWM Discussion Paper no. 17. March 2009.

Purdue Online Writing Lab (2013). "Sentence Fragments". Last edited 21 February 2013. https://owl.purdue.edu/owl/general_writing/mechanics/sentence_fragments.html

Rajah-Kanagasabai, Camilla, and Lynne D. Roberts (2015). "Predicting Self-reported Research Misconduct and Questionable Research Practices in University Students Using an Augmented Theory of Planned Behavior". *Frontiers in Psychology* vol. 6, no. 535, May 2015. https://www.researchgate.net/publication/275650234_Predicting_selfreported_research_misconduct_in_an_augmented_Theory_of_Planned_Behavior.

Ratner, Carl (2002). "Subjectivity and Objectivity in Qualitative Methodology". *Forum Qualitative Sozialforschung / Forum: Qualitative Social Research* vol. 3, no. 3. http://www.qualitativeresearch.net/fqs-texte/3-02/3-02ratner-e.htm.

Raz, Hilda, and Jeffrey Lependorf (2004). "The Place of Belletristic Writing in Scholarly Publishing: The Council of Editors of Learned Journals Keynote Addresses MLA Convention 2003". Edited and introduced by Michael Cornett. *Journal of Scholarly Publishing*, July 2004, pp. 184–99.

Ringenberg, William C. (2016). "Academic Freedom: an Interview." Christianity Today.com. September pp. 74–75.

Rolls, N., and P. Wignell (2013). *Communicating at University: Skills for Success*. Darwin, Australia: Charles Darwin University Press.

Rujoiu, Octavian, and Valentina Rujoiu (2014). "Academic Dishonesty and Workplace Dishonesty: an Overview". "Proceedings of the 8th International Management Conference: Management Challenges for Sustainable Development" (6–7 November 2014, Bucharest, Romania), pp. 928–38. Accessed 16 August 2015.

Russell, Tony, Allen Brizee, Elizabeth Angeli, Russell Keck, Joshua M. Piaz, Michelle Campbell, Rodrigo Rodriguez-Funtes, Daniel P. Kenzie, Ausan Wegener, and Maryam Ghafoor (2016). "MLA Formatting and Style Guide". The Purdue OWL, Purdue University Writing Lab. Last edited 12 September 2016.

Savage, Alice, and Patricia Mayer (2012). *Effective Academic Writing*. 2nd ed. Oxford University Press. 978 0 19432347 5.

Schensul, Stephen L., Jean J. Schensul, and Margaret D. LeCompte (1999). *Essential Ethnographic Methods: Observations, Interviews, and Questionnaires*. Book 2 in Ethnographer's Toolkit. Walnut Creek, California: Alta Mira Press.

Schroeder, Carrie Jean (2000). "Dangling and Misplaced Modifiers". The Write Place, St. Cloud State University. Last updated 18 August 2000. Accessed 10 November 2016. http://leo.stcloudstate.edu/grammar/modifiers.html.

_____, and Donella Westphal (2000). "Connotations". Created for St. Cloud State University. Last updated: 23 August 2000. Accessed 23 August 2000. http://leo.stcloudstate.edu/grammar/connotations.html.

Schuon, Frithjof (1953). *The Transcendent Unity of Religions*. Translated by P. Townsend. London: Faber and Faber.

Seligman, Martin E. P. (2002). *Authentic Happiness: Using the New Positive Psychology to Realize Your Potential for Lasting Fulfillment*. New York: Free Press.

Senate Standing Committee on Education, Employment and Workplace Relations. (2013). "Effectiveness of the National Assessment Program – Literacy and Numeracy Interim Report". Retrieved from http://www.aph.gov.au/Parliamentary_Business/Committees/Senate/Education_Employment_and_Workplace_Relations/

Naplan13/~/media/Committees/Senate/committee/eet_ctte/ naplan_2013/interi m_report/report.ashx.

Senge, P. M. (1990). *The fifth Discipline: The Art and Practice of the Learning Organization*. New York: Currency Doubleday.

Seyler, Dorothy U. (1994). *Understanding Argument: a Text with Readings*. McGraw-Hill College. 1 January 1994. ISBN-10: 0070564388.

Shekhovtsov, Anton, and Andreas Umland (2009). "Is Aleksandr Dugin a Traditionalist? 'Neo-Euroasianism' and Perennial Philosophy". *Russian Review* 68, October 2009, pp. 662–78.

Shryack, Jessica, Michael F. Steger, Robert F. Krueger, and Christopher S. Kallie (2010). "The Structure of Virtue: An Empirical Investigation of the Dimensionality of the Virtues in Action Inventory of Strengths". *Personality and Individual Differences* vol. 48, pp. 714–19. ScienceDirect/ journal homepage: www.elsevier.com/locate/paid.

Silvia, Paul J. (2007). *How to Write a Lot: A Practical Guide to Productive Academic Writing*. Washington, DC: American Psychological Association.

Smith, Pete, and Chris Rust (2011). "The Potential of Research-based Learning for the Creation of Truly Inclusive Academic Communities of Practice". *Innovations in Education and Teaching International* vol. 48, no. 2. May 2011, pp. 115–125.

Snartt, M. (2012). "Does NAPLAN tell Us Something about Our Students, or Do Our Students Tell Us Something about NAPLAN?" *Australian Educational Leader* vol.34, no. 2, pp. 51–53.

Snooks & Co. (2002). "Methods of Citation", chapter 12 of the *Style Manual for Authors, Editors and Printers*. 6th ed. University of Tasmania Library Guides, http://utas.libguides.com/ld.php?content_id=21757697.

Stankiewicz, Mary Ann (1997). "Perennial Promises and Pitfalls in Arts Education Reform". *Arts Education Policy Review*, vol. 99, no. 2, Nov/Dec 1997. H:\EBESCO Complete Files\Perennial promises and pitfalls in arts education reform EBSCOhost.htm.

State University of New York Press (2006). "The Scholars are Heirs of the Prophets". /ReligionKnolwledgeScienceFiles/Scholarsare%HeirsofProphets2061252.pdf.

Sternberg, Robert J. (2009). "Ethics and Giftedness". *High Ability Studies* vol. 20, no. 2, December 2009, pp. 121–30.

Stevenson, Olivia (2009). Review of *Academic Writing and Publishing* by James Hartley. *Psychology of Education Review* vol. 33, no. 2, pp. 35–7.

Stolley, Karl, Allen Brizee, and Joshua M. Paiz (2013). "Best Practices for Research and Drafting". Written for the Purdue University Online Writing Lab. Last edited 7 January 2013.

Strunk (1918). *Elementary Principles of Composition, The Elements of Style*. Wikisource, accessed 18 February 2017. Page last modified 15 November 2014; available under a Creative Commons Attribution-ShareAlike License. https://en.wikisource.org/wiki/The_Elements_of_Style/Principles.

Susan Bell, Susan (2008) *The Artful Edit: On the Practice of Editing Yourself*, W.W. Norton. Database: Academic Search Complete, http://search.ebscohost.com/?authtype=cookie,ip,uid.

Sweeney, Teresa, and Fran Hooker (2005). "Strategies for Writing Effective Conclusions". Home Academic Resource Center Writing Tips. Webster University Writing Center. https://www.Sweeney,+Teresa,+and+Fran+Hooker+Strategies+for+Writing+

Effective+Conclusions%E2%80%9D.+Home+Academic+ Resource+Center+

Sword, Helen (2012). *Stylish Academic Writing*. Cambridge, Massachusetts: Harvard University Press.

Taylor, Steven J., and Bogdan, Robert (1984). *Introduction to Qualitative Research: The Search for Meanings*. 2nd ed. New York: John Wiley.

Tate, Thomas (2000). "General Strategies for Revising and Editing on Computers". the Write Place, St. Cloud State University.Last updated 25 May 2000.

Tonkin, Humphrey (2010). "Navigating and Expanding the MLA International Bibliography". *Journal of Scholarly Publishing*, April 2010. DOI: 10.3138/jsp.41.3.340, */EBSCOhostFiles/ NavigatingandExpandingtheMLA.pdf.*

Toor, Rachel (2012). "Becoming a 'Stylish' Writer". *Chronicle of Higher Education* vol. 58, no. 40. Database: Academic Search Complete, *http://search.ebscohost.com/?authtype=cookie,ip,uid.*

Tschichold, C. (1999). "Intelligent Grammar Checking for CALL". *Language Processing in CALL: Special Issue of ReCALL*. Hull: CTICML, University of Hull.

Tutwiler, Sandra Winn, Kathleen deMarrais, David Gabbard, Andrea Hyde, Pamela Konkol, Huey-li Li, Yolanda Medina, Joseph Rayle, and Amy Swain (the Committee on Academic Standards and Accreditation) (2012). "Standards for Academic and Professional Instruction in Foundations of Education", draft paper presented to the educational community by the American Educational Studies Association. 3rd ed. *Educational Studies* vol. 49, pp. 107–18. DOI: 10.1080/00131946.2013.767253.

University of Carolina Upstate (2017). "Evaluating Information - STAAR Method: URL and What It Can Tell You". University of Carolina Upstate Library Guides. Last updated: 15 March, 2017. Accessed 27 March 2017. http://uscupstate.libguides.com/STAAR_Web_Evaluation.

University College Dublin Library (2011). "MLA Referencing Style". Accessed 17 September 2016. *https://www.ucd.ie/t4cms/Guide70.pdf*

University of North South West Sydney (2016). "The American Psychological Association Referencing System (a Guide)". Last updated 28 June 2016. Accessed 17 September 2016. DOI: H:\Guide to Academic Writing Files\Document\APA Style\The American Psychological Association (APA) Referencing System _ UNSW Current Students.html.

University of Southern Queensland (2016). "Harvard AGPS Referencing Guide". EBSCOhost Login. Retrieved 6 October 2016.

University of Sydney (2012). "Harvard Style Referencing Guide: Introduction to the Harvard Author-Date Referencing Style." Harvard_Complete.pdf. EBSCOhost Login. Accessed 18 September 2016.

University of Sydney Learning Center (2012). "Writing in an Academic Style". Accessed 1 October 2016. Writing in an Academic Style.pdf.

University of Tasmania Library (2009). "Referencing and Assignment Writing: Harvard". University of Tasmania, Australia. http://utas.libguides.com/referencing

University of Western Australia Library Guides (2016). "APA Citation Style: Introduction". Last updated 14 March 2016. http://guides.is.uwa.edu.au/ap.

Walbridge, John (1999). *The Leaven of the Ancients: Suhrawardi and the Heritage of the Greeks.* SUNY Series in Islam. New York: State University of New York Press. ISBN-10: 0791443604.

Weber, Ryan, and Allen Brizee (2013). "Strategies for Variation". Purdue University Online Writing Lab (OWL). Last edited 1 March 2013, https://owl.purdue.edu/owl/general_writing/academic_writing/sentence_variety/index.html

Webster's Collegiate Dictionary. 6th ed. (1985). "Euthanasia". Massachusetts: Merriam Webster Publishers, p. 429.

Wei, Yu Hong, and Graham Davies (2011). "Do Grammar Checkers Work? A Report on Research into the Effectiveness of Grammatik V Based on Samples of Authentic Essays by EFL Students". Paper presented at EUROCALL 96, Dániel Berszenyi College, Hungary. https://www.camsoftpartners.co.uk/euro96b.htm

Wells, Jaclyn M. (2009). "Introductions". The Purdue OWL, Purdue University Writing Lab. Last edited by Allen Brizee on 23 March 2009.

_____ (2009). "Transition Words". The Purdue OWL, Purdue University Writing Lab. Last edited by Allen Brizee on 23 March 2009.

_____ (2013). "Purdue OWL Engagement". Purdue OWL, the OWL at Purdue University. https://owl.english.purdue.edu/engagement/2/2/60/.

_____, Morgan Sousa, Mia Martini, Allen Brizee, and Ashley Velázquez (2016). "Proofreading Strategies to Try". The Writing Lab and the OWL at Purdue and Purdue University. Last edited 9 February 2016. Accessed 3 December 2016. https://owl.english.purdue.edu/owl/resource/561/01/.

_____, Morgan Sousa, Mia Martini, Allen Brizee, Ashley Velázquez, and Maryam Ghafoor (2017). "Finding Common Errors". the Writing Lab and The OWL at Purdue and Purdue University. Last edited 7 February 2017. Accessed 22 December 2017. https://owl.english.purdue.edu/owl/resource/561/02/.

Westphal, Donella (2004). "Plagiarism". Created for St. Cloud State University. Last updated 26 May 2004. http://leo.stcloudstate.edu/research/plagiarism.html.

_____ (2000). "Active and Passive Verbs." The Write Place. St. Cloud State University. Last updated 8 February 2000.

Wheaton College Writing Center (2009). "Style, Diction, Tone, and Voice". Accessed 11 October 2016. Style\Style Only Files\Style, Diction, Tone, and Voice _ Wheaton.html.

Wikipedia (n.d.). "Diction". Accessed 11 February 2017 https://en.wikipedia.org/w/index.php?title=Diction&oldid=731051895.

_____ (n.d.). "Editing Grammar Checker". Under the Creative Commons license. Accessed 9 January 2017. https://en.wikipedia.org/w/index.php?title=Grammar_checker&action=edit&section=3.

_____ "*The Elements of Style*" Retrieved 23 January 2017. https://en.wikipedia.org/w/index.php?title= The_Elements_of_Style&action=edit&section=4.

_____ (n.d.). "Grammar/ Usage". Available under the Creative Commons Attribution-ShareAlike License. Accessed 1st October 2016. https://en.wikipedia.org/wiki/Grammar//https://en.wikipedia.org/wiki/Usage.

_____ (n.d.). "List of Commonly Misused English Words". Available under the Creative Commons Attribution-ShareAlike License. Last modified on 14 September 2016. Accessed 10 November 2016.

_____ (n.d.). "MLA Handbook". Accessed 9 January 2017.

_____ (n. d.). "Parenthetical Referencing". Text available under the Creative Commons Attribution-ShareAlike License. Accessed 14 September 2016.

_____ (n.d.). "Usage". Available under a Creative Commons Attribution-ShareAlike License. Accessed 1 October 2016. https://en.wikipedia.org/wiki/Usage.

Wilson, Michael (2014). "Critical Reflection on Authentic Leadership and School Leader Development from a Virtue Ethical Perspective", in *Educational Review* vol. 66, no. 4, pp. 482–96. http://dx.doi.org/10.1080/00131911.2013.812062.

Wing, Alan M., and Alan D. Baddeley (2009). "Righting Errors in Writing Errors: The Wing and Baddeley (1980) Spelling Error Corpus Revisited". *Cognitive Neuropsychology* vol. 26, no. 2, pp. 223–26. Psychology Press of the Taylor & Francis Group. http://www.psypress.com/cogneuropsychology DOI: 10.1080/02643290902823612.

Winston, Mark, D. "Ethical Leadership and Ethical Decision Making: A Meta-analysis of Research Related to Ethics Education". Revised date July 2015. *EBESCO Complete Files\Ethical leadership: A meta-analysis of research related to ethics educa.htm.*

Writing Center (2010). "Conclusion". The University of North Carolina at Chapel Hill. 1 January 2010.

_____ (2010). "Writing an Effective Conclusion". The University of North Carolina at Chapel Hill. Accessed 14 November 2016.

_____. (2009). "Introductions Guide" University of North Carolina.

_____ (2014a). "Editing and Proofreading". University of North Carolina. Licensed under a Creative Commons

Attribution- Non-Commercial-NoDerivs 2.5 License. Accessed 14 November 2016.

_____ (2014b). "Gender-Inclusive Language". University of North Carolina. Under Creative Commons Attribution-NonCommercial-NoDerivs 2.5 License. Accessed 20 February 2017. http://writingcenter.unc.edu/handouts/gender-inclusive-language/.

_____ (2014c). "Style". University of North Carolina. Under Creative Commons Attribution-NonCommercial-NoDerivs 2.5 License. http://writingcenter.unc.edu/handouts/style/.

Writing Center (2017). "How-to Guides". University of Colorado. http://www.ucdenver.edu/academics/colleges/CLAS/Centers/writing/resources/Pages/guides.asp x.

Writer's Web (2014). "Writing Effective Conclusions". University of Richmond. Updated 1 October 2014. http://writing2.richmond.edu/writing/wweb/conclude.html.

Writing Studio (2014). "Tips for Writing a Good Conclusion". Colorado State University. 1 January 2014. http://writing.colostate.edu/files/classes/7998/file_b4a54838- fc40-1691-86bb6f50fa6b3141.pdf.

Wyrick, Jean (2014). *Steps to Writing Well*. 12th ed. Boston, Massachusetts: Wadsworth Cengage Learning. ISBA-13: 978-1-133-31131-7.

Zinsser, William (2009). "Visions and Revisions: Writing 'On Writing Well' and Keeping It Up-to-date for 35 Years". *American Scholar* vol. 78, no. 2. Database: EBSCOhost Academic Search Complete. Retrieved 23 January 2017.

INDEX

A

Abstract 139, 147 – 8, 365 – 6, 379
Academic:

    academic community 4, 7, 63 –6, 68, 82, 147

    academic conventions 1 - 2, 25, 286, 289, 343, 379

    academic dishonesty 7, 83 – 7, 108, 433, 441

    academic essay 436

    academic integrity 83, 87

active voice 294, 296, 332

addressing negative and positive consequences 161, 165

adjectives 254, 263

    adjective endings 265 - 6

    adjectives formed from verbs 263

    order of adjectives 265

adverbs 9, 232, 254, 266, 305, 327

analysis (of data) 40, 55, 57, 59. 61, 440

    numeric analysis 58

    textual analysis 59

APA (American Psychological Association) style 4, 8, 10, 93, 176, 178, 180, 181, 186, 192, 194, 364 – 369, 375, 402

In-text citations in APA 181,

List of References in APA 369

articles 251

    definite article 251

    indefinite article 251

B

bad diction 308 – 9
binding 380

C

case study 3 – 4, 139 – 40, 149

cause-and-effect essay 389

Christianity 72

Citations 8, 10, 27, 69, 84, 92, 105, 378

classification and partition essay 128

clauses 232 – 235, 254

    adjective clauses 256

    adverbial clauses 256

    dependent clauses 235 – 236, 255 – 259, 352

    independent clauses 275, 322, 352 - 353

    noun clauses 255

clichés 333

cohesive devices 343

comma splices 314 – 5, 321, 323

comparison and contrast essay 130 - 1

Complexity (of language) 290

computer checkers 359

conciseness 302, 344

conclusion 159, 365

conclusion techniques 159, 161

    echo 161 - 2

    summarize 161, 182

    offer solution 161, 163

    give warning 161, 164

address negative and positive consequences 161, 165

look to the future 161, 165

give advice 161, 168

give opinion or speculation 161, 166

recommend action 161, 167

answer question(s) 161, 169

ask questions 161, 170

make prediction 161, 171

discuss future developments 161, 172

point out limitations 161, 172

connotations 307

containers 221, 227 - 8

contribution(s) of the research 140

contributors (in MLA style) 218, 223, 227

coordinating conjunctions 309, 326, 352

D

dangling modifiers 324 - 5

data 140, 406

data analysis (numeric / textual) 55 - 59

data sources 37 - 40

primary sources 40

secondary sources 38

data quality 54

data treatment 55 - 7

presentation of data 56

processing of data 55

deduction 124 - 5

definition essay (sample essay) 384

descriptive essay (sample essay) 382

diction 308 – 9

documentation 220, 278, 289

E

Editing 348, 354

English forms 236 - 7

continuous forms 237

perfect forms 238

perfect continuous forms 238

English tenses 236

Present Tense 237

Past Tense 237

Future Tense 237

ethical considerations 45

Essays 127, 131

Definition essays 128

Descriptive essays 129

Narrative essays 130

Comparison / Contrast essays 130

Cause and Effect essays 132

Classification and Partition essays 133

Process essays 133

Opinion essays 134

evaluating internet sources 21 - 2

evaluating print sources 21

evaluating URLs 23

F

final copy 379

final draft 379

formality (of language) 291

fused sentences 315, 322 - 3

G

gender-sensitive language 345

giving advice 168

giving warning 164

give opinion 166

grammar checkers 357
graphics 366, 369, 373, 377, 405

H

Harvard referencing and citations style 370, 374, 403
higher education 83, 86
higher-order thinking (HOT) 290

I

Impartiality 291
Induction 124
Interviews 41 - 5
in-text citations 176, 181, 193 – 5, 216, 223, 345
introduction 115, 117, 135, 365
Islam 71

L

Language 314
    language clarity 288
    language complexity 290
    language formality 291
list of references 176, 178, 186, 193, 205, 379
literature review 139 - 40
looking to the future 161, 165
loose sentences 296

M

main body 31, 113, 118, 139
making predictions 161
methods of data collection 41
    interviews 41
    observations 46
    questionnaires 52
    surveys 50

methods of development 127
misplaced modifiers 325
misspelt words 315, 329 - 30
MLA (Modern Language Association) style 216
    MLA concept of containers 221
    MLA core elements 218
    MLA Handbook 8th Edition 217

N

narrative essay (sample essay) 130
neutrality 291

O

Objectivity 291
Observations 46 - 9
offering solutions 161, 163
opinion/argument essay 128, 134 - 6
outline 31

P

Padding 333
Paragraph 118
    body of the paragraph 120
    paragraph development 124
    paragraph structure 118
    paragraph unity and coherence 121
parallel structures 326, 354
paraphrasing 90, 95, 97
parenthetical referencing 180
passive voice 241 – 3, 332
perennial tradition 72
philosophy of education 75
phrases 245
    prepositional phrases 245
    noun phrases 246

gerund phrases 247
infinitive phrases 248
phrasal verbs 24
verb phrases 249
plagiarism 81 – 4, 86, 88, 90 - 105
unintentional plagiarism 86
Plato's philosophy 75
point out limitations 161, 172
positive psychology 73
process essay 133, 394
proofreading 346 - 7
punctuation 267, 352
full stop 273
comma 268
colon 274
semicolon 275
apostrophe 282
brackets 277
quotation marks 276
parentheses 277
hyphen 279

Q

quantity expressions 327
questionnaires 52, 54
quotation 98
long quotation 100
short quotation 99
punctuating quotations 101

R

reading strategies 27
recommending action 161, 167
redundancy 302, 331
referencing 176, 180
relative pronouns 259, 333
repetition 331, 335
research methods—qualitative 36

research methods—quantitative 35
revising by computer 354
run-on (*fused*) sentences 262

S

search-and-replace computer check
facility 359
sentences in English 232
simple sentence 233
compound sentence 234
complex sentence 235
sentences of equal weight 299
sentences of unequal weight
301
sentence length 303
sentence fragments 261, 315 – 6,
319, 321, 352
sentence openings 304
sentence rhythm 303
sentence variety 236
slang 306, 308 - 9
sources of data 38 - 40
spell checker 355
style (academic Style, bad style)
286 – 7, 305, 331
subject-verb agreement 238 – 9,
349 - 50
submission 379
subordinating conjunctions 235,
257 - 8
summarizing 90, 93, 95
summary 95, 162 - 3
surveys 50 - 1
synthesizing 90

T

tense 236 - 9
tense forms 237

topic sentence 119, 365
thesis formula 290
thesis statement 114 – 6, 118, 135
tone 288, 310
triteness 308

V

vagueness 308

verbs; active verbs, passive verbs 241, 317
visual illustrations 151 - 7
voice 232, 239, 310

W

word choice 309
wordiness 302, 309, 333 - 4
workplace dishonesty 87

www.ingramcontent.com/pod-product-compliance
Ingram Content Group UK Ltd.
Pitfield, Milton Keynes, MK11 3LW, UK
UKHW041304160125
4146UKWH00004B/7